El Salvador

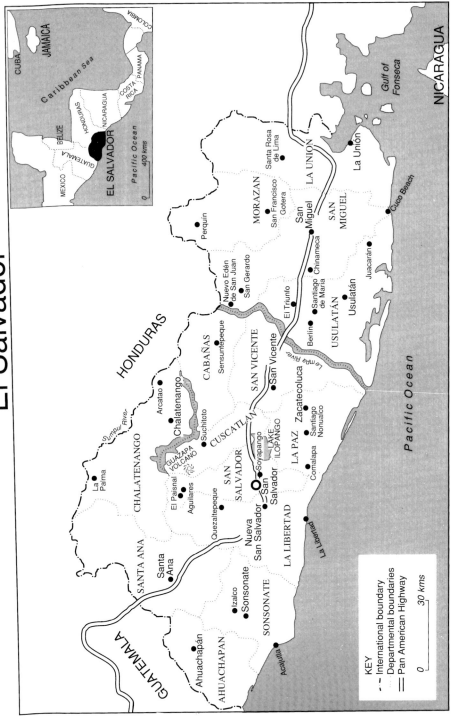

KEY
- –·– International boundary
- ······ Departmental boundaries
- ═══ Pan American Highway

0 ⊢———⊣ 30 kms

Morazán

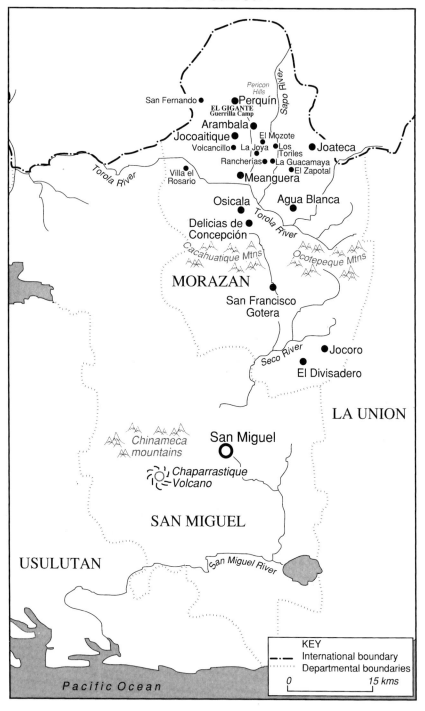

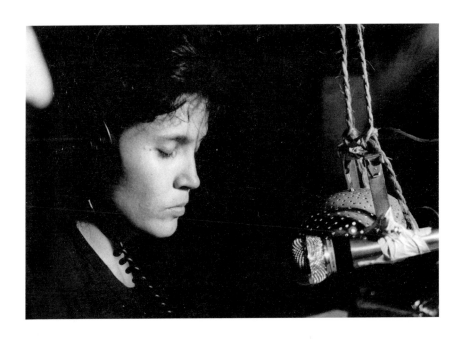

top: Comandante Luisa.

bottom: The Radio Venceremos production collective putting another show together at La Guacamaya.

top: Leoncio Pichinte, Butterfly, Santiago and Marvel at the Ojo de Agua camp.

bottom: Radio Venceremos' air-raid shelter.

top: Santiago interviewing Comandante William Pascasio (Memo).
Behind them stands ERP leader Joaquín Villalobos (Atilio).

bottom: In Perquín. From left to right: Joaquín Villalobos, Luisa, Santiago
and Leti.

top: Mauricio calibrating the Radio Venceremos equipment from an air-raid shelter.

bottom: Guns, guitars and violins: The Torogoces of Morazán, the guerrillas' favourite band.

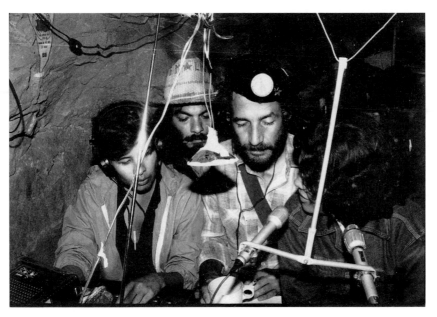

top: Guerrilla advertising: "Everyone should listen to Radio Venceremos".

bottom: Broadcasting in the Bat Cave. From left to right, Marcela, Apolonio, Santiago and La Morena.

The monitoring team in La Guacamaya, tuning in to everything from The Voice of America to Radio Moscow.

'*Rebel Radio* is an exciting tale of life in the rebels' zones of control during El Salvador's decade-long civil war - as told by the young men and women responsible for running the guerrillas' radio station, Radio Venceremos. Their account is an almost Homeric drama of war, violence and death filled with stories of extraordinary courage, political intrigue, "macho" derring-do, youthful hi-jinks, passionate love, clandestine sexual liaisons and the ordinary and not-so-ordinary events of daily life in the mountains of Morazán. If you ever wondered what it was like to be a young guerrilla in El Salvador, this book is for you. *Rebel Radio* is a tribute to the courage, inventiveness, vitality and audacity of the Salvadoran people.'

Robert Armstrong, co-author with Janet Shenk of *El Salvador: The Face of Revolution*

'These remarkable stories should be required reading for those pessimistic about the struggle of ordinary people against power, and for journalists wishing to rediscover pride in their profession. The work of Radio Venceremos is legendary and the stories of how it became so are rich in humanity, wit and, above all, heroism.'

John Pilger, award-winning filmmaker and author of *Heroes* and *Distant Voices*

'These remarkable stories tell a tale of almost incredible courage and ingenuity in the struggle to keep the spark of hope alive in a country being turned into a living Hell. It is a real tribute to the human spirit.'

Noam Chomsky, author of *Turning the Tide: US Intervention in Central America*

'Every day for 12 years, El Salvador's *Radio Venceremos* broadcast as an underground guerrilla radio station. From bunkers under aerial bombardment, on the run from government troops, outwitting high-tech jamming - the radio fought for a space on the airwaves, just as the guerrillas fought for a space in the country's politics. It became the main public voice of opposition in the middle of a bloody civil war, challenging the regime's control of the media through censorship and fear.

The story of *Radio Venceremos* is a story of courage and self-sacrifice, of humour and above all of success. The guerrillas were never defeated, the radio never silenced.'

Jon Snow, television broadcaster

The story of El Salvador's Radio Venceremos

José Ignacio López Vigil

Translator Mark Fried

LATIN AMERICAN BUREAU • CURBSTONE PRESS

First published as *Las Mil y Una Historias de Radio Venceremos,* by José
Ignacio López Vigil, UCA Editores, San Salvador, 1991

Published in North America by Curbstone Press
Published in the UK by the Latin America Bureau

Cover photo: from forthcoming film of the Radio Venceremos story,
       directed by Manuel de Pedro; historical adviser, Santiago
Cover design: Andy Dark

Printed in the U.S. on acid-free paper by Bookcrafters

Curbstone Press is a 501(c)(3) nonprofit publishing house whose operations
are supported in part by private donations and by grants from ADCO
Foundation, J. Walton Bissell Foundation, Inc., Witter Bynner Foundation for
Poetry, Inc., Connecticut Commission on the Arts, Connecticut Arts
Endowment Fund, Lannan Foundation, LEF Foundation, Lila Wallace-
Reader's Digest Literary Publishers Marketing Development Program,
administered by the Council of Literary Magazines and Presses, The Andrew
W. Mellon Foundation, National Endowment for the Arts, and The Plumsock
Fund.

Library of congress Cataloging-in-Publication Data

López Vigil, José Ignacio.
  [Mil y una historias de Radio Venceremos. English]
  Rebel radio : the story of El Salvador's Radio Venceremos / by José
Ignacio López Vigil ; translated by Mark Fried.
      p.   cm.
    ISBN 1-880684-21-7 : $19.95. — ISBN 0-906156-88-2 (pbk.)
      1. El Salvador—History—1979-   2. Radio Venceremos (El Salvador)
  3. Insurgency—El Salvador—History—20th Century.   I. Fried, Mark.
  II. Radio Venceremos (El Salvador)   III. Title.
  F1488.3.L6813   1994
  972.8405'3—dc20

                                                    94-33187

CURBSTONE PRESS, 321 Jackson Street, Willimantic, CT 06226

Contents

Cast of Characters

Of the many people mentioned in this book, the principal voices heard are (in the order of their appearance, and by their *noms de guerre*):

Jonás   Commander Jorge Meléndez, military leader of the guerrilla front in Morazán and a member of the PRS political commission. Taught theatre and acting before the war.

Apolonio   A Salvadoran electrical engineer, he helped set up the station in 1980 and stayed on as a Venceremos technician.

Abel   A Salvadoran technician, he helped set up the station in 1980 and stayed on as a member of the station collective.

Mauricio   A Salvadoran technician, he helped set up the station in 1980 and stayed on as a member of the station collective.

Santiago   A Venezuelan radio broadcaster, he became the Radio Venceremos anchor-man in 1981 and remains so today.

Luisa   Commander Mercedes del Carmen Letona headed the radio collective in its early years. She is a member of the political commission of the Party of the Salvadoran Revolution (PRS) and of the political-diplomatic commission of the FMLN.

Atilio   Commander Joaquín Villalobos is PRS secretary general, leader of the Revolutionary People's Army (ERP) and a member of the FMLN General Command.

Evelin /Butterfly   A Salvadoran student activist, she became a Venceremos broadcaster in 1981.

Marvel   Originally a filmmaker from Venezuela, Hernán Vera became a Venceremos broadcaster in 1981.

Morena   A Salvadoran activist, she joined the Venceremos collective in 1982.

Leti   A peasant woman from Morazán and one of the first radio operators among the guerrillas, she became head of the Venceremos collective in the mid-1980s.

Marcela   Peasant farmer who joined Venceremos after being elected mayor of "liberated" Villa El Rosario. Operated the mixer, subsequently transferred to FMLN's press office.

Marvin   A Salvadoran print journalist, he became a Venceremos broadcaster in 1982.

TRANSLATOR'S NOTE

Two terms which have special meaning for the Salvadoran guerrillas and which may not be familiar to the English reader have been left in Spanish. They are:

compa (also the diminutive *compita*) short for *compañero* or comrade, it refers to a member or sympathiser of the FMLN, and also to a lover or spouse.

cuilio a common term for the enemy, it refers to any member of the Salvadoran Armed Forces.

REBEL RADIO

Introduction

All I had from Radio Venceremos was a poster on the wall and a poorly-recorded cassette, but I was fascinated by the legendary station. What sort of people worked there? How had they managed to keep a clandestine station on the air for so long, broadcasting from the depths of Morazán?

Whatever seems far away turns up right next door. While I was looking for them, they found me. They asked me to give them a course on radio production. A course for a guerrilla radio station? I accepted. Wherever and whenever, I'd be there.

I suspected that I would be the student. I could show them a few techniques, help them try out different formats. But they were the ones with the unique experience, built up over ten years of war, of doing radio with a microphone in one hand and a gun in the other, broadcasting underground and amid flying bullets.

After the workshops, they told me stories. They told me about the first programme they ran from Parra de Bambú, and how they broke through the army's encircling noose. How they tricked the enemy's goniometers, and how the correspondents reported from the front lines. I met the station's founders, heard about their love affairs in the Bat Cave, and learned the still relatively unknown truth of Monterrosa's death.

They were incredible stories. At first I listened with my mouth hanging open, then I turned on my tape recorder. Later I organised their testimonies chronologically, according to the different stages of the war. Stringing their stories together, this book was born. It's their book, not mine. They conceived it, gave it life in the heat of night-time conversations into a hidden mike. I just helped out with the birth.

Is the book about radio? About communications? I don't know. Radio Venceremos is present in all the stories, that's for sure. Each story touches on basic elements of what in Latin America we call popular and alternative media. Naturally, the working conditions were extreme, barely imaginable to broadcasters in air-conditioned studios with "Silence" written on the door.

Let's just say these are chronicles of the thousand and one adventures lived by the *compas* who made this radio station possible. Stories that aren't intended to prove anything. The book shows, it doesn't tell. It's up to the reader to discover the moral of each story.

Sometimes the voices overlap. An event is told by two or three people who lived through it. The fact is, I didn't worry much about who was doing the talking, only what they were saying. I respected the Salvadoran way of speaking, with all its "vulgarities". Guerrillas and soldiers tend not to speak by the dictionary. I hope the context explains the very Salvadoran expressions they use. If not, and you're not from there, ask any of the thousands of Salvadoran exiles dispersed throughout the world. They'll tell you what *volado* means, and where *La Ciguanaba* appears. And they'll tell you other stories as surprising as those collected here. I don't believe there's enough ink in the world to write them all down.

José Ignacio López Vigil
Tenth Anniversary of Radio Venceremos

Section I
The General Offensive

Enter the Viking

Jonás[1] turned up at my house in Mexico.

"We've got to have a radio station," he said. "We'll bust our balls to get it."

In El Salvador at that time, at the end of the seventies, things had turned black as ants. The repression was brutal. Print media was no longer effective. If you had a leaflet in your bag, it could cost you your life. Was it worth risking the lives of those handing leaflets out, to say nothing of those accepting them? Maybe that's why the idea of a radio station took root — they can't frisk you for a voice.

There was no place for us in the media. The left-wing papers had been closed down. *La Crónica del Pueblo* and *El Independiente* had both been bombed. They had begun to dynamite Monsignor Romero's[2] radio station. Journalists were being threatened, murdered, gagged, no one could tell anyone about anything. Our brief takeovers of radio stations were something, but not much.

"We need technical support," Jonás insisted.

I had a few contacts at the University of Guadalajara. That's where we found Toño, an electrical engineer, a dreamer, one of those people who never makes any money because he spends his life looking for meaning in what he does.

Toño worked in a cockroach-infested hole behind an auditorium. There he had all sorts of old equipment: half-built television sets, stripped-down tape recorders, a shitload of tangled wires and, presiding over the disorder, his desk.

"We need a radio station in El Salvador," Jonás told him. "An AM station that can be heard right in the capital city. That's our idea."

Toño fell in love with the project. Before we'd even finished telling him about it, he was looking for a map of El Salvador to study the mountains, calculate distances, heights, valleys, the topography of our little country. The first task we faced wasn't so much learning the ropes as getting hold of equipment. There were legal complications. You can't simply buy a radio transmitter just like that. You need a permit, a licence, a lot of stuff. And since we figured they would try to jam it, Toño suggested we try a short-wave communications radio, which he would try to adapt for AM broadcasting by crystallising the end of the band...

"Whatever, but let's do it now," Jonás interrupted.

From that moment on, Toño spent every waking hour searching for equipment. Through contacts he had — and he never told us who — he got hold of an old transmitter, a very old transmitter, but a good one. He took it out of a fishing boat. A *Valiant Viking*. It had a viking stamped right there on the metal cover. It was small, but solid, weighed a good sixty pounds. And it was reliable, as we discovered later on.

Once he had the transmitter, Toño set to work to adapt it. He shut himself away in his workshop, hooking up buttons and soldering circuits, and managed to adjust it for AM. Then he began doing tests. He'd put on music and go off in his car to tune in and test the signal's reach and the quality of the sound. That guy was having the time of his life, it was written all over his face.

"How are you doing?" I greeted him one day.

"It's ready," he said. "The Viking works. It's going to talk more than an old parrot."

"Toño, how does it work?" I asked, worried already.

You see, neither Jonás nor any of us knew anything about electronics. Nothing at all. We had trouble turning on a transistor radio. So he began trying to train us. That is, to train me. The first time, Toño was just like every other technician. They start giving you instructions and talking about ohms and resistance and watts and volts, and they keep you sitting there as if you knew what was going on, as if you had the same background. At last I admitted: "I don't understand anything."

So we agreed he would explain each step so that even a little kid could do it. On the Viking's side there were a whole slew of buttons. He put a number on each one. And in a notebook he wrote: "First, you push such-and-such a switch up. Second, you push such-and-such a switch down." And so on. Because down there no one was going to understand it any other way. Those little numbers travelled down with the transmitter, and they were still there years later, when the Viking fell into enemy hands. We never took them off.

Then we had to figure out how to ship it. I bought a small trailer and did some alterations. For the transmitter I built a hiding place: a box with a sink bolted to the top. Since I couldn't trust a carpenter to do it, I sawed it myself. I took the exact measurements, and the hollow box with its fake sink turned out really splendid. All set? Well, no, because when it came time to pack it up, it wouldn't fit. The Viking was nice and square, but in the back it had a thing that stuck out, like an old plug. This can't be important, I thought. Zip, I pulled it out, and the transmitter fitted perfectly. Problem resolved, I set off for El Salvador. My buddy and I were happy as could be, driving down to the place, still in Mexican territory, where we handed it over to others.

"Be careful when you wash your hands!" I joked with the guy I gave it to.

We weren't going to cross the border. The plan was to get others who weren't Salvadoran to take in the transmitter. I'd travel down later by plane. Once the equipment was safely in the country, I'd turn up with the infamous manual, because I was to be the instructor! It was my job to explain how the hell to run that sucker.

At last, months later, the day we were waiting for arrived. We all met on a farm in Quezaltepeque. Everyone from the party who had anything to do with the radio station was there — Joaquín first in line. We put the transmitter in a small empty house. We hung the aerial from one tree to another — a bipolar aerial that was so long it almost reached beyond the edge of the farm. Then we connected up the cables. Everything was perfect. The moment of truth had arrived. I went into action. The first step... The second step... With the manual in my hand, I gave the orders.

"Ready?" asks Joaquín.

"Ready." I say.

"But this isn't working. Nothing's happening."

"Nothing's happening?"

"Nix."

I kept looking through that manual and everyone kept looking at me. Joaquín, Jonás, half the national directorate. I started getting anxious. And what tends to happen in such circumstances happened: everyone knows, everyone gives an opinion, everyone sticks his finger in.

"Look, that tube barely gives off any light."

"No, *hombre*, it's not the tube. It's this thing over here..."

"Tighten that screw, look how loose it is..."

Do this, do that, nobody paid me the slightest heed. I stuffed the manual in my pocket so they wouldn't even remember to ask me.

"It's the tube," someone decided. "Stop the chatter and let's change the tube."

"What if that burns it out?" said another.

"Listen brother, if you don't play, you can't win."

In a little while, someone was off to San Salvador with the "bad" tube to buy another. He went and returned. They changed the tube on the Viking and it still didn't work. So they continued debating what might be wrong with the machine, and decided it was broken. That's when I remembered the little thing I'd pulled off in Mexico. The truth is I didn't dare mention it. But I couldn't keep quiet either.

"Look, I took something off it, a plug, because it didn't fit in the box. But I don't think that shitty little piece..."

I was dying. Luckily, no one thought what I said mattered. They kept on pushing and pulling on the machine, trying it and getting more and more frustrated. It gave no sign of life. All our great plans had been crushed.

"César," Joaquín says to me, "what did you say about a plug? Could that be it?"

I don't think he'd even finished asking, and I was already getting ready to go back to Mexico. When I explained the disaster to Toño, he laughed: "You've got to be kidding, that's a bridge. The bridge that completes the circuit! It's like taking the spark plugs out of a car! Okay, where did you put it?"

For some reason, I hadn't thrown the little bridge away. I found it and sent it to San Salvador, and they tell me — I wasn't there to see for myself — that the Viking worked beautifully.

Broadcasting under Blankets

The very first broadcasts took place in '79. We painted graffiti calling on people to tune in to our new station on Tuesdays and Fridays, and ran off leaflets announcing that the Salvadoran people now had their own voice, their own station, the People's Revolutionary Radio.

At first we went up on a little hill near the city to go on air. There was no other way. We hooked up at six in the afternoon — for how long? Ten minutes, maybe fifteen. A mix of commentary, revolutionary music and combative messages: agitation.

By 22 January, 1980 we were transmitting from the National University. That day we'd organised the first big demonstration of the recently created Revolutionary Coordinating Body of the Masses. Damn, it was incredible! Over 300,000 people in the street, the largest mobilisation ever. People began gathering at eight in the morning in Cuscatlán Park. They just kept coming, a sea of men, women, youth, unionists, militants with banners asking for democracy and attacking the Christian Democrats and their civilian-military junta, imposed by the gringos.

At about 9.30am the crowd started to march, but since there were so many it moved very slowly. When the ones in front reached the National Palace near the cathedral, the ones at the back were still at the El Salvador del Mundo statue. The march didn't go straight downtown, it snaked all around the side streets — it must have been ten kilometres long, more or less. And there were people on the sides. All along the march there were cars with loudspeakers tuned in to our station so that everyone could hear.

We were back at the university broadcasting. Every so often a comrade would phone to tell us how the demonstration was going. We also listened to what the other stations were saying. That was the way we worked back then, pirating off other correspondents because the RRP, our station, was completely clandestine.

Transmitting from the university required some complicated manoeuvring. We usually went on air at six o'clock when the most students would be around. We'd put the aerial up on the roof and connect everything. Then we'd slip through a back door into a little room — a little closed off corner on the first floor, like a storeroom. We'd leave a tape recorder outside playing loud music to distract people, and several of us would keep watch to make sure no one came near. Then those of us with the loudest voices would take the microphone and begin the programme. We had to cover ourselves with blankets to muffle our chants, otherwise they carried into the hallway outside. It was boiling hot anyway, so broadcasting under wool blankets, like ghosts, was a real ordeal.

On the 22nd it was my turn to be the fan. The Viking overheated a lot, it wasn't made to transmit for such long periods. But with the excitement of all that was going on, we stayed on air an hour at a time. Our first hour-long programme! And there I was with a piece of cardboard fanning the Viking so that it wouldn't pass out. When the announcers stuck their heads up for air I'd fan them too. Mariana[3] was there, full of enthusiasm, announcing, reading messages, greeting all the organisations represented on the march.

Then a helicopter circled overhead and we thought they'd located us, so we turned off the transmitter and ended the broadcast.

"Let's go out into the street", I said, "and see what's happening."

What was happening was a terrible massacre. When we got to the US Embassy, we met people streaming the other way.

"They're killing!" they screamed. "Don't go down there!"

But since we were armed, we went on anyway.

"We're going to get it sooner or later anyway," one *compa* said. "Let's blow them to pieces!"

"Don't even think about it. They're shooting from the rooftops."

It was inexcusable — criminal. That huge mass of defenceless people targeted by sharpshooters firing from the roof of the National Palace itself. Other snipers were on top of the theatre and other buildings nearby. Even people who ran to the church got machine-gunned. Some died in their blood on the cathedral steps, others were trampled by the crowd. About a hundred were killed that day, never mind the wounded.

"You've got to take the station elsewhere," the leadership told us. "Increase its signal so that it reaches the whole country. Add short wave so that the whole world will know about the murderers who run this country."

We spent the rest of the year looking for a technician who could adapt the equipment, and a secure place to broadcast from. We found it in Morazán.

Inspired by the Monsignor

Monsignor Romero's radio station[4] was across the street from the archbishopric. Father Rogelio Pedraz was the director and he asked Goyo[5] if he knew of anyone trustworthy who could install a ten-kilo piece of equipment that had just been donated.

Goyo said, "My brother Apolonio just finished studying electronics in Germany."

Yes, I returned with my diploma and landed a good job in the communications department of CEL,[6] but it didn't mean anything to me. I wanted to give the technical things I'd studied overseas some social content. So after I met Rogelio and began to help out at YSAX, I was happy. At least I was doing something, supporting those who could do more than me.

That's when Rubén, another technician, a friend I'd met in Germany, came back to the country.

"It's Sunday," I told him. "Let's go to the cathedral."

"Are you drunk?" he asked. "Since when do you go to mass?"

"You should hear Monsignor Romero's homily. He's going to speak today."

Rubén was awestruck when he heard the Monsignor fearlessly chastise the forces of repression, raising his voice to condemn the attacks, speaking for those who could not speak. He decided to help me. The Monsignor's brave words were like a little motor that kept us going at his station, despite the friends and relatives who'd tell us, "You'd better get out of AX."

The noose was tightening day by day, but we felt we had to keep helping the Monsignor reach thousands of homes in the capital and in much of the country each Sunday. What affection and admiration that man evoked; you could listen to his sermon as you walked down the street, hearing it through the windows of every house, as if it were the only station in San Salvador!

The connections that happen in life: besides Goyo, I had another brother, Rafi, who had already joined the guerrillas. And just then the *compas* were looking for a technician to run the Viking they'd brought from Mexico. They wanted to set up a clandestine radio station to transmit from the university campus. So Jonás contacted me and asked if the bipolar aerial they had was appropriate. I told them it would work, but since the equipment had been adapted for broadcasting in AM between 1580 and 1540 KHz, the aerial ought to be about 90 metres long. And it would be no mean feat to hang such a huge aerial off the roof of the university!

Well, I helped them do it. A whole group of us went along because you need a lot of muscle-power to stretch taut such a long cable. We took the measurements and found it would fit across the roofs of the three buildings of engineering school. One group climbed up on the middle building carrying the middle of the aerial, where the insulator was. Two other groups went up on the other rooftops to pull it tight. We bolted one end down and then stretched it from the other end. We used a board to push and push until it was straight. Then we bolted it down. And we left it there.

When it was time to transmit all we had to do was thread a cable onto the female connector at the centre and throw it down to where the Viking was hidden. Afterwards, just unthread it and that was that. That's how we were able to broadcast the historic march of 22 January.

Later on I couldn't continue working with the organisation because CEL sent me abroad on a training course. Rubén, my friend, stayed to help out at YSAX. Since by then I'd met Marianella[7] and had done translations at the Human Rights Commission, I took a lot of material with me about the situation in my country to spread the word overseas.

I returned to El Salvador a few days after the assassination of Monsignor Romero. The news hit me between the eyes. I could neither believe nor accept it. I was a pacifist. I worked in YSAX because I was convinced that the Monsignor could find a way out of the country's disastrous crisis. A whole lot of people shared that same hope. When they killed him, that was when I said yes to everything the *compas* proposed. I said yes to armed struggle. The death of the Monsignor helped clarify my beliefs. Not only in my case. I think the same thing happened to many others.[8]

I went to work on the transmitter. Mateo, who was my contact, brought me a huge box in the parking lot of a supermarket. Inside was the Viking. I had to adapt it for short wave because they had already decided to take it to Morazán. In those days I lived in an apartment near the zoo. I took the equipment home, looked it over, and realised that it could work perfectly well on other bands. The Mexican technician had changed the crystals so that it would work only on AM, but the equipment had everything it needed to broadcast on short wave. Only the tuner was broken, creating a short circuit. I had to repair it and than guess how it all worked, because there was no manual or anything. The instructions that César had brought from Mexico had been lost. My brother Rafi helped me and, between the two of us trying all the switches, we managed to figure it out.

I had still not gone underground. When I went out to the CEL office, I'd hide the transmitter under my bed. Or rather I'd put the bed on top of the transmitter, because to hide the Viking I had to build myself a special bed out of wood, one that would fold up like a big sandwich. When I came home, I'd open it up, take out the equipment, and Rafi and I would get to work testing it. Rafi would go out with his short wave radio, I'd put on classical music and he'd check the reception.

"It's buzzing over here," he'd tell me.

"Now you can't hear shit," he'd say next.

Day after day we worked at adjusting it until we got a good sound. The *compas* were thrilled when we told them the equipment worked fine. But it would work even better if we had a 300-watt amplifier, since the Viking could only put out 50 watts.

So we bought one in Panama, and while I was there I also bought several walkie-talkies, planning already for military communications on the two-metre band. Then I had to bring them all through customs at the Comalapa airport!

"What's this?" the customs agents asked, pointing to the walkie-talkies, which I had taken apart so that only the keypads were visible.

"They're remote controls for TVs."

"And what's this?" they asked, pointing to the amplifier which was so well packed and repacked that all you could see were a few buttons.

"A sound system for a party, *hombre*. Are you going to tell me you've never seen one before?"

"Show us the receipts."

"I haven't got them. I was robbed in Panama."

Of course I did have them, but well hidden. Imagine — on the receipt it said "Communications equipment". They kept me there for about an hour, hanging around and growing desperate. They wanted a bribe, of course.

"What's the story?" I pretended to be angry, "If there are taxes, then tell me how much. But I don't have the receipts."

"But to work out the taxes we need the receipts."

"So how can we settle this? Listen, I work at CEL, understand? For the government! The people from the company are waiting for me outside. Call them in here, ask them, see what ought to be done, but let's get on with it!"

Since they couldn't get either a receipt or a bribe out of me, they had to let me go.

I grabbed my bags and didn't look back. The *compa* waiting for me outside was as pale as I was.

"I've got everything," I told him happily.

To the car and home to unpack the treasure. Now we had an amplifier for the Viking! Before sending it to Morazán, two *compas*, Chefe and a girl, came to be taught how to use it. I'd numbered all the switches with little paper tags, and written up a manual explaining each step from turning it on to turning it off. I made it all very simple, thinking of the people who were going to be using it, and I took the precaution of making a photocopy.

We were also on the lookout for enough equipment to start a military communications network on the fronts. Since we couldn't buy these things, we figured we would requisition them. I walked the streets looking at the rooftops and wherever I saw a communications aerial I'd note down the address. Later, the commandos would go and take them. Everything ended up at my apartment, which was looking more and more like a storeroom: the Viking, six little Honda generators (one for each front), Yagi aerials, aluminium tubes, coaxial cables... Now we had all the implements, but we had to train the implementers. So we planned a course in military communications for future radio operators, to be held on the last days of the year.

A nun arranged for us to stay in a house on the outskirts of San Salvador. We spent 30 and 31 December there. We had the liberated radios, the walkie-talkies from Panama, the home-made aerials. They got a blackboard for us, and we held the classes in a nice cool corridor. Everything was as clean and orderly as could be.

"Boys and girls," they used to call us, "lunch is ready."

We ate in a spotless room with white tablecloths. They stuffed us full, we talked for a while, and then back to class. At three in the afternoon, they'd be back: "Boys and girls, would you like a snack?"

They brought us coffee and cookies. It was fantastic.

The eve of the 31st — New Year's Eve — was just what the doctor ordered. While the fireworks were going off in the street, we were inside doing tests. With so much noise, it was a perfect simulation of a battle. One student would take a radio to one corner of the house, another to the other.

"Eastern Front calling the Guazapa Front," one would say. "Do you read me? Over."

"The shit's coming down hard!" answered the other. "Shout louder, sonofabitch!"

Abel and Mauricio, who already knew something about radio and electronics, led the classes along with me. The participants included Oscar, Babyface and Samuel, who's now in the South, and a nun who went on to do political work in San Vicente... There was also another nun learning to be a radio operator and encoder who was killed a few days later in Cutumay Camones.

The course was over. At the beginning of January 1981, with plans for the offensive under way, we said good-bye. From my apartment things disappeared one by one: the Honda generators, the radios, the aerials... Everything went to the front lines.

The Pee that Changed my Life

I'm a filmmaker. I studied film in London and came to Central America to make a movie. I couldn't even find El Salvador on the map. When we got to the border, travelling by land from Mexico, I had to ask where we were. I should say we, because the two other Venezuelans I was travelling with knew as little as I did.

That was August of '79, or September, I can't remember. San Salvador was a pressure cooker. There was a meeting going on at every corner. There were demonstrations of 200,000 people. We went to have breakfast at the market, and on a street about four blocks from the university I had to slam on the brakes. We couldn't get by. Strewn across the street were twelve arms. Human arms. All left arms, chopped off with a chain saw, tied together with a banner of the Popular Revolutionary Bloc. That's what the death squads did — and do.

On another street I came across half a body, just from the waist down. Also cut with a chain saw. It was grotesque, you could see perfectly how they cut through the muscles, the bones, right above the belt on his pants, like canned meat. I found out later that Major Roberto D'Aubuisson and his death-squad cohorts boasted about decapitating and mutilating hundreds of young people with chain saws in the grounds of an abattoir called "Mataderos, SA", owned by the Lemus O'Byrne family.

That was San Salvador. The country made a deep impression, and I started falling in love with it. But we were on our way elsewhere, to Nicaragua, to make a film. Back in Caracas we were in an alternative film group called Chaos. We were all leftists, activists, and the crisis of the Venezuelan Left had hit our group. The guerrillas had failed, we had no funding, we just didn't know what to do, so to feel useful we did solidarity work for the Sandinista Front. One day some foundation money landed in our laps — these things happen — on a Wednesday. That Thursday was July 19, the day of the Nicaraguan revolution.

"Wonderful!" we said. "We'll go to Nicaragua and make a film about how a revolution takes off."

We bought movie equipment in New York, we bought a van all fully equipped, and we travelled down overland, Pancho, Richard and I. We spent a few days in San Salvador just to get everything ready to go on to our destination: Managua. We went to the Nicaraguan embassy to get visas, and it took forever because the Sandinistas who had just come to power hadn't quite figured out how to do these things.

"What visas?" they said. "Come back later on, nobody knows about visas here."

Hoping to save time, we left the van at a gas station so they could wash it and change the oil. But that took forever too. So I went out for a walk and I passed by the Hotel Alameda. That's where most of the foreign journalists stayed, and since we had press cards from Venezuela I thought: "I'm going to go in to take a leak. At least I'll get to see where my colleagues stay."

I go in and ask the receptionist for the washroom. She's very nice, of course: it's right over there. And in the washroom I run into my old black friend Big League. He was my political officer back in Venezuela, one of Douglas Bravo's men.[9] I hadn't heard tell of him since he escaped by tunnel from Modelo Prison.

"Goddamn!" I say. "What are you doing here?"

"Peeing, pal, same as you."

Emotional embraces in the bathroom. And when we start telling stories about what one or the other has done, Big League cuts me off.

"Listen, have you got a car?"

"Of course."

"Then you know what? While we're talking, keep me company while I go do a *volado*."

It was the first time anyone had invited me to do a *volado*. In San Salvador, a *volado* can mean just about anything. It could be to go have a cup of coffee, get there, sit down, what'll you have, a cup of coffee, two cups, chit-chat, what a pretty girl, do you like the food here, would you like another cup of coffee, no, I've had enough, let's go. What about the *volado* we were going to do? We just did it. A *volado* could be that: to check on movements near a particular spot, or have a waiter give you a letter. A *volado* could also be getting in your van, stopping over there where that little blue car is parked, the door opens, in come seven G-3 rifles onto the floor, the door closes, you get going, and you don't stop. In '79 for that sort of *volado* you had to have blood colder than an iguana's.

"Who's with you?" Big League asks me.

"Pancho and Richard."

"Better still. I need three for another *volado*."

"But we're about to leave for Nicaragua. Right now."

"What are you going to do in Nicaragua?"

"The revolution triumphed, my brother!"

"What kind of shit is that!" Big League began his attack. "You guys just show up for the party, right? The revolution's over in Nicaragua. Here is where it's got to be made now."

"But our movie..."

"What movie? The real movie is right here, right now, in El Salvador. You've got to watch the fruit mature to enjoy it when it's ripe."

What else could I say? He convinced me. That pee changed the course of my life. All three of us, because Big League took the whole group. We stayed on in El Salvador another two weeks. And then another two. We went to Nicaragua, not to make movies, but to make contacts. We returned to San Salvador. We filmed demonstrations. We filmed bodies. We filmed takeovers of churches and embassies. We put out a magazine. We set up a photography project and an archive. We founded the COMIN, the International Information Command. We helped lay the foundations for the big offensive that was coming.

Announcer Wanted

One day Commander Ana Guadalupe[10] called us in and said: "Look, we're going to start a radio station. A guerrilla radio station. We have the equipment, but no staff. Which of you three does announcing?"

Pancho, Richard and I eyed each other, trying to pass the buck. We had a radio programme in Venezuela called "Chaos on the Air". But what she was proposing was evidently something quite different.

"You, Hernán?" Ana Guadalupe says to me sweetly.

"I'm a filmmaker," I protest.

"Well, get busy because you have to get this project moving. And there isn't much time. So start hunting — find someone."

We were in Managua. I went home to the house of the woman who was my girlfriend at the time. She worked in popular education putting on puppet shows. When I told her about it, she said, "There's a great programme on the *Voice of Nicaragua*. It's got a strange announcer. I'd swear he was Venezuelan."

"Another Venezuelan? Aren't there enough of us already!"

"I bet he is, but I can't quite place his accent. His name is Santiago and he's got a good voice, good tone, good..."

"Good balls is what he'll need if he's going to the front lines!"

Since we were nuts, we just called up Santiago and went to speak to him. He was Venezuelan all right, from Mérida, but he was in love with Nicaragua, had been since the earthquake when he went to help out with disaster relief. Then he left, came back, and when the revolution triumphed, he stayed to work. Santiago is a radio man. A handyman who can do everything, which is what he does best. We liked him so much that after a few words we started spinning the same web that Big League spun for us: "What are you doing here? It's all over here. Let's go to El Salvador, that's where the shit's flying.

***

One day Richard, one of the Venezuelans, shows up with my book *The Clandestine Jails*[11] and says: "Sign it."

"Who is it for?" I ask.

"We found an announcer for the station. Someone called Santiago."

Delighted, I took the book and wrote something like: "We're waiting for you. Drop what you're doing and come with us." Richard said that this little touch would ripen the fruit. He sent it right over to the Atlantic Coast where Santiago was helping set up a repeating station for the *Voice of Nicaragua*. I don't know if he read much of the book, or just the note I wrote, because he was back in Managua in one bounce.

"The man's here," they told me. "You've got to talk to him."

I had an appointment with a group of Germans from the West German solidarity committee in the same place and at the same time they were going to firm it up with Santiago. So my *compañero* Chico[12] saw him.

"Well?"

"This is just what I've wanted to do my whole life!" Santiago shouts with his usual enthusiasm. "A guerrilla radio station! When does it go on air?"

"Yesterday," Chico tells him.

"Okay, give me a week and I'll get out of all my commitments here."

But the funny part is how Santiago viewed us. He'd already met the three Venezuelans, but no one from the FMLN. He says that when he first walked in, he saw a woman — that was me — with a group of white guys counting dollars. That was the Germans who'd brought a big donation from their solidarity campaign "Arms for El Salvador". Then they sent him into a little room and in a minute a kid in blue jeans and sneakers walked in and introduced himself as "Comandante Chico". All Santiago could think was: "If this guy's a commander... Well, he must be."

I think we had to tear out part of Santiago's heart and mend it with another. Because he was really hot on Nicaragua, in love with his work and with Sandino. It was like one revolution stealing the boyfriend of another.

***

And he stayed. His vow to work with us was, as they say, sworn on a dozen Bibles. He accepted, got it together, and within a week he was in San Salvador — and from San Salvador on to Morazán. He's been there for ten years and he's still just as dedicated, crazy and passionate about the station as he was on the day we met.

Crossing the Torola River

From Santiago's "Travel Notes":

At customs, after a few questions about the motives of my trip, I get by without any problems using the false passport. Two *compañeros* take me to the capital. Down the highway we see a group of parked cars. At one side a group of women are crying beside the body of a young man whose arms have been torn off. On his breast there is a sign:

Killed for being a subversive.

Death Squad

At noon we arrive at the safe-house in San Salvador, where Commanders Clelia[13] and Mariana are meeting with the heads of the commando units and militia that will take part in the nationwide general offensive the FMLN is planning. After the meeting, they go over the plans for setting up the radio station. The transmitter has already been sent to the north-east region.

Clelia explains: "The biggest problem for the station will be its military defence. The country doesn't have big mountain ranges where we could hide a radio station. There are towns with army detachments all over the place; the territory is criss-crossed by highways and roads. So the grassroots character of the struggle will have to provide security. The people will be for the station what the mountains are for the guerrillas."

When the meeting is over, Clelia and Mariana serve everyone *tamales*; it's Christmas eve. I tell Clelia how much she looks like Commander Luisa.

"Of course, we're twin sisters."

The next day, we head off with two *compañeros*, Alí and Gustavo. We pass the fortifications of the US embassy just as a caravan of armoured cars is entering.

"That's Napoleón Duarte going in there, the president of the Christian Democratic military junta."

Later on we make contact with another of our travel companions. He's a Belgian priest who has lived in El Salvador for many years, Father Rogelio Ponseele. Until today he has been the parish priest of Zacamil and other poor *barrios* of the capital, but he can no longer stay there. The death squads are after him. Several bombs have been placed in the parish house. Some eleven priests, one bishop and dozens of catechists have been murdered. Rogelio doesn't consider leaving the country. Today he begins a new stage in his life, carrying out his pastoral work in the zones controlled by the guerrillas.

When we go through the poor *barrios* of San Salvador, we see groups of soldiers and policemen doing house-to-house searches. Several people are beaten with rifle butts and put in the backs of military trucks. They all have their hands tied behind them at the thumbs.

"Tomorrow they'll turn up tortured and murdered on some beach or in a garbage dump," Rogelio comments. "Today in one spot alone they found 14 decapitated bodies. They want to use terror to stop the rebellion."

We continue the trip past volcanoes and flat valleys, great extensions of coffee groves, and then cotton fields. Most of the country's arable land is controlled by a handful of rich families. When we reach the city of San Miguel, Manlio Armijo (a.k.a. "Juan") is waiting for us. He's one of the supply chiefs for the guerrillas in the eastern zone.

"We sent the radio transmitter to Morazán on December 17!" he tells us.

In neighbouring houses twinkling coloured lights illuminate Nativity scenes. Down the street a group of elderly women dressed in black and carrying candles accompany two caskets to the cemetery. Two boys murdered by the death squads. Soldiers from the Third Brigade leave the barracks each night dressed as civilians, in search of their victims.

At this time of night the highway is deserted. Near Santa Rosa de Lima, Manlio slows down and pulls over to the side of the road. His headlights shine on a child sitting on a rock.

"Hey kid! Climb aboard!" Manlio shouts.

"I can't, I'm waiting for my grandma."

"Jesus, you stupid ape, don't you recognise me?"

"Oh! I didn't recognise the car, I thought you were soldiers!"

The boy picks up a full branch of bananas and jumps into the back of the pickup.

"The security squad is waiting," he tells us. "Let's go!"

A shadow jumps into the middle of the road. It's a boy, practically a child, holding a rifle. He makes signs. His name is Patango and he's part of the unit of nine *compañeros* who will take us to the camps. One of them gives me a Browning pistol and some bullets. He offers another gun to the priest.

"No thanks, *compa*," Rogelio says. "I don't need it."

From nearby houses we hear loud barking. Each of us picks up our backpack and Manlio gives us a hug good-bye.

"Santiago, we'll see you after the triumph. You know we'll be listening to you on the radio. Give my best to the *compas* in Morazán!"

We begin a long march. It will take two days to reach La Guacamaya. The moon hasn't risen and we have to walk in the dark, feeling our way down the path, tripping and getting scratched by thorns. Because of the army's proximity, we can't use flashlights. After three hours of climbing up and down, we stop at a peasant's house. The entire family gets up to offer us bread and coffee, while the grandfather gives us information on the movements of the soldiers.

When dawn is near we reach Hechoandrajos, the first camp. We rest all day and when the sun sets we begin climbing the mountains of Ocotepeque. We walk without stopping and at four in the morning, sore and exhausted, we reach the banks of the Torola River. We take shelter from the cold in a small house and, without waking the inhabitants, we spread a plastic sheet out next to the embers of the fire and fall into a deep sleep. When we awake it's daytime and a young peasant woman is making coffee. Unperturbed, she steps carefully over the three strangers she found sleeping in the middle of her small hut. To the first *compañero* who wakes, she hands a gourd of steaming coffee and a *tortilla* with salt.

"Boys, all I can offer you is a few *tortillas* because we've run out of beans."

We cross the Torola. From here on it's guerrilla territory. Farther on we pass empty schools, houses and mills, abandoned two months ago when the army launched a big operation. Thousands of *campesinos* fled from their villages. Some sought protection in the guerrilla camps, where they were put to work at different tasks; others sought refuge in Honduras.

Several hours farther on we reach the Sapo River, where we bathe and then, refreshed and energised, we climb a rocky cliff on the way up to La Guacamaya. Another hour and we arrive at the camps. The broad flat field which houses the command centre is buzzing with activity: fighters come and go carrying messages; in the kitchen *tortillas* are being patted out and beans stirred in their pots.

"Welcome brothers," Commander Galia[14] greets us. "Put down your backpacks, you're just in time for coffee."

"Put more *tortillas* on to toast!" someone shouts.

A *compañero* comes out of the house and smiles as he stretches out his hand to the newcomers. It's Joaquín Villalobos, "Atilio", one of the five members of the FMLN General Command.

10 January 1981

The Viking had gone to Morazán in October. But as I found out from Payín Perica later on, in Hechoandrajos they had to pack it up again as soon as it arrived because a military operation had been launched in the entire region. The *compas* called it the "October invasion". For several interminable days they had to carry the transmitter everywhere.

To make matters worse, the two boys Apolonio trained in his apartment in San Salvador, who were to bring the instruction manual, were told not to carry any paper with them because it was dangerous. Nothing written. Naturally, by the time both they and the Viking arrived in La Guacamaya, they'd forgot everything they'd learned. Luckily, Santiago joined us around then, and since his dad had been a ham operator, he knew something about radios. Or at least he said he did.

***

Of course, the problem was that Santiago, who was so enthusiastic about the whole idea, told Chico he could do anything, so Chico told him to travel at once because at that very moment they needed a technician to get the station on air. When he got to Morazán, they handed it over to him: "Here is the equipment."

Santiago: "But, I'm not an engineer... I don't know much about this. What I know about is how to talk."

"To talk!" they said, "We've got plenty of big mouths here! Well, look brother, even though you don't know how to, just do it. That radio has to be broadcasting on 12 January, understand?"

***

So Santiago started hanging the aerial from the trees, trying to calibrate the equipment, trying to get some sound out of it, but it just wouldn't work. One day went by, then another, the date set for the FMLN's general offensive was approaching fast and the Viking wouldn't say Boo.

"Hurry up, pal. That has to be running for the twelfth!"

Santiago was so anxious that he blew all the spare fuses. The equipment went on and off, it gave off more sparks than the fireworks at a fiesta. But not a sound. *¡Puta!* is what you'd hear more than anything else during the last days of December. The station was really small — just a transmitter, a little Honda generator (untested because the gasoline we needed to try it out hadn't arrived), a pocket tape recorder, and a cassette by the Chilean folk group Quilapayún. That was everything, but to get it to work without the manual was a bitch.

We also didn't have a name for the station. It hadn't been baptised. Late New Year's Eve, Atilio and a group of others sat down to eat *tamales* and solve the world's problems.

"So what's it going to be called?" one asked.

"The Mute," another joked, "because that piece of junk won't make a sound."

"Freedom..."

"Liberation..."

"The voice of the people..."

"It's got to be a verb," Atilio insisted.

"What do you mean a verb?"

"An action word, for struggle. What do we want?"

"To win," said one.

"Then We *Shall* Win!" said Atilio, "That's it: *Radio Venceremos*."

The name fitted just right because besides its meaning it was one of the songs we had on our one and only cassette:

> *Venceremos, venceremos*
> *mil cadenas habrá que romper...*[15]

So we'd killed two birds with one stone, the name and the theme song. Everything was ready, except that the transmitter wouldn't transmit...

***

Others would have given up but Santiago kept at it, absorbed by the task. The commanders were deep into planning the offensive to begin on the twelfth, when suddenly they heard a scream.

"It's working!" whooped Santiago and Walter and everyone. "The needles are moving! It's modulating!"

They ran to find a receiver, tuned it in, and sure enough, there it was on air, the first song broadcast on Radio Venceremos. With his characteristic stubbornness, Santiago had managed to make the transmitter work. He did it because he had to. That happened, if I remember correctly, on New Year's Day, 1981.

The signal was very weak, I don't know if it even reached the Torola River, five kilometres away. It almost seemed like a toy. But we were broadcasting! We started doing tests and you could hear Santiago talking; he'd put on some music; he'd adjust it here and there. We seemed to have it. Everything was set, except for the incredible noise the generator made. To quiet it down, Santiago decided to dig a hole for it, like a foxhole. Two hours later it overheated and burned out.

"Is it ruined?" came the worried question from the recently euphoric crew.

"It's ruined," Santiago confessed.

"So now what do we do?"

"Now we're fucked but good."

***

It was a race against the clock. It went on air on the first of January, and burned out on the second. Since we had barely ten days left, we sent an urgent message to San Salvador and on the ninth Mauricio the technician showed up. He arrived like one of the three kings, carrying a new generator. It was smaller than the one that burned out, but it worked well. He also brought tools, spare parts and, best of all, he brought along the instruction manual we had so often dreamed of, which the ever-cautious Apolonio had taken the trouble to photocopy.

I'm talking about the ninth. The offensive was supposed to begin on the twelfth, but there were last minute changes. Early that Saturday, the tenth, Jonás turned up at the camp. He came to Morazán to take charge of our Francisco Sánchez Northeast Front. And he brought the news that the offensive would be moved up.

"It's today," Jonás said. "This afternoon the attacks will begin all over the country. Venceremos' first broadcast has to be today."

***

The news gave everyone a burst of energy. Orders, munitions, grenades, cables, contact bombs, maize and beans, boots and medicine, all started flying. There wasn't time to design the first programme, we had to improvise. The first priority was to make aerials for military communications, to guarantee a link between the commanders and the columns which that very night would march off to attack the base at San Francisco Gotera. Hurriedly, we drew up a code for communications, and readied the walkie-talkies needed for coordination in combat. At dusk, the sound of orders being given could be heard all over the camps. In orderly formation the squadrons began to march off, rifles across their chests, with the conviction of those who go to war to win. They would learn to fight by fighting. Near the Sapo River we heard the final chant: "For those who have no bread, no shoes, we promise to win!"

***

That night after nine o'clock, we turned on the generator Mauricio had brought, revved up the Viking, plugged in the microphone, and made our debut on air with these words:

Brothers of El Salvador and the world: At this moment Radio Venceremos, the voice of the FMLN, begins broadcasting from somewhere in El Salvador to accompany the Salvadoran people step by step in their march towards final victory over centuries of oppression.

Right then, hundreds and thousands were fighting throughout the country: in the streets of the capital, in Chalatenango, in San Vicente, in Usulután, Cuscatlán, La Paz, San Miguel, Cabañas... Barricades were going up, the army was being ambushed, roads were blockaded. In Santa Ana, a group of patriotic officers took control of the Second Infantry Brigade headquarters and joined the offensive.

Salvadorans, patriots, revolutionaries, lay and religious, civilian and military: the duty and privilege of achieving the liberation of our country has fallen to us. The days and hours to come will be decisive. We must harvest the fruit of the seeds sown by our fallen brothers during fifty years of struggle. We carry on our shoulders a great responsibility. The future of our country depends on the discipline, skill, decisiveness, and heroism with which we carry out this great popular insurrection and offensive. The great battle beginning at this very moment will continue until total victory is achieved. We have a message for the soldiers and troops fighting on the side of the enemy: Does it make sense to sacrifice yourselves and die for a cause that is not your own but that of a handful of rich men? The new society will guarantee a place for you. Abandon your posts. Don't kill your brothers. Join the struggle of the people. Don't fight against history. Ours is not a struggle for vengeance or reprisal. It is a struggle to achieve true peace, justice and liberty. Our forces fight to build and not to destroy. Close ranks everyone and fight, until we win or until we die!

Commander Joaquín Villalobos,
Message on Radio Venceremos, 10 January, 1981

Atilio finished talking and Rogelio began. From that day, 10 January, from the very first programme on Venceremos, there has been no conflict between Christianity and revolution.

A people tired of so much suffering has decided to rise up in arms to win its freedom. The members of this popular army are mostly Christians who have come to the defence of a people trapped in an unparalleled Calvary. Violence is legitimate when it is used to defend an entire people. Brothers, the people are right.

Father Rogelio Ponseele,
Message on Radio Venceremos, January 10, 1981

The Chickenshit Journalist

On 9 January, just before the offensive, I took the afternoon flight from Managua to San Salvador. As a journalist, I was supposed to cover the events of the 10th and the 11th in the capital, and from there go up to Morazán, to the command centre, to take video footage of the Northeast Front's military actions.

After I left the airport, I stopped at the intersection past La Libertad where you pick up the highway for San Salvador. There's a gas station there where boys sell fish. I bought a big red-mouthed porgy to eat with my friends on the propaganda team, Skinny Gustavo and the German guy Paolo. I'd also brought along a couple of bottles of rum. We deserve a nice going-away party before going off to war, I thought.

My contact was Pepa, one of the people in charge of propaganda. At ten in the morning she came and told me: "You're going right to Morazán. Don't do anything here in the capital. Tomorrow I'll let you know if they'll meet you in Santa Rosa de Lima or in Las Minas or somewhere else, and what your password will be, but get everything ready for tomorrow."

Nelson Arriete, another Venezuelan who worked in the organisation, was driving Pepa around in our infamous filmmakers' mini-van. When Nelson was about to leave, I told him to come back later on. I'd cook up the fish and we could give ourselves a send-off. I was going to Morazán and who knows when the hell we would see each other again. I was feeling sentimental, you know?

That's what we did. The shit started at five in the afternoon, and there we were taking it easy, licking our lips over the porgy and getting shitfaced on Nicaraguan rum.

At dawn on the 11th, Nelson and I were inside the safe-house listening to gun battles in the street. Pepa hadn't come. That had us really worried, but all we could do was wait. Finally, at about seven that night, the telephone rang: "Is Nelson there?" said a soft voice on the other end of the line.

That was strange, very strange, because nobody knew Nelson was there. When you conspire, secrets are your best friends. Something had gone wrong.

"It's for you," I said.

"For me?" answered Nelson suspiciously, as he took the phone.

"The *cuilios* showed up where Pepa was," the voice on the phone said. "Don't go there."

We called up a *compa* in Mexico and asked him to call that number and make sure. A few minutes later, he called us back to say that a child answered. For sure something had gone wrong.

Later on we found out that in that house they had captured Commander Clelia, Pepa and Mateo, the head of communications, who talked and gave names. My video archive was stored in that house, and they found it. Our legal status as "Venezuelan journalists" was over.

We spent the night of the 11th on tenterhooks, waiting like idiots for the police to kick down the door. To go into the street would have been ridiculous because it was a battlefield. If you weren't going out to fight, you had no business being there. No cars went by, no one went out, there was nothing but danger.

That night went by and nothing happened. At six in the morning, when the curfew was lifted, we decided to leave for Morazán. We didn't have a contact, but we figured we could work things out along the way. Paolo, Skinny Gustavo and I took off. Nelson didn't want to go.

In San Vicente, the FPL[16] had set up the strangest barricade I'd ever seen. Two kilometres of cars! One after another after another, all parked right up against each other across the road like cobblestones, an impenetrable wall.

"Stop your car there," the *compa* told me.

"We're going to Morazán," I told him. "We're from the press."

"Well, the press only gets this far," he pointed towards my place in the barricade. "Why do you want to go to Morazán, my friend? If you want to see the war, it's right here."

Which was just what I wanted, to be where the guns were thundering. To film the war. Morazán or San Vicente, it was all the same to me.

"You head on back," I said to Gustavo and Paolo. "I'm staying here."

"What do you mean here?" they exploded. "These guys are from the FPL!"

"So?"

"We're from the ERP!"[17]

After two hours of spewing sectarian spittle, one of those chance things happened and a guy came up to say hello. He was an officer.

"How are you? How are things going?"

"Badly. You won't let us through."

"Say 'we'. We're all the same, the FMLN."

"Well if that's how it is, then give us a chance. I've got a movie camera and I have to get to Morazán."

He gave the order. And in a Herculean effort they moved the cars, one by one, while I drove down the gutter, scraping along, until we got to the other side. By then it was four in the afternoon.

Barely a kilometre beyond the guerrilla barricade was a military checkpoint.

"How did you get by?" a *cuilio* asked us.

"I'm a journalist, understand? The press!"

"But nobody goes through here..."

"So tell me, what are you doing here?" I was getting more and more obnoxious. "The guerrillas are right over there! And here you are shooting the breeze! It's hard to believe! Excuse me!"

That's how we got to Santa Rosa de Lima. The streets of the town were silent, desolate. Several bodies were lined up in front of the local military command, on the porch. On another corner, we saw the bodies of another four *compañeros*. In all that incredible silence, we drove up the road to Las Minas. I knew my way around those parts somewhat, I'd been there before. But now we'd lost our contact and our way. We stopped the car at a fork, and while we were discussing what to do, a group of guerrillas surrounded us. We identified ourselves and everyone started smiling. Adán, the officer in charge of the zone, was there and explained what happened. They attacked Santa Rosa at six in the morning, but failed to take it. They'd been infiltrated and the enemy knew all about their plans. They fought well anyhow, and even drove the soldiers back to the command post, but they had to retreat and they lost a lot of people. By chance again, the rendezvous point was right there, where we had stopped.

We began the retreat towards Hechoandrajos and reached the village as it was getting dark. While I rested, I turned on my seven-band radio and looked for the news.

Two Venezuelans, collaborators of the ERP, have been captured. Journalists Nelson Arriete and Hernán Vera...

"Do you know them, *compa*?" they asked.

"Of course. The second one is me."

I started laughing. I was sitting there in the yard of a peasant's house in Morazán, the most secure place in the world. Nelson had indeed been captured and I was worried about him. But being a journalist would protect him. Press is press, no? I also figured they put out the news that way so I would come out to deny it. And then they could grab me. But I was happy to be in Morazán, finally in the guerrilla camps I had so often dreamed of.

Man, I was euphoric and I wanted to talk! The problem was that in Morazán the *campesinos* go to bed with the sun. At seven or seven-thirty, everyone is asleep. But I stayed up talking with one and then another. They gave me a *nailon* to sleep on. That's the guerrilla's bed, a sheet of plastic your size. You use your backpack for a pillow, pull out your blanket, and you're ready. Everyone sleeps right up against one another. Body heat is worth a lot, and no one sleeps alone; you look for company, for proximity to others. But what I wanted was to talk, so I kept up my chitter-chatter. By midnight only the sentry was awake.

"Look, I'm not supposed to talk," he said to me in a low voice. "Don't you people sleep in the city?"

Left without a choice, I had to go to bed. I went out to the yard, one of those yards that are so common in peasant houses around here, round with a stone wall. I looked at the pile of *compañeros* sleeping under the dew, the entire yard filled with people and blankets. In the moonlight I managed to spot a free space waiting for me in the middle of the yard. These *compas* really are considerate, I thought. These are the things we in the city have to learn, hospitality, the small details, a willingness to think of others. These people don't even know me and they saved me a place. Or perhaps it's because I'm a journalist... I took out my blanket, stretched out my plastic sheet and lay down. I was exhausted after all the day's excitement and marching.

When I awoke, everyone was already up. I opened my ears first, and heard everyone laughing at me. When I got up, I saw I was covered in chickenshit, shat on all over. That spot hadn't been left for me or for the press. It was right below the tree where the chickens roosted.

A War on Adjectives

On 14 January, at about six in the afternoon, I arrived at La Guacamaya. I found Santiago and it was an emotional encounter, bear hugs. Santiago thought I'd landed in jail; he'd heard it on the news.

"So you've finally shown up, numbskull! You've got to help me."

"Oh no. I make movies and don't forget it. You take care of the radio, and I'll take care of my films."

"But Hernán, look..."

"We'll talk later. Show me around. Introduce me to the *compas.*"

The place was called La Parra de Bambú. It was at a crossroads in the village of La Guacamaya, where there was a little house like all the peasant houses of the region, with a tile roof, clay walls and dirt floor. The name came from the leafy vines that grew on one side. In the back, in the yard, they showed me our three bomb shelters. The shelters are like little tunnels, deep ditches about three metres long, covered with logs and a mound of dirt. At each end there's an entrance. In case of aerial attack or mortar shelling, that's where we save our skins.

Near the house, at the top of a small hill, they'd set up another shelter for the transmitter. We broadcast the programmes from there. The shelter was just big enough for the little table that held the Viking and another for the announcer and the few gadgets we had then. A cable ran from there to the street, about twenty metres away, where we had the generator. There I said hello to Mauricio the technician, who was trying to rebuild the generator Santiago burned out by mistake. I also met Evelin, his *compa*, who ran the front's internal communications network, called the "orange radio", which at the time was quite rudimentary. I greeted Walter, Commander Walter, and his 14 men whose mission was to protect the station: Ismael, Servando, Isra, Somoza... They introduced me to Julito Perica, Payín Perica, Chepito Perica, Minchito Perica, all brothers and all members of the Venceremos security squad.

"And now", Santiago laughed, "I'll introduce you to the staff: me."

Santiago was the announcer, script-writer, engineer, everything. Because the other *compañeros* were busy with the offensive, with the attacks. In those early days, Venceremos was Santiago.

"And what do we do tomorrow?" I asked.

"Tomorrow we go to mass."

It was the first time I'd ever been to mass. In my whole life I'd never gone to church. I knew nothing at all about liberation theology. I'd never heard a priest talk like those who preached at the funeral of Monsignor Romero or that of the leaders of the FDR.[18] Before those funerals, talk of God and revolution didn't impress me, it bothered me. The mixture, like rice and mangoes, challenged my way of thinking. I couldn't absorb it so quickly. But neither could I deny what I was seeing and hearing.

Now here I was in a guerrilla camp, and Father Rogelio Ponseele was celebrating an open-air mass for all the people: the *campesinos*, the combatants, Jonás. Felipe and his friends, who had yet to adopt the name "Los Torogoces", sang the "Peasant Mass". Santiago recorded it all for the radio, and I, with my video equipment, happily sought out the best shots. For the very first time I saw a classic guerrilla with a beret, a string bag, and a FAL on his back, taking communion. It was...truly marvellous.

After mass, I was still euphoric. Jonás called me over. For sure it had to be to congratulate me on my good video work, I thought.

"Pack that shit up," he said. "Give it to Walter and he'll bury it."

"What?"

"Those cameras weigh a ton and the army's on the way. We're going to have some fighting here for sure."

"But the video project..."

"What comes first, comes first, brother. And what comes first is the war."

"But what about me? What do I do?"

"For the time being, you help Santiago on the radio."

That was the end of my career as a filmmaker. It lasted one day. And the next day I started working with Santiago on Venceremos. Torturing myself with Santiago, to be more precise.

"Write a commentary, a rousing one," Santiago told me.

I picked up my sheet of paper and pencil, sat under a tree and started writing, pondering the state of the offensive, exalting the bravery of our men, their incredible fighting capacity, their extraordinary audacity, their fantastic discipline... When I finished, I gave it to Santiago. He read it, crumpled it up and threw it on the ground.

"That's a piece of shit. Start again."

"A piece of shit?" I asked, holding myself back.

"That's right. A shit sandwich."

"Why is it no good, if I might ask?"

"It's no good because it's no good. You've got nothing but adjectives and you don't say anything concrete. That's political doubletalk. Nothing but hot air. Do you know what everyone's calling you in the camp?"

"What?" I asked, about to blow.

"'Marvel'. Because they show you the kitchen and you say it's marvellous. They show you the river and it's a marvel. They give you some soup and it tastes marvellous. Marvel is all you ever say."

"Who gave me that name?"

"Jonás, your marvellous commander. And now, you're going to rewrite your marvellous commentary, and make war on all those adjectives, *hombre*."

My work! My ideas! My intellect crumpled up and thrown on the ground! Four years studying in England and this countryman of mine, who thinks he's the fucking Queen of Sheba, tells me I'm nobody! This went on for a long time: I'd write and Santiago would crumple it up. I'd rewrite and Santiago would take a red pencil to it, zip, zip, zip, of fifty lines only ten would make it through.

"What I crossed out is no good. Do it without adjectives."

Later on, twenty would get through. Then more. Little by little, it sunk in, and Marvel ended up winning that endless battle with his way of thinking.

The First Guerrilla Sugar Mill

A little bit beyond the clinic, near Red Point, which is where we had the command post, we built a mill for grinding sugar cane. We did it during that same month of January, practically in the midst of the offensive. It was an incredible effort on Jonás's part.

Jonás was always first, and I'm not kidding. He was always ahead of the rest. The first to get up, the first to run outside, the first to bathe. He was also the first to hear of any news.

"Did you hear what the VOA[19] said?"

"No, I don't listen to gringo stations."

"You've got to listen to the VOA, sonofabitch! If you don't know the enemy, how are you going to beat him?"

Now he had the idea of a sugar mill stuck between his eyebrows. "We've got to grind our own sugar! If we can't be self-sufficient, how are we going to run this war?"

That was his thing, and he kept on insisting until they got hold of the metal piece, the great big one that turns and grinds. They made the pegs out of wood, brought oxen and built the whole mill. Don Arquímedes was put in charge of the business. And Jonás asked Venceremos to broadcast the inauguration of the first guerrilla sugar mill, live and direct.

***

In the command post, long meetings were held to evaluate the offensive. Evidently, the genocide in the cities had traumatised the masses, worn them down and demobilised them. The expected insurrection did not materialise. However, the 10 January offensive was seen as a necessary step in consolidating the rearguard and building a popular army within those zones. Now the task was to resist, to grow and to advance.

In the United States, Ronald Reagan, who had just become president, threatened to turn his war machine against the continent's liberation movements.

***

The inauguration was set for 27 February. That was some party! No one would have guessed we were at war! We didn't want to use animals for the first batch. We turned it ourselves, crushing the first sugar canes in our mill. The ceremony began with applause, gunshots in the air, words of commitment from Don Arquímedes, and an enthusiastic speech from Jonás: "This mill will provide the calories for our guerrilla fighters!"

***

Did we lose? Did we win? Our view of the offensive left no room for defeat. For us it was about moving from an insurrectional moment to a war. It was intended to establish the rearguard for the war. Relatively few left for the fronts from that astounding movement that brought 300,000 people into the streets of San Salvador in 1980. What the offensive did was to rouse the countryside. People who to that day had worked clandestinely or semi-clandestinely came out, took up arms and made it their career. They joined the guerrilla war.

Although we didn't take power, the offensive was victorious. Or rather, it was strategic. It allowed us to make the leap from insurrection to war. From small groups of urban guerrillas, we formed a popular army, harvesting the fruits of incredible organising work in the countryside, and embracing the enormous task of arming the people right under the army's nose. We managed to consolidate our rearguard, and that allowed us to wage war.

***

We all worked hard turning the new mill around and around. The screeching of steel, the chants, great shouts of joy all went out over the air on Venceremos. Soon the cane juice began to flow and everyone got a taste of our first batch. Once the juice was boiled in big pots and we began producing brown sugar and molasses, we'd be economically self-sufficient. That was Jonás's idea: each pound of sugar we didn't have to buy would be money saved for other things. Revolutionary war costs money, arms are expensive, and *colones* don't grow on trees. Moreover, every turn of that mill was putting people to work, relieving the unemployment of so many landless peasants.

Rather than saying we made a mistake in gauging the willingness of the people to rise up on 10 January, I'd say we made a mistake not having done it a few months earlier. If we had done it a few months before, if we had resolved the problems that held back our unification, we'd have taken power. But the offensive, although late, was extremely important in terms of maintaining the viability of a revolutionary alternative.

Commander Joaquín Villalobos
July 1989

If you can make one you can make a hundred, so the idea caught on. In the villages, at the fronts, people seized on the idea, and dozens of sugar mills began appearing all over Morazán.

Footnotes

[1] Commander Jorge Meléndez, head of the Francisco Sánchez Eastern Front and member of the political commission of the Party of the Salvadoran Revolution (PRS).

[2] Oscar Arnulfo Romero was archbishop of San Salvador from 1977 until his assassination in 1980.

[3] Commander Ana Sonia Medina, member of the PRS political commission.

[4] YSAX, known as AX.

[5] Monsignor Gregorio Rosa Chávez, auxiliary bishop of San Salvador, and currently chief of the Department of Social Communications of the Latin American Episcopal Conference (DECOS-CELAM).

[6] Lempa River Hydroelectric Commission.

[7] Marianella García-Villas, president of the Human Rights Commission of El Salvador, murdered by the death squads on 14 March 1983.

[8] On 18 February, 1980, the White Warrior's Union (UGB) of then Captain Roberto D'Aubuisson dynamited Monsignor Romero's radio station. On 23 March, YSAX was on the air again, thanks to spontaneous donations. That was the Sunday that the Monsignor called on soldiers to disobey orders. The following day, 24 March, the military high command announced that the archbishop had placed himself outside the law. That afternoon, while he celebrated mass in the chapel of a cancer ward, where he had a room, Oscar Arnulfo Romero was assassinated with a bullet in the heart.

[9] Douglas Bravo was leader of the Party of the Venezuelan Revolution (PRV) which waged a guerrilla struggle in the 1960s.

[10] Ana Guadalupe Martínez, a.k.a. Commander María, a member of the political commission of the PRS and the political-diplomatic commission of the FMLN.

[11] In *The Clandestine Jails*, Commander Ana Guadalupe Martínez narrates the tortures and humiliations she suffered as a prisoner of the National Guard in San Salvador in 1976.

[12] Commander Claudio Rabindranath Armijo, member of the political commission of the PRS and of the general staff of the Modesto Ramírez Central Front.

[13] Lilian Mercedes Letona, who was later freed and then died on a special mission in September 1983.

[14] Sonia Aguiñada, member of the PRS central committee.

[15] 'a thousand chains must be broken'.

[16] Popular Liberation Forces, one of the five organisations that make up the Farabundo Martí Liberation Front (FMLN).

[17] People's Revolutionary Army, another of the five FMLN member organisations and principal sponsor of Radio Venceremos.

[18] Democratic Revolutionary Front, a coalition of centre-left organisations. On November 27, 1980, the members of the FDR's executive committee were kidnapped from the legal aid office of the archbishopric of San Salvador by members of the National Police and the army. They were: Enrique Alvarez Córdoba, president of the FDR; Juan Chacón of the BPR; Enrique Barrera of the MNR, Manuel Franco of the UDN; Humberto Mendoza of the MPL; and Doroteo Hernández of the MERS. In the early morning of the next day, near Ilopango, their bodies were found strangled with barbed wire, having been tortured and shot many times with military calibre bullets.

[19] The Voice of America, the US government radio station.

Section II
Building the Rearguard

Another Fifty Knee-Bends

We'd get up at five in the morning, when the stars were still out, and we'd start training: running, running, running... On the first day, those of us on the Venceremos staff were told we weren't a combat unit. We only had to know enough to defend ourselves. The station's security squad was made up of real fighters, but those of us who worked in production and on the air just had to be fit enough to march so we could avoid the battles.

Jonás ran the training programme. Jonás is a man of war. He aimed to harden us and build a team. Nearly all of us were city kids and he had to bring us together, to mould us, almost like kneading bread, and make us into a single body. On every march we chanted: "We're a single man, we're a single arm, a single head, a single leg..."

He'd say, for example: "Let's run over to that fence." If we all ran and one got there first and the rest afterwards, the one who made a mistake, the dunce, was the one who ran ahead. Because the goal was to get there all at the same time. If we all ran and one fell behind for whatever reason, the one who failed, who didn't fulfil his mission, was the entire group that had gone ahead. Because no one can be left behind. That was the idea. It turned out to be exhausting.

"Halt!" Jonás yelled. "Are you tired?"

"Nooooooo!" everyone answered.

"Yup," said a low voice.

"Halt!" bellowed Jonás. "Who said he's tired?"

"Me," I said.

"Fifty knee-bends, everyone."

And down we went, squatting, standing, squatting, standing... three, four... eleven, twelve... thirty-three, thirty-four... forty-eight, forty-nine... fifty.

"Halt!" screamed Jonás. "Are you tired?"

"Nooooooo!" everyone groaned.

"Perfect. Then let's go on. Let's run twenty times around the camp. Let's go, double time! One, two, three, four... One, two, three, four... One, two, three, four."

And there you'd see us, like mules at a sugar mill, going round and round. Jonás ought to be more considerate, I thought. We've come from the asphalt and the buses, we're not used to this.

"Halt!" Jonás again. "Are you tired?"

"Noooooo!" everyone again.

"How many more times can you do it?"

"Twenty!" screamed Santiago at the top of his lungs.

"No, *hombre*, how can we do twenty?" I was about to pass out, soaked in sweat down to my tail.

"Halt! Who said no?"

"I did, *comandante*," I confessed.

"How many more can you do?"

"More? One more...if I really try."

"One? Really?" Jonás' eyes bored into me, he looked like a wild animal. "Fifty more knee-bends!"

"All of us?" Santiago asked.

"All of you!" Jonás yelled.

Everyone gave me the dirtiest look you could imagine. And the story started all over again, squatting, standing, squatting, standing, squatting, standing... thirty... forty... fifty.

"And now, are you tired?"

"Noooooo!"

"So, how many more times around the camp?"

"Twenty!" Santiago wheezed.

"Demagogue!" I whispered.

"Halt!" Jonás' eyes gave off sparks. "Who said that?"

"I said that...that I can't take another knee-bend or another knee in the pants! I came here to do radio!"

"You came here to make the revolution," Jonás cut me off. "Listen and listen sharp, you sons of corncobs, what do you think, that war is a piece of cake? War is war! I know you come from the city, that you're not in shape... Well you can get in shape. Another twenty times around the camp!"

And that's how it went: Whoever didn't want any soup, got his bowl filled to the brim. And the next day, the same thing. Then the even numbers had to carry the odds. Ready? You've got to be ready to carry the wounded. But when the evens carry the odds and your partner turns out to be, for example, Father Rogelio who weighs 220 pounds. Imagine carrying that big white guy piggyback! And there was no let-up with the running, the push-ups, the sit-ups, the knee-bends... In ten days my legs were like steel. I could run in the dark. My ankles were incredibly strong.

It wasn't easy for those of us from the city to keep up with the *campesinos* of Morazán, weather-beaten fighters who knew how to do everything. Isra was one of those men, one of the special ones. After a training session, Isra would say: "Excuse me, *comandante*, I'm going to look for a *garrobo*."[1]

"How long?" Jonás would ask.

"Half an hour."

And half an hour later, there was Isra with a great big *garrobo*. He knew everything about the countryside and the mountains. One day he asked me: "Would you like to eat rabbit?"

"But isn't it against the rules to use up bullets?"

"Come on!"

It was about twelve noon. We walked some twenty minutes from the camp until we came to a little hill in a cactus field.

"Don't make any noise," he whispered. "Here it is."

I watched that tall, strong man turn into a cat and sneak ahead without moving a leaf. He approached a little cave, stuck in his hand, and bingo! He had a rabbit by the ears. Without a shot, not even a stone. Nothing. He simply observed the habits of that rabbit and knew where the animal took its nap.

One day I said to myself: Shit, I'd like to bring something to the kitchen, a rabbit, a *garrobo*, something. Food. I see Isra and I feel a mixture of admiration and envy. Any day at any time, winter or summer, night or day, Isra turns up with his FAL and his backpack always dirty from working, always sweaty. You'd never see him when he'd leave, only when he'd come back, always when he'd come back.

"Cook this," and he'd let an armadillo, an agouti, or a big green *garrobo* fall on the table.

It can't be so hard to catch a *garrobo*, I thought. What's wrong with me? I see them sunning themselves. Why don't I try? I've got to do something about this or I'll be useless forever. One morning after the jogs and the knee-bends, I casually asked Isra: "Where do you go to hunt *garrobos*, *compa*?"

"Are you going to hunt *garrobos*?"

"Yeah."

"You won't get lost? Do you want me to go with you?"

"No. I want to do it myself. Just tell me more or less where."

"Well, from that stream you go down..."

I went. I went and I came back. A whole morning and nothing. All afternoon and still nothing. One day nothing and the next even less. Could all the *garrobos* in the world have already been eaten?

"Didn't you catch anything?" Isra asked, poking fun.

"Nope. I didn't find anything."

"Listen, do you know what *garrobos* eat?"

"What they eat? Well...no."

"How the hell do you think you're going to find them then? First find out what they eat, *hombre*, and where those fruit grow. Then you just sit there waiting. Or do you think they're going to fall on your head and you just have to grab them by the tail? No, pal, that isn't how it works. So you don't know what *garrobos* eat and you want to eat them! By the way, do you know where they sun themselves?"

As Isra spoke I started relating everything to the pile of shit I'd studied in high school: reptiles' cold blood, the warm blood of mammals. Isra knew nothing about cold or hot, but he knew which season the *garrobos* spend in the sun and which one they spend in their caves. Which fruit they eat and where they find it all year round. Which fruit they like more, and that it's in season only in April and May. From Isra I learned the basics of culture: how to relate to the world. Isra trained me to live.

War Correspondent in Meanguera

Santiago was the anchor and I was the roving correspondent. Santiago would stay in the camp at Punto Rojo, and I'd go along with the combatants as a reporter. The first time I recorded a battle was when we attacked the little town of Meanguera, which, like most towns in Morazán, was occupied by the army. Memo[2], one of my heroes, was in charge of the operation. Second in command was Pedro, another great fighter. I carried a microcassette recorder and several of those tiny cassettes that look like toys, and a pistol in my belt.

We approached Meanguera in absolute silence. I remember hearing the horn of the early morning bus warning the last passengers to hurry up. We waited until the bus pulled out.

"At this very moment we are advancing on Meanguera," I started recording my live report. "Today is March 2nd, it's five in the morning and it's barely..."

"Shhhh! Shut up!" a *compa* hissed. "You're going to give us away."

"At this very moment the *compañeros* ask for silence, because we are only a few metres from..."

"Shut your trap, idiot!"

But I was there as a journalist. Santiago, my teacher, had given me great advice: Remember that you are the eyes of those who are going to listen to the show. Describe everything you see.

As soon as the bus left, five of our men launched the assault. The idea was to attack the main trench across from the corner of the schoolyard where we were hiding. But the day before, the *cuilios* had dug another little trench in the middle of the road. And when our men jumped to attack the main one, they fell into the one we didn't know about. The soldiers there threw a fragmentation grenade at them. Boom!

I didn't know about this, so I carried on with my reporting full of enthusiasm: "Our forces have captured the main trench and are advancing on the town of Meanguera. You can hear the explosions..."

Then I saw Pedro, the second in command, running the wrong way, with his back and his pants all bloody, pierced by shrapnel. And behind him came Memo, carrying someone seriously wounded. And over there lay another, already dead. The explosion I heard was the *cuilios'* grenade, and it destroyed our assault. It also destroyed my morale, because this was my first time on a battlefield.

"Who's unarmed?" Memo asks urgently.

"Me," a *compita* says and Memo gives him a FAL.

"You, what have you got?" he asks me.

"I've got a pistol."

"Take this," and he gives me the RPG-2 the wounded man was carrying.

When I found myself holding that huge rocket-launcher, the one they call the "Chinese club", I froze. The only thing I knew about RPG-2s was what happened in the camp a week before. A *compa* was cleaning one, stupidly having left the grenade inside. He wiped it with a cloth and it went off. We were at the station about 100 metres away when we heard the boom. We threw ourselves on the ground. The alarm went out. Any explosion in the camp means an attack. A minute later the security squad came by like souls fleeing from the devil, carrying the wounded *compa*. His feet, his legs, even his chest were burned to a crisp. It went off so close that it was the gases that killed him. That's what came to mind when Memo handed me the rocket-launcher.

"But I'm here as a reporter, you know..."

"Take it."

I turned off the tape recorder and started thinking: Is the safety on? Does it even have a safety? I can't touch this beast, it's going to go off. Where do the gases come out? Why do they give this to me? I was panic-stricken. I hadn't a bitch of an idea how that club worked. Fuck the club, and fuck the Chinaman who invented it! I put the recorder in my pack and, what else was I to do? I picked up the RPG-2. Memo went on ahead and was lost from sight. In the blink of an eye he was back at our post.

"We have to counterattack," Memo orders. "Who has the RPG-2?"

"I do, but..."

"And what about the grenades?"

"I've got them," says Sandra, a 14-year-old kid.

"You and you, follow me."

Memo is a tiger. A big man, muscular, he jumps over walls, crawls under fences, shoots his machine gun, grabs an RPG-2 and fires. And Sandra, a girl from Morazán who has been a guerrilla all her life, who attacks as well at night as during the day because she can see in the dark. She leapt after Memo like a hare. And I brought up the rear: what an unequal trio.

"Sandra," I say to her, "do you know where the safety is on this thing?"

"Shut up. Don't be such a wimp."

So I just listened to their directions, their orders amid the clatter of gunfire. Follow, climb up, squat down, come on, hurry up, jump, crawl...

When at last we got to the right position near the barracks, Memo tells me: "Give me the RPG-2."

He takes it, sits down, and turns to me: "Jesus! You could've killed me! This shit doesn't have the safety on. And you running up and down with it! You like to take risks!"

"No, really, I..."

"Wise up, Marvel!"

Well, Memo took that rocket-launcher, aimed carefully and bang! The big papaya landed right inside the barracks. He handed me the club, now unloaded. That was a different story, right? I slung it over my shoulder, happy as could be, took out my tape recorder and started reporting again.

"At this very moment the planes are flying over us, but they aren't shooting..."

Back then planes were sent more for psychological effect, and to coordinate the reinforcements that were being rushed over. We'd managed to surround the troops in the local command centre. And with contact bombs we were making them shit in their pants. I remember one *compa* who tossed those bombs so easily, as if they were ripe guavas: boom! boom!

Memo came back to where Sandra and I were crouching. A medic had taken out another of our wounded and his FAL was free.

"You don't have a gun?" Memo realises.

"This pistol."

"What are you going to do with that toy? I can't carry two rifles, so take the FAL."

"Why don't you leave me the medic's carbine instead?"

Memo must have seen my face, because he let me keep the little carbine. That was something at least.

"Stand there," Memo orders me.

He put Sandra about fifty metres away, and a third *compa* beyond her. We were at the edge of a little cemetery.

"For sure their reinforcements are going to come from this side. You cover the road. When the *cuilios* show up start shooting to let us know. Nobody runs from here, understand?"

Memo takes off and Sandra tells me again that I can't run away, that I mustn't be a wimp. What could I do? I covered the road. If they shoot me, I've got the cemetery right here. I took up my post, got my carbine ready. And since my job was to wait, I pulled out the recorder and continued reporting. You could hear gunfire close by. But you could also hear birds singing.

What I'm going to tell you is silly, but at that moment what had me worried was that the recording wasn't going to seem real because of the birds. You see, birds don't stop singing even in the middle of the biggest gun-battles. It was stupid, since no one could ever distinguish that little sound on our crummy short-wave radio. But the tweeting really pissed me off, because they would think the report was faked, that it didn't take place right at the scene. I started listening to the recording with the earphone. Can you hear the birds? Yup, the sound was so sharp you could distinguish it perfectly. Dammit! Who's going to believe that this tape with bird-effects was recorded in the middle of explosions and gunfire? No producer in the world would think to put bird song in the background of a battle scene.

There I was, lost in these idiotic thoughts, when... snap, crack, I hear sounds behind me. Next to the cemetery there was a cornfield with the stalks dried and bent over. I turned slowly around. More steps and a shape moving. This wasn't in the script, they're coming up behind me. But such is the luck of a loser, he even trips over his ass. I tried to calm myself and suddenly I remembered to take the safety off the carbine. With the trauma of the RPG-2 I'd kept it on. Some sentry I was with my gun jammed!

It was obvious they were approaching from behind. I thought: For the first time in my life I'm going to kill someone. Or he'll kill me. In a metaphysical split-second, it all crossed my mind: to kill or not to kill, life and death, being or not being. The only thing for sure, I thought, is that if I keep on thinking like this they're going to bust my ass. I look at Sandra and see that she's like me, on full alert. I hear the noise again. I can see something crawling towards me. I've got it in my sights. Your time's up, sonofabitch. I hope Sandra doesn't shoot first because I couldn't stand the embarrassment. If I don't come through, they're going to make fun of me for the rest of the war. And I'm about to pull the trigger when out comes this black pig, dark like charcoal, biggest I've ever seen! I've never told anybody about that before. Especially Sandra.

That was my first time in combat and my first experience as a war correspondent. When the micro-cassette was full a messenger carried it to the station. It had to arrive before six o'clock to get on the programme. So I explained this to the boy and told him: "Give it to Santiago." And that kid took off like a bullet, with unbelievable speed, running across the bush, working out his route by eye — what in Morazán they call "in direction". In the direction of that guava tree you see there. I don't see anything, just a sea of green. There where that vine is, you see? All branches look alike to me. But our messengers always made it to La Guacamaya incredibly fast to deliver cassettes to the station. And there would be Santiago, happily putting the story on air.

The mobile unit of Radio Venceremos, as always, is on the front lines, accompanying our people at war. Today we broadcast the assault on Meanguera!

That time in Meanguera we weren't able to take the barracks. And look how the world works: it was because we didn't have a radio. At our command post, Jonás was listening to the enemy communications. He had a PATROL radio, the commercial ones that have a police band. Jonás had one, but Memo didn't. And there was no way to get the information back to Memo. So Jonás, about three hours away from Meanguera, was listening to the sergeant in the barracks under siege:

"If in five minutes the reinforcements aren't here, I'm going to surrender. I've got eight men dead, I don't know how many wounded, I've got no munitions, they're coming at us from all sides..."

"Hang in there," his commanding officer ordered, "the reinforcements are on the way!"

"No!" the sergeant whined. "You want me to die here like a pig!"

Memo, foreseeing that reinforcements were on the way, decided to retreat when the fall of the base was a question of minutes. If he'd had the report of the demoralisation of the troops inside, all he would have had to do was drop an RPG-2 on them and that would have done it. But in the early days we didn't have radio communications. We were still learning. To do radio and to make war.

Surround and Destroy

In March, barely two months after we went on air, the army ran out of patience and launched an unusually large operation in Morazán. Their objective was to destroy the command post and the station. They knew perfectly well that Radio Venceremos was in La Guacamaya. They didn't have to figure it out, the station was public knowledge; you could walk right by it at the crossroads of Parra de Bambú.

"Hello, Doña Tencha," we'd call out from the house. "How's the family, the kids?"

Everyone knew where we had set up the station. Of course in that village every last person was part of the organisation. There were no informers.

"Look, *muchachos,*" a visiting neighbour told us, "here are some *tamales* for you so you can talk pretty. Your programme is lovely. We always listen. Hey, send me best wishes tomorrow. It's my birthday!"

At first, everything was small and homemade. Even though we had bomb shelters, we often recorded outside. We cut some branches for shade, brought out the table, several stools. By that time we were doing two additional broadcasts — with a lot of the same material, of course — in the morning and at noon. But the programme that was fresh, our prime time, our infallible commitment, was every day at six in the afternoon.

Jonás set that goal. At six o'clock, rain, thunder or mortar-fire, the show had to go on. At six o'clock, Santiago had his mouth ready, Marvel had his report written, Apolonio had the equipment working, Walter had the whole security squad on alert.

The enemy's goal was to annihilate us. They deployed several battalions to surround our camp at La Guacamaya. It was no joke. They sent 1,600 troops in a pincer movement which moved closer every day. Counting all of those who had guns, we didn't even number 150. What's more, those 150 fighters had to protect the command post, the station, the internal communications operation, the clinic with the wounded... it was like a giant fighting a dwarf. Even so, the commanders decided to resist, to defend the strategic rearguard at all cost. Riding on this, to a great degree, was the future of the war — and of the station.

They closed in. Only the Sapo River lay between them and us. We were within a FAL's range, about 500 metres, so close that the *cuilios* could easily hear the Venceremos generator. At quarter to six — vrooooooom, to make matters worse the muffler was broken — we'd turn it on and the soldiers would start cursing. We could hear them.

"They turned that shit on again, didn't they? Now we'll teach them!"

And mortar-fire would begin to rain down. Thirty, forty, fifty shots one after another. Once we counted 132.

"Maybe that'll shut you up, sons of bitches!"

Our response was Santiago's defiant voice, at six on the dot:

This is Radio Venceremos, the official voice of the FMLN, transmitting its signal of freedom from Morazán, El Salvador, territory in combat against oppression and imperialism...

Santiago and I buried ourselves in the bomb shelter and, incredible as it seems, we did the broadcasts live, while the shit fell all around us. The programme was live every day with natural sound effects, because even though the mortar blasts didn't break the logs of our shelter, they filtered through on air. Since the *cuilios* monitored our station, we gave them the pleasure of listening to the blasts they hoped would destroy us.

A lot of noise and not much progress. The pincer movement was bogged down. Days went by and the line of fire didn't move a millimetre. It seemed impossible to defend so much terrain with so few men. Our flank, for example, barely had eight *compas* to defend it. Only eight, and they kept a whole troop of soldiers at bay! No one could get through. The *compas* stood firm, in the trenches day and night. There they ate, they slept, they shat; no one moved from there. The women in the kitchen brought them their pile of *tortillas*, beans, rice. It looked like a movie: our *compas* blasting away with their guns up front, and us blasting away with our tongues at the back, doing radio under flying bullets.

Sometimes I'd go up to the line of fire to do some reporting.

"What's up, *compañeros*? How's it going?"

"Great," they'd say, "if they dare to cross we'll kick the shit out of them! Tell the *cuilios* that over the radio!"

I'd record short interviews and head right back to the shelter, dodging mortar shells and bullets, to put them on air. Of course, broadcasting right under the enemy's nose was key to keeping up morale among our troops. And it was very demoralising for the enemy, since they were using up tons of munitions and getting nowhere.

That's what we were doing when one afternoon, at about four o'clock, Chepito Perica stuck his head into the shelter. He was the cook and he looked terrified; his eyes like two fried eggs.

"The *cuilios* are right here!" he says, his voice a thread.

"Of course," say Santiago and I, "they've been here for days."

"They broke through! They're inside!"

"Look Chepito, we're in the middle of recording something right now. It's four o'clock and we're not done. Don't bother us. Go tell Walter about it."

"Do you want to see them?" the man insists.

I stick my head above ground, and sure enough the suckers are right nearby, on a hill inside the camp. They'd broken through our line of defence!

"Santiago, the *cuilios*!" I whisper.

Santiago sticks his head out and sees the column of soldiers approaching through the thicket.

"We've got to save the station!"

The station, all of it, fit into a suitcase. We packed up the equipment without a sound and slipped out to the crossroads. Santiago ran to tell Walter, the head of security.

"The *cuilios* are here!" he wakes Walter up.

"Don't make jokes, I haven't shut my eyes in four nights."

Walter slept inside a wall. He'd dug a cave and filled it with straw, like a manger for baby Jesus. He slept there with his *compañera* Mabel, who got killed later on.

"If you don't get up, I'll take your gun," Santiago tells him and grabs the gun.

At that Walter leaps out of his manger like a cat, jumps into his boots and in a second he has three men with him preparing a new defence.

"You, to the clinic," he tells us. "Watch over the equipment there."

On the way to the clinic, we ran into Jonás. He'd already sensed the danger by listening to the enemy communications. He'd caught a powerful signal close by and figured they had penetrated the area. It was actually only a few soldiers who had been ordered to explore the river and had got lost. Somehow they ended up in our camp. They had to run like turkeys, because we tried out our new homemade mortar on them. The first blast, because it was the first, landed I don't know how many metres from where they had stumbled in. But when the *cuilios* felt us stepping on their tails, they knew it wasn't friendly fire. They left in a hurry. That made Jonás mad: we had them in our hands and they got away. Despite the fright, we went back to our work and, disciplined as we were, we finished getting the programme ready. At six o'clock we were broadcasting the news of the flight of the intruders.

That very day we moved from Parra de Bambú to the clinic. The bomb shelter there was larger and more secure. Since the shelling didn't let up, we spent all day underground, like armadillos. Santiago set up his hammock inside the shelter and wouldn't get out of it. We could no longer broadcast live, so we recorded the show on cassette. We put on music, we made announcements, everything was fine up to that point. The problem came later, when we had to take the tape over to Parra, where we left the Viking, our transmitter, underground. Every afternoon we'd play Russian roulette. Who would take the cassette? Who would run those interminable hundred metres between our shelter and the transmitter? Every day at quarter to six, as dusk closed in, we'd say good-bye forever.

"It's your turn today, Marvel," Santiago would tell me.

I went on even days, Santiago on odd ones. We might have last-minute problems with the programme, even though it was recorded, or we might have to read some urgent news over the air. Apolonio, the technician who had joined us and who performed daily miracles to keep the equipment running, kept us company. Someone from the security squad also came along. We went out with our heads down, in silence, each one praying to his own saint. He who lives in fear of death dies a thousand times, I'd repeat to myself. But that didn't do anything for the chill up my spine.

When we reached the generator, the moment of truth would arrive. Apolonio would yank on the cord, that beast would start burning diesel, and the three of us would race to the bomb shelter. Because as soon as the *cuilios* heard the put-put-put of the generator, they'd start swearing and shelling us. But by then we'd have the cassette set up and once again Radio Venceremos was filling the airwaves throughout Morazán.

We set the generating plant up at the edge of the main road where lots of people went by. During the battle we dug a hole in the embankment and stuck it inside. We kept the transmitter, the Viking, in a good shelter. But we had to leave the aerial outside, right? So we tied long ropes to the ends. When we wanted to broadcast, we tossed the ropes over notches high in some evergreen oaks to make a pulley, and we raised the aerial up. After the programme, we let it down and laid it on the ground. That hid things a bit. El Mozote was quite close by, and from the heights of El Mozote you could see the aerial.

They tore it to hell, anyway, up or down. Since it was a big aerial, about twenty metres long, the mortar fragments kept breaking it. There were so many explosions, they even broke the coaxial cable that connected the aerial to the equipment.

"Apolonio! Get over here and tie some knots!" Santiago would shout to me.

When the fire would let up, I'd peek out, run over, tie up the broken pieces of aerial without soldering them, just a little knot, because what counted was to get back on the air. After the programme, I'd do proper repairs.

***

24 March 1981: Still surrounded by the army, we marked the first anniversary of the assassination of Monsignor Romero. Father Rogelio planned a big mass in the village of El Mozote, about thirty minutes by foot from La Guacamaya. My job was to record the mass and then run back as fast as I could to broadcast it at six o'clock. Since the enemy knew all about the event, that day they went to town with mortar fire. Did they think they could kill the memory of the Monsignor? They bombed us too. It was the first time that a Fuga Magister plane attacked the camp. We lost two *compañeros* who had just come from San Salvador and were training for the special forces. The bomb fell right in their trench, and we couldn't find any trace of them. They got pulverised.

In the midst of that violent bombardment, we set off for El Mozote. I remember Rogelio, that big man, so red and so tall, stumbling over furrows, surrounded by a large group of gun-toting guerrillas. They took us to the church where another crowd awaited us. The whole town was there, so many they spilled out the doors. I stayed outside for a while, bought cigarettes, interviewed some peasants, and then went in. I will never forget that church doorway, its arch of greenery and the little well-trimmed pine hedge in front. And that crowd of civilians and guerrillas asking Jesus Christ to take the side of the oppressed, their side. At the back, behind an altar filled with flowers and lit by candles, was Father Rogelio. He wore a white alb and a red stole. I don't know if he was thinking of the Monsignor's blood when he got dressed. It also looked like the FMLN flag, red with a white star.

***

What was our relationship like with the priests, with the Popular Church? Good from before the beginning. Because Carmelo, Whitey César, Rafael Arce Zablah, the most brilliant thinker the organisation ever had... all of them were students of Father Miguel Ventura. I don't believe there is a leading political cadre in Morazán who did not enter this struggle by the door of the Christian base communities. Not one, except maybe Joaquín Villalobos, who joined along with Rafael Arce and belonged to a group of young Christian Democrats.

Did we accept Rogelio? The word "accept" doesn't fit, because that priest was no stranger to the revolution. No one complained about attending the mass or about broadcasting it on Venceremos. Look, on 10 January Joaquín and Rogelio both spoke on the very first programme the station broadcast. Santiago and Rogelio travelled together, arrived the same day in La Guacamaya. Today they are still the closest of friends.

No one has been treated differently because he is a believer. When we began developing political schools, the subject came up. I remember a fierce debate among the commanders about materialism and idealism.

"Cut it out. Here everyone has his own philosophy. The priests have theirs, we have ours. And we all have the same right to express our points of view."

No one ever put a hand over Rogelio's mouth, nor did it ever occur to anyone to do so. Neither has Rogelio ever put his hand over the mouth of a Marxist. What we've done is to sleep, die, fight together. That's what we've lived, it's what's real. The rest hardly matters.

***

I approached the altar to record Rogelio's sermon. He was remembering how Monsignor Romero, the day before he was gunned down in San Salvador, called on the soldiers to disobey their officers when they were sent to kill their own people, their own brothers. The Monsignor had sent a letter to the president of the United States asking him to stop military aid to the Duarte government.

"The ones who killed the Monsignor are the same ones who are bombing us!" Rogelio preached.

As soon as the mass was over we were on our way back to La Guacamaya. I had to get back before six so that thousands of other Christians could join in the commemoration of Saint Romero — as many already called him — over the airwaves. On the way I saw something unbelievable: the fields were burned, reduced to embers. They'd dropped white phosphorus bombs.

At the camp Santiago was anxious to get the programme on the air. He listened to the beginning of the tape and got even more excited because he wanted to accompany it with the sound of bells.

"Without bells it won't sound like a mass!" Santiago was obsessed.

"And how the fuck are we going to make bells if there aren't any?" I asked, disgusted.

I think it was Chepito who found a piece of a 120mm mortar shell in a ditch, a huge piece of twisted steel. We tried banging it with a fork, clang, clang, and it sounded better than the Vatican. That's how we did special effects.

***

That day, 24 March, the bombing started when I was heading down to the clinic. It was twice as bad as usual, because they wanted to ruin the Monsignor Romero anniversary. I took cover behind some rocks nearby. Planes and artillery were dropping tons of bombs, an almost pathological attempt to wipe us out.

When the rain of lead let up, I went over to Parra de Bambú. The aerial was a pile of debris. Shrapnel had broken it into seven pieces. The cable to the transmitter was just as bad. One piece of shrapnel had pierced the generator's gas tank. Another had hit one of the logs of the Viking's shelter. You could see where it hit. In other words, one of the bombs had fallen within ten metres of the station. The whole area was flattened, the trees knocked over, the roof of the house knocked off, in ruins. I set to work tying knots straight away. Since the gas tank was perforated, I filled it only part way, up to the hole. When Marvel got back with the tape of the mass in El Mozote, I had everything ready to go on air.

***

Reckless? I'd say it was more a question of honour. To defend our position at La Guacamaya despite that damned pincer movement was a challenge which we accepted and won. I think in the first days of the war it was those apparently rash things that defeated the enemy. We had an unbending will to win. The will of a mule. That's what kept the enemy from finishing us off. That first year was decisive; they could have killed us all. Not any more. Those were the months in which we established our rearguard and consolidated our strength in order to then go on the offensive.

To hold a mass in El Mozote, or turn on the radio in Parra de Bambú, was a question of combat morale. It was a way to make the army feel that the seventy mortar shells they just sent over weren't worth a piece of cheese, that we didn't give a shit. We'd only shut up if the bomb fell right in our mouths. That determination won us the war, because war is much more than bullets. The victor isn't the one who kills the enemy, nor the one who captures more arms, nor the one who downs more helicopters. The victor is the one who achieves the political objectives which led him to start the war in the first place. And one of our objectives is freedom of religion in El Salvador: words should not get you killed, thinking should not be a crime. Celebrating mass in El Mozote, right in their face, was a taste of victory, like winning ahead of time.

To the Black Road

We wanted to pinch the pincer. The commanders planned a manoeuvre using reinforcements from other fronts to sneak up behind the soldiers who were strangling us at La Guacamaya. They were supposed to be on the way, but they hadn't arrived, so we had to drop that plan and take seriously the saying that when you're surrounded you're as good as buried.

Twenty-one days resisting! We couldn't hold out any longer. Our provisions and munitions were running low; we'd even run out of gasoline for the radio. We had to break the siege and move elsewhere.

"When?" we asked Jonás.

"Get everything ready for tonight."

The idea was to march all night to reach the Black Road, the paved highway that goes up to Perquín and divides Morazán in two. That was the edge of the noose. If we could get across the road before dawn, we'd be home and dry. But to do that, we had to move the command post, the radio station, the clinic with the wounded, the explosives workshop — and all the residents of the area! If the peasants stayed behind, the army would soon be in to massacre them, claiming they were guerrilla supporters.

We had no choice. We packed things up and got people organised. Leoncio Pichinte, the station's political officer, and Walter, the head of security, started giving orders, putting someone in charge of every task.

"What about Pedrito, what will he do?"

Pedrito was a soldier we captured in combat a few days before the siege. He was our first prisoner of war and, since there was no place to put him, they locked him up at Venceremos. The jail was a little house with a guard to keep an eye on Pedrito; they'd just sit around all day and shoot the breeze. One day during the siege, we were in a jam.

"Who's going to take food to the front lines today?"

The women from the kitchen had been told not to do it since the mortar barrages made crawling to the trenches too dangerous.

"I'll go," Pedrito offered.

Walter was uneasy. Would he try to escape? But Pedrito seemed humble enough.

"Don't you try to get away, you hear?" Walter warned him. "If you run, I'll kill you."

"No, *compa*, don't worry. I just want to help out."

That's how Pedrito started, as a food-carrier, and since he did the job okay, now they called on him for the march. He and Isra were the two strongest men in the camp, the best backs.

"You two will carry Venceremos, take turns with the load. Pedrito, you take charge of the transmitter. Isra, you take charge of the transmitter and Pedrito."

We split up the rest of the baggage. Julito Perica carried the archive of cassettes. Santiago and I carried the suitcase with the tape recorder, the mixer and the cables. Apolonio, the aerial. We hid the battery. When we got where we were going — if we got there — we could find another.

The march was set for midnight, twelve sharp. But one *compa*, wounded by a 50-calibre bullet, was getting gangrene in the foot.

"How many hours will we march?" Eduardo the doctor asks.

"All night and part of the morning," Jonás tells him.

"This guy won't make it. He'll die on us."

"Suppose you operate on him now. Will he make it?"

"Maybe."

"How long will it take?"

"Half an hour."

"Do it in fifteen minutes. We can't wait any longer."

Eduardo took the wounded man down into a bomb shelter, and with the last bit of anaesthesia we had left he amputated his foot. They packed him quickly into a hammock and the great caravan set off — a little late.

The night was dark as a raven's wing. In absolute silence, the endless line of people started moving. Hundreds of *campesinos* with their belongings, sacks of corn on their backs, women carrying coffee pots, *comales* for cooking *tortillas*, huge baskets on their heads, old pots and pans, four wounded people in hammocks, dogs, chickens, all sorts of things. The children had to be kept quiet with sheets or breasts. At times you'd hear a cry, and an officer would come running.

"Señora, shut your kid's mouth," he'd whisper. "If not, they'll shut all of ours for us."

Morazán has the rockiest paths in the world. I don't know how God managed to put all the stones left over from creation here. It's no joke. When it's two in the morning on a moonless night and you trip over those boulders, you slip, you stub you toe, another falls on your foot... I hate the stones of Morazán. I lost half my skin on them.

We continued bushwhacking and soon we saw the first of the soldiers' camps. It was on a hill, so close that we could see their lamps and canvas tents. We had to follow a little stream right by them, so close that if the guard sensed our presence and woke up, we'd have a bloodbath. One by one, our hands on the backpack of the person in front, holding our breath, we crept past the *cuilios* and they didn't see us. Later on Rogelio told us that was how the Hebrews marched across the Red Sea to escape from the pharaoh.

We advanced, but slowly. Too slowly, because of the large number of civilians along with us.

"Hurry up, hurry up, hurry up, hurry up..." Jonás repeated the chant in a hushed voice, moving ahead at the edge of the path. Memo passed him in the opposite direction.

"*¡Por la gran puta!* Jonás, we can't go on like this! Daylight will catch us! We've got to tell all these old folks and little kids to step aside so our men and the radio can go first."

"What about the people?" someone asked.

"The lives of these people depends on those of us who carry guns. If the guerrillas don't get across the Black Road, no one will survive, not them nor us."

So they decided to rearrange the column. Instead of everyone marching all mixed together, the civilians would march at the back and we would go on in front. I didn't like it, because it seemed like we were abandoning our people. But we had to make sure we crossed the Black Road. We had to open fire on the enemy, open a hole in the noose, and escape through it whoever could. At the pace we were travelling, they'd kill us all.

At about four-thirty in the morning we reached La Joya, a village near our destination. Our group went on ahead with Jonás and in the faint early light we could make out the *cuilios* guarding the paved road. Their silhouettes could be seen on the banks at the side of the road. The moment had arrived. Our best men leapt out and set up their guns on the shoulders of the road. The shooting began. Pedrito, the ex-soldier, was one of the first to go across. With the Venceremos transmitter on his back, he ran and jumped across to the other side. That day Pedrito won his stripes; from then on no one had to guard him.

Our people started crossing under fire. Rogelio went across like a soul in purgatory. The wounded went across in their hammocks. All of the radio's security squad crossed. I got across. As Santiago crossed, the gunfight worsened. Santiago pulled out his .38 pistol and started shooting too.

"What are you doing?" Jonás swore at him. "What good is that shit? Run and don't look back!"

When a lot of people had got across, the real battle began. Half of us ended up on one side of the road, the other half on the other. We lost two *compas* covering the retreat of the rest. By now it was dawn, and the peasants who hadn't managed to cross, seeing the situation was impossible, dispersed on their own to the nearest villages. There they could hide among the residents. Only a few got captured. From that experience we learned that the best cover for civilians is the people themselves.

In the midst of all the madness, Jonás said "You from Venceremos, get going to Guarumas right away. Look at the time. Do you think you can get everything set up to go on air at six o'clock this afternoon?"

"We'll have to," we told him.

We marched for another two hours and reached the Araute River near the bay they call El Cadejo. There we set up the aerial and placed the Viking in a clearing, without a thought to building any sort of shelter. Since we didn't have a drop of gasoline, we sent Julito Perica to find some in a cache nearby. And at six on the dot — a bitter surprise for General García,[3] who was already announcing our annihilation — Santiago's voice resounded over Morazán.

Welcome, Butterfly

I studied journalism in San Salvador. Or rather, I was a "student of" journalism, because we had so much to do that we never studied. The last thing we attended were classes. My real mission was to do political work at the university, and we managed to build up a sizeable revolutionary presence there. I'm talking about '78, '79, when the 28 February Popular Leagues were founded. There I was, sticking my nose into whatever I could: strikes, occupying churches, occupying embassies... I was always agitating. Ever since I was little I was never ashamed to speak up. Or to shout. My father wanted his daughters to get involved in everything.

In getting involved in everything, I ended up pregnant, so the ERP got me out to Costa Rica, where I worked on solidarity. Even with my big belly I kept on agitating. I had my son and a few days later I began harassing them to let me return to El Salvador. You see, I wanted to follow the struggle from close up.

"Okay, you're going in," Bruno the chief told me.

"To do what?"

"To work on Venceremos, what else?"

I reached the front on 12 March 1981. As I entered the camp I heard a woman's voice.

"Halt!"

I'd never seen a woman guerrilla before and she made quite an impression. I got all excited. She looked beautiful with her uniform and her M-16.

"How was the trip, guys? Come on in!"

The *compa* pointed out the path to Las Trojas where they had a provisional camp. There I met Morena, who later worked at the station too, and a whole bunch of others — most of them later died in combat.

The next day we went down to the river to bathe. I didn't know how to swim and the pool was deep, a big pool with a whirlpool in the middle. So the *compas* tied a rope around my waist and threw me in. When they saw me flailing around, they pulled me out again. Meanwhile, Morena was cooking up *tamales* and we were all getting ready to stuff our faces. That's just what we were doing, happy as clams, when at about ten in the morning we heard gunfire. Everybody scattered. Since I didn't know the terrain and didn't have a gun or anything, they stuck me in a cave near the river. They also put Joel in there, a young doctor who had made the trip with me. We were the two new ones, just arrived, and they gave each of us a grenade.

"Look," Morena tells us, "you're going to stay here until we come to get you. But if the enemy finds you, your mission is to set off these two things and die."

Shit! It's ugly to be sitting in a cave with a grenade in your hand, waiting to blow yourself up along with the first *cuilio* who shows his face, right? But we had no choice. The *compas* didn't have enough guns and we wouldn't have known how to use them. So we sat there. Two hours later, Morena was back, this time laughing herself silly, and she called to us: "Come on, dopeheads, let's finish the *tamales*."

"What about the enemy?"

"We whipped them. We got the commanding officer between the eyes and the rest of them got wounded and fled. We even got their rifles!"

From Las Trojas they called up the *compas* from Venceremos in La Guacamaya.

"Evelin's here," they told them.

"Well, keep her there," they said. "There's no way to get through."

Those were the days of the siege around La Guacamaya, so we waited a week and then marched to Ojo de Agua to greet the *compas* who had just beaten the army by crossing the Black Road. Really young boys were coming in carrying their guns, fresh from a brush with death, telling a thousand stories about the battle. I didn't know anyone and no one introduced me, so I stood there like a store-bought chicken, quiet as could be, next to one of the posts holding up the kitchen roof. More than anything, I watched a girl who was pushing buttons and sending messages by walkie-talkie. It was Leti, one of the first radio operators on the front.

At last someone remembered me.

"The folks from Venceremos are already here. Go with them. They're getting ready to broadcast the programme."

I went to a clearing and there was Santiago installing the little equipment he had: a worn-out tape recorder, a microphone and a few cassettes in an old box.

"Evelin!" Santiago recognised me and went on sticking in cables and setting everything up to go right on air.

I always had my mouth up to a loudspeaker at student demonstrations, but I'd never done real announcing.

"Look," Santiago handed me a paper, "these are the slogans for today."

"What do you mean today?"

"Right now. Stand here next to me."

"What do I do?"

"Shout loud."

Apolonio turned on the equipment, Santiago greeted the audience, and I started shouting like crazy. That's what they'd asked me to do, right? I even raised one foot to wind up and shout even louder. *¡¡¡Rrrevolución o* *muerrrte!!!* That day the programme was shorter, only fifteen minutes, because we didn't have much gasoline. But before it was over, Jonás showed up and kept looking at me with an awful face. Santiago signed off and Jonás asked him: "Who's the girl?"

"Evelin. An announcer."

"A hysteric you mean!"

Jonás stormed off and I stood there, frozen with my foot in the air. That was my debut on Venceremos. Later on I got my feet on the ground, we all became friends, and we didn't have any more disagreements. The only thing was my name. Since there was another Evelin in the camp working in communications, they mixed us up and messages got crossed.

"I'm going to call myself Arlen," I told Santiago.

"It doesn't fit you," he said. "You're like a soul with wings, happy, always singing on any trail. Your name should be Butterfly."

"Fine," I accepted. "I like it."

But Leoncio Pichinte, the head of our collective, didn't. He said it didn't fit with the station's serious image.

"The name doesn't go out on air, *hombre*," said Santiago.

"But word travels on the front and everyone will know. Butterfly! What is this naming yourself after an insect?"

"If you're worried about animals, look at your own name first, Leoncio the lion."

Repeat anything enough and you win. The name got more and more popular among the people, and soon even Pichinte wouldn't call me anything but Butterfly.

The People are our Mountains

The new camp was called Ojo de Agua, a pretty spot at the foot of Cacalote Hill. We had a house and set up the radio equipment on the porch, where it was cool. I remember Santiago searched desperately for a microphone stand and couldn't find anything better than a crucifix from one of the bedrooms. We tied the microphone to it and that's how we broadcast, eyeball to eyeball with a crucifix. It turned out to be so practical that we took it everywhere with us.

Our collective had grown with the arrival of Butterfly. No one could match her for loud and cheerful pandemonium. And no one could figure out how such a little woman had such strong lungs. Without a second thought, and despite certain reservations on Jonás's part, we put her on air. She didn't need much rehearsal. Right away Butterfly became the woman's voice on Venceremos and Santiago's co-anchor. Rafi Rosa also joined up, "the broadcaster who touches the hearts of working women" we called him, kidding him about his seductive voice. He took charge of a segment targeted at the popular movement.

We were growing in numbers and equipment. We got a big new generator that allowed us to boost our signal. No longer were we the crummy little station of the first days; we were putting out 600 or 700 watts. We started hearing from listeners in Honduras and Mexico; we even got an illegible postcard from a Japanese ham radio operator. In those first few months they still hadn't started jamming our signal, so we could be heard clearly all over Central America.

What really took off were the battle fronts. The enemy hadn't killed the dog in time and now it had rabies to deal with. The failure of their pincer movement on La Guacamaya proved our capacity to hold territory. Much of Morazán, where we installed the radio station, was now guerrilla-controlled. Popular power was spreading like wildfire; day by day the military, political and economic structures necessary for large-scale war were being developed.

***

Consolidating the station depended on consolidating the terrain. What is El Salvador? Such a small country, a little thumb; I hiked across it myself twice that year, 1981. From the mountains of Morazán you can see the lights of the capital twinkling. It's a country filled with people, six million in that little plot of land. What does that mean? It means that here you can't even hide your thoughts. In Morazán, if they catch you with a can of gasoline you're dead because they'll assume you're taking fuel to Venceremos. Many anonymous heroes died trying to bring us a gallon of gas. In the same way, if they catch you with an inch of coaxial cable, you can kiss this cruel world good-bye.

So how was it possible, how is it possible, to conceal an entire station in such a small place? It couldn't be done without a very strong political organisation, a lot of grassroots collaboration, and territory broadly controlled by the guerrillas. But not empty territory. We broke completely with the traditional notion that rearguards should be built in unpopulated and isolated zones. Our mountains have been the people themselves. We were born amidst the masses and we continue resisting and winning this war by linking ourselves to the masses. The more population a region has, the more secure we feel there and the stronger we become. That's why speaking of Venceremos as a clandestine station is very relative. We never used that word, we don't like it when friends or enemies label us clandestine. At least, not in the early stages. Later on, when the war got more complicated, things had to become more compartmentalised.

***

Every morning all of us on the Venceremos team would run to El Centro, the spot where we broadcast the first afternoon after breaking free from the army's siege. That's not a place, it's paradise. Green grass, cows grazing, sheep, birds, a crystal-clear river — and us, we'd throw ourselves head first into those pools of transparent water.

"So, what story should we come up with today?"

"Let's go to the dairy farm!"

Tape recorder in hand, we'd head off to one of several dairy farms we ran to supply our field hospital and our camps. We were even making cheese! In Limón, for example, you could see fifty cows and the *compas* peacefully milking them. One day we wanted to do a report on it, but a downpour kept us inside.

"It doesn't matter, I'll be the cow," said Santiago.

"Don't kid around."

"Why not? Let's record it. You'll see, it'll come out just the same: Mooooooo!"

"Then I'm going to be the milkman," said Rafi.

"I'll be the milk," Butterfly stepped in. "Pss, pss, pss..."

Barely able to keep a straight face, we introduced the programme:

Here we are at a revolutionary dairy farm with a special report for all of you...

At the swimming hole we decided on stories and editorials. We thought up so many crazy ideas! Several *compas* would show up all sweaty to tell us about the ambush they had just carried out. We'd say: "Come on and do it again for the radio," and we'd tape the ambush as if it were happening at that very moment, like a live report. The steps, the hushed voices while they were watching the road, the enemy car approaching, the sound of the explosion... It was a docudrama, but acted out by the same people who had been in combat a few moments before. It was real, but with a bit of a timelag.

"Let's interview the people from the military school. What do you think?"

"And how many times have they been on the show already?"

"True, but this time let's have only the women from the school speak. The feminine voices of the war!"

"Great! Let's go."

While the enemy was launching big operations to try to dislodge us from the zone, we were setting up a military school in Agua Blanca, an open field where all the helicopters in the air force could have landed! We visited the school and felt proud to see 25 men and women in perfect formation, presenting arms, singing the national anthem. When they heard themselves afterwards on Venceremos they were as excited as little kids. That school was also a political symbol: our combatants didn't train in Cuba. They trained here, in the territory we controlled.

This was a very creative time; we were always trying out something new. One day we went to the primary school to interview students for the show. Then Santiago had an idea: "Let the kids take the radio by assault!"

That's exactly what they did. That crowd of monkeys burst into the camp all excited. And while Rosita gave them juice and sweet bread, they shouted slogans, sang songs and told riddles. We recorded it all. Later we had the two sharpest ones, two brothers Chiyo and Pajarillo, stay to put the programme together. At six o'clock, Santiago went on air with a note of alarm in his voice:

Attention, listen up, Radio Venceremos is in danger! It's been taken over! In a few moments we will have more on the attack we suffered this morning!

A musical bridge, and Santiago continued, laughing:

And here are the people who took over our station! The children from the Francisco Sánchez Northeast Front Primary School! I'll leave you with your announcers for today, Chiyo and Pajarillo!

That day Santiago and Butterfly didn't broadcast a word. Everything, from the greeting to the sign-off, was done by the children. And you should have heard the ease with which those two kids gave the military and international news, and introduced their schoolmates, telling all about their life in the school!

There was always that two-way street: we'd go to where the people were and we'd bring people to the station. Both ways increased people's participation. "Clandestine" Radio Venceremos attended the inauguration of the health school, did reports on the Nivo explosives factory, broadcast from the cornfields of the militia, took the microphones to the tailor's, the shoemaker's, the potter's workshop, to the new press and propaganda collective. We even did a special programme at the old folks' camp. All the elements of the new society we were building took part, raising their voices on the station that didn't want to speak to the people so much as have the people speak.

Tamales in Villa Rosario

We approached the first positions little by little, silently, without giving ourselves away. It was about four in the morning and you could already see candles in the houses, you could already hear women slapping *tortillas*, the aroma of freshly-made coffee... I had a tape recorder in one hand and a megaphone in the other. I was supposed to report for the radio and call on the soldiers to desert.

Soon after the shit began, the surviving soldiers and paramilitary forces were left holed up in the local military command. Carmelo⁴, our commanding officer, told me to accompany a squadron. They would take me to where I could shout to the *cuilios* to give up and surrender. I was to tell them we'd spare their lives.

I walked behind the squadron. These squadrons are made up of boys with incredible strength and agility and skill. There I was trying to keep up with them. We headed off, circled around the town. Villa El Rosario is very small. It has a plaza in the middle, the church at the centre, the town hall and the military command at one end, and a couple of streets with houses. That's all. Like I said, we skirted around the town because the main unit of *compas* were attacking the enemy's command post from the front. We were to move in from behind, through the backyards to the church, climb up into the belfry and from there shout to the stubborn ones who had not yet surrendered.

The backyards of the houses in Villa were separated by short stone walls with a little corridor in between belonging to no one. My squadron flew over both walls in one jump. Already out of breath, I managed to get one foot up, haul myself up, and climb over to the next wall, but on one of those damn walls I got distracted, slipped, and cracked my right shin so hard my eyes flooded with tears. Fucking rock! I twisted around to rub my leg, threw the megaphone on the ground and started making signs to those ahead of me. But they just waved back: "Come on!" they hissed.

Bathed in cold sweat from the shock of the blow, I decided I didn't give a fuck. I'm sitting down right here. Those Tarzans have to come back and get me, because their orders are to take me along. But no, on they went, cheerful as ever as the bullets flew by.

I was parched from pain, my tongue glued to the roof of my mouth. What a thirst! Since I was in the backyard of a house, I tried to peek in between the planks of the kitchen wall. Through the cracks I managed to spot a jug. Water! At least there was water. I got up, forgetting all about the scrape on my shin, and slipped into the kitchen. I didn't see anyone. With the gunfire, everyone had taken refuge under their beds, there wasn't a civilian around. There I was moving towards that sweating pitcher of water. And there was a dipper beside it, just like it was waiting for me. I drank my glass of cold water. I drank another. When you're with the guerrillas you look at things anew, and you discover what really counts. The pleasure I found in those two glasses of water I couldn't possibly describe to you.

Then, since I've got a golden horseshoe up my ass, I look around and see another large clay bowl, all blackened from the fire and covered with a board. I take off the cover and it's filled to the brim with *tamales*, just off the fire, hot, all piled up, not a single one eaten yet. Then I think of old Federico, my political officer. I remember that I'm supposed to look out for my comrades and make sure they respect private property, the home, the land. I remember, but I stick in my hand and pull out a tamale. I eat it. One is nothing. I sit on the floor and I eat seven *tamales*. Long live the Virgin and her rosary! When I can't find room for another *tamale*, my conscience speaks up. You deadbeat! I get up, put seven more in my pack, and go out into the yard. Now I leap over walls with a decisiveness hitherto unknown. At last I see my squadron coming.

"Yo man!" they say. "Where were you? We thought the enemy had caught you."

"The belfry!" I say. "You haven't taken the belfry yet? Let's go!"

We get to the corner of the church. We have to climb up one of those huge stone buttresses. One of the *compas* scrambles up that bloody belfry in two steps and holds his gun down to help me. Once I'm there among the bells, I turn on the megaphone to exhort them to surrender, and right then, rat-a-tat-tat!, a 50mm machine gun almost slices us to pieces. The *compa* throws himself to the floor, I fall after him on my head, megaphone and all. The *compa* grabs the megaphone and starts shouting: "It's us! You're going to kill us!"

It turns out that the machine gun was ours, set up high on the outskirts of town to keep the enemy at bay. Since the machine-gunner hadn't been told about the belfry action, he thought we were the *cuilios*. He did the right thing, because that was a vital position. In war, there are basic principles, permanent ones: whoever has the heights, has the advantage. Where there is a height, your objective is to take it or keep the enemy from taking it. That belfry was the highest point in Villa.

We climbed down and walked around the town once more trying to get close to the command post from the other side. On the way I gave a *tamale* to each of my seven companions in the squadron. It was a case of being charitable with other people's things, but it eased my conscience. We reached the corner of the little barracks where the soldiers were holed up. I raised the megaphone:

"Soldiers, you're poor too. You're fighting against your own people. It makes no sense to defend the interests of a few colonels who never come to die with you. You're surrounded. Give yourselves up. Your lives will be spared. We have four prisoners already and they aren't complaining. One of them is wounded and he's being taken care of. There's still time soldiers. Surrender before it's too late!"

Some gave themselves up, others refused. So we had to assault the building. I don't remember how many died there. We took a lot of prisoners and several of them ended up joining us. They were part of the civil defence, young boys forced by the local commander to perform guard duty. One night a week, or something like that, they had to patrol with the army. If you don't do it, they say you're a guerrilla sympathiser and that makes your life in the town very difficult. In many cases these civil defence people are really our sympathisers, they give us information: the hour the guard changes, how many guns there are, if you come in tomorrow at such-and-such o'clock I'll be in that trench, from there you can advance to the next... Or from the moment the gun battle begins they start demoralising the rest with "Let's give in," and "They've screwed us now."

The soldiers that are more brainwashed won't surrender. The soldier that has done things against the people, who has committed crimes, fears the vengeance of people who know what he has done, and he won't surrender. Those are hard ones to get out, worse than pulling a tooth.

We took Villa El Rosario. In such cases, the first thing we do is bring everyone out into the plaza. The political officers explain the reasons for our struggle, they dialogue with the people. I was one of them, but while they organised the meeting, I went to find the house of the *tamales*. My conscience was weighing on me. I met the man, woman and children in the doorway. It struck me how clean they all were, the kids' shirts were very clean.

"Excuse me," I say.

"Come in," the man says. "Sit down. Would you like a cup of coffee?"

"Thank you."

"And a few *tamales*?"

"Yes...that is, no. *Tamales* no."

"You don't like them?"

"No...that is, yes. That's precisely what I've come to speak with you about."

"Tell me, tell me."

"Well, look. In the heat of the battle I..." and I told him the story.
"But if you like *tamales* so much," and the man began to wave to other *compas* passing by. "All you boys come into my house and share these among everyone."

This man was an evangelical, the minister of the church. He would not accept any payment for the 14 *tamales* I pinched, and I had gone there to pay for them, you know. I felt remorse, a political remorse. Because if 500 guerrillas did what I did, imagine what that would do to the population, the awful example that would set.

Meanwhile, back in Ojo de Agua, Santiago was dying from dysentery. He was so weak he couldn't get off the latrine. His diarrhoea was so uncontrollable that he shat all over himself in his hammock. During the takeover of Villa, Santiago had to do his announcing lying down, and since he gets excited when he's on air, and when he gets excited he talks loud, every time he raised his voice he lost everything. A shout and a shit, that's how it went, and poor Butterfly at his side, announcing too, didn't have enough hands to hold the microphone and wipe up her co-anchor.

But more than dysentery, what was killing Santiago was envy. I sent him heroic dispatches, interviews with combatants, reports on captured weaponry, revolutionary songs sung by the people...

"Come back Marvel," he told me over the radio itself. "Now it's my turn."

"Don't be crazy, you're sick," I sent word to him by means of a courier. "Besides, you're the star announcer, (this was my best argument), you've got to be there to make sure the show goes on."

So he started working on Jonás, and in the end he got his way. About three days later I got an order from Jonás: "Return urgently. There are to be changes."

When I was about halfway there I met the man, Santiago himself, like Don Quijote de la Mancha mounted on a lame mare and tied to the saddle. Literally tied on.

"Santiago!" I say.

"Shut up you bastard," he answers, and he continues on towards Villa.

I think he got better without any medicine, just from the excitement. In the town they were organising a true people's government. The judge and the mayor had run away, and from among all the residents they named a new local governing council. They did a survey to find out people's needs, then decided to provide hot meals for old folks without family, to have free medical care, collective lands for planting vegetables, corn and beans, even a community newspaper.

Our idea was to stay, the longer the better. It would demoralise the enemy still further after their defeat at La Guacamaya, and it would enable the community to consolidate its structures of production and self-defence. The resistance was fierce, we had to fight off over a thousand troops that pressed us from the south, but days and days went by and they couldn't dislodge us. We took Villa on 16 April and on 1 May we were still there. The Labour Day celebration was really something, and Venceremos broadcast the whole thing. In the plaza, everyone together, civilians and guerrillas, swore in Marcela as the elected mayor of a liberated village. They sang, told jokes, even ate *tamales*, and later in the afternoon, the order was given to pack up and go. The army had begun mortaring the houses and we couldn't fight that, so we had to evacuate the population and let the *cuilios* capture empty terrain. For two weeks in a far corner of Morazán, we had experienced life in a revolutionary society. Tomorrow it would be the whole country, and forever.

Sapodillas[5] for All

We moved to El Zapotal. More than a guerrilla camp, it was an entire village of our own. Over here in a big old hacienda house, we set up the kitchen. Over there in another beautiful house, the transmitter and the workshop. Behind that, the *compas* who worked on press and propaganda. By the main path, in a spotless little white house surrounded by mango, avocado, chirimoya and sapodilla trees, we set up the Venceremos studios and the monitoring room. It couldn't have been better, because, in addition, Santiago and I had both got hold of horses. Everything was peaceful and wonderful.

To make things even better, a few days before, during the resistance in Villa El Rosario, we got some great news: *The General Command has decided that from this day on Radio Venceremos will be the official voice of the Farabundo Martí National Liberation Front.*

"What a responsibility! This shows how much trust the leadership has in our collective."

"But it also shows the need to strengthen it. I mean, ideologically, of course."

"But given the backwardness of people's consciousness..."

And on we went talking hot air. Look, what I like best in life is talking politics, and Santiago, if he doesn't beat me, he's an easy tie. We did a lot of arguing in those days. We argued over everything, down to the last comma of the editorial. We discovered revisionism in every proposal and nonsense in every opinion. That didn't include our own, of course. We argued so long and hard that the sun would go down and we still wouldn't have taped the programme. We'd turn on the equipment at ten o'clock at night, at eleven, at whatever time it was, and we'd keep working amid papers and microphones without ever looking at the clock.

"Don't work so hard, boys," Isra would arrive. "Look, the brain is like a sapodilla. You have to pick it when it's ripe."

Isra, a typical *campesino* who always carried his machete and his gourd, would bring us an exquisite papaya dessert to sweeten our discussions. Another day he'd make us crab chowder, always finger-licking good. But his best dish, the one that would disrupt any recording session, was iguana eggs. When Isra showed up at midnight with a frying pan filled to the brim with fried iguana eggs, prepared according to his simple recipe of oil and salt, I can assure you that no rich man in this world has ever experienced such gastronomic delight.

That's when someone else who loved to gab showed up, Leoncio Pichinte.

"What's up, comrades?"

And he'd launch another great debate until three in the morning on the political moment or on the commentary we ought to give the next day. I suggested we ought to tell the soldiers stories about Vietnam and encourage them to shoot their officers.

"But another goal is to reach the officers," Pichinte would say.

An ethical debate on our politics would ensue. It had a lot to do with the logic of ideology.

"Speaking of consciousness, Pichinte, we've got a lot on our plate now we're the official voice of the FMLN. I'm not one to gossip, but some of the *compañeros* ought to strengthen their class consciousness. We've got to make a qualitative leap."

"Don't confuse lard with butter, Marvel. It's not a leap, it's a process of accumulation."

"Aren't you clever! That depends on..."

We argued with unbridled passion. That was our duty as intellectuals, to debate ideas and broadcast them on the programme, and to help the station collective grow. We spent the entire night debating — or fell asleep in the process.

I remember one morning I left the little house where we slept and nearly tripped over a big ripe sapodilla, split open on the ground. I ate it all up on the spot. When I looked up, I saw that the branches of the tree were filled with more sapodillas than I'd ever dreamed of. I started throwing rocks and more rocks to see if I could stuff myself with at least a couple more. My arm was falling off and I hadn't managed to knock even one down when Isra arrived.

"Boy, you sure like sapodillas."

"That's right. What about you?"

"Who doesn't?" and he sat down to watch me throw a few more stones. "Would you like to eat sapodillas?"

"Of course. Do you think I'm doing target practice?"

"You're not going to eat sapodillas like that. All you're going to do is give yourself a sore arm. Let's bring down the sapodillas!" Isra was getting excited. "Go get a bag, and I'll start climbing."

I went into the house and took from my pack the plastic bag where I kept my notebooks.

"That's the bag?"

"Yeah, what's the matter?"

"I think I've got another," Isra told me and he started back down the tree with all the patience in the world. Off he went and came back with three burlap sacks.

"Take these."

That's when I fell out of the other tree, the ideological one. We were going to harvest sapodillas for the entire camp! With a long pole that peasant started knocking down the fruits that were starting to ripen at the ends of the branches. Thud, thud, thud... When we had about 300 sapodillas...

"The bags are full," I shouted from down below.

Isra came down from that big tree and with that same patience said: "Will you wrap them up, or shall I?"

"No... I think maybe you'd better put them away."

Isra picked up the burlap bags. Then he wrapped the fruits up to ripen so that everyone would have one to eat.

Burned like a Dog

August 10-81

The paved highway swings back and forth between two big hills, Gigante and Pericón, before it reaches Perquín, a small town of cobblestoned streets amid pine forests and rocky cliffs — and home to the National Guard garrison which our forces begin attacking early in the morning as part of a new military campaign. After a few minutes of combat, the soldiers abandon their trenches and take refuge in the little barracks.

11 August 1981

The commander of the garrison under siege calls for air support to cover their retreat. Three Fuga planes start bombing the outskirts of town, but it doesn't ease the pressure from the guerrilla forces. The Army High Command decides to drop bombs on the town itself, one of which falls to one side of the barracks, causing the death of a child and wounding several civilians.

12 August 1981

Taking over Perquín is just part of the plan. The goal is to draw troops towards the north of Morazán and attack them as they are deployed. As expected, the company based in La Guacamaya heads off to help the one in Perquín. It gets wiped out.

14 August 1981

At noon, a column of 200 soldiers led by armoured personnel carriers crosses the bridge over the Torola River and tries to break through our lines. That's where our ambush awaits them and there too, with the combatants, is the mobile unit of Radio Venceremos. Rafi, microphone in hand, is nervous, not because he sees the soldiers and the long snout of the tank's cannon, but because it is his first time reporting.

15 August 1981

After five days the FMLN flag still flies over the villages we've taken. A few kilometres away lies the garrison at Jocoaitique, virtually under siege by our forces. Leading the units in that zone, Walter (José Santos Méndez), the chief of security for Radio Venceremos, falls in combat.

17 August 1981

The station's mobile unit broadcasts the conversation between Joaquín Villalobos and 32 prisoners of war. Joaquín, in the name of the General Command, assures them that their physical and moral integrity will be respected in accordance with the Geneva conventions. The soldiers, convinced by their officers that the guerrillas dismember any who surrender during combat, are surprised at the treatment they receive.

20 August 1981

The FMLN announces that after having held Perquín for ten days and having achieved our political and military objectives, the forces will pull out of the town in order to begin new offensive actions. The count: 83 soldiers killed or wounded, 32 taken prisoner. Among the US materiel captured: 55 rifles, two machine-guns, a military radio, and thousands of rounds of ammunition.

***

The *compas* recovered Walter's body, took it to Perquín and buried him right there in the centre of the plaza. It was a heartfelt ceremony. A lot of the townspeople came because everyone knew Walter and they loved him dearly. Jonás, clearly moved, gave the eulogy for our *compañero* killed in combat.

What did the army do? As soon as they took back Perquín, after a siege of several days, they brought everyone out into the plaza.

"Who was at the funeral of that communist?"

Some remained silent, others used the phrase that's always used to avoid reprisals: "They forced us to be there."

The officer shouted: "I'm the boss in this plaza! Dig it up!"

They dug Walter up and right there, in the plaza of Perquín, they threw gasoline on his body and burned it. That's what the gorillas did.

Sometimes they tell us that on Venceremos we shouldn't use terms like "gorillas" to refer to some army officers, but that description has a real meaning. A gorilla is an officer who doesn't have the two inches of human forehead they need to show that they respect the customs of the people. That if you violate those customs you antagonise the people, and in the end it's counterproductive. How would a peasant from Morazán react if you dug up a human being and burned him as if he were a dog? Communist or not, that is intolerable. Some officers are so filled with hate that they commit acts of stupidity worthy of gorillas.

If the army only knew how many peasants left that macabre ceremony to travel down the back ways that only they know and arrived, angry and pained, at our guerrilla camp to tell us about what the gorillas had just done!

"You should have seen it, what a sorrowful sight! They dug him up! What sort of heart could commit such a crime?"

"Okay, calm down."

"No, it's not that, what we came to ask is, when are you coming back? Because we can't let this pass, *compas*, this is too much."

When a *campesino* says that something's "too much", the straw has already broken the camel's back. He's ready to die and to kill.

"What can I do to help, *compas*?"

From then on, that's a man who is giving to the revolution the only thing he controls: his life. Many joined up after the desecration of Walter's body.

A Rifle's Been Stolen

The commanders called out the entire front for a meeting at the military school. Even the old folks have to be there, they said. Early in the morning, without knowing what for, people started arriving from the hospital, from the sugar mill, from the explosives workshop, from the arms workshop, the medics, the logistics team, the communications team, Los Torogoces musical group, the Radio Venceremos team. A multitude.

Everyone in military formation. Jonás strode up and announced that the commanders, after having evaluated everyone's conduct, wanted to offer public recognition, a homage, to those they considered to be exemplary. They asked Roque of the logistics team to come forward. They asked Alberto, an excellent and selfless doctor, to come forward. Several others were asked including someone from the Venceremos team.

The atmosphere was happy, until Jonás, who knew what was coming, took the floor again.

"But there are also cases of which we should be ashamed," he began earnestly. "Just as we have applauded the exemplary ones, we are going to bring forward those who by their undignified behaviour have tainted the honour of us all. I'm referring to Victorino."

We all turned around to look at him. Victorino was one of the most beloved *compas* among us. He was from the Nivo workshop, a fierce combatant, one of the best explosives experts on the front, a maker of contact bombs, a good friend. Who wouldn't have put their hands in the fire for him? And there he was in front of us all, suffering his greatest humiliation. Jonás told the story:

"We noticed that a carbine was missing. It's not easy for me to tell you this, but we've investigated and Victorino was the one who stole it. We called Victorino, we asked him, he lowered his head, cried, and said yes he had stolen it. We asked him why and he said that he needed the money. He sold a weapon, a rifle! He sold one of the rifles for which Lito[6] died, for which many more in San Salvador died because they didn't get them soon enough. You know that when someone falls in combat, like Walter in Perquín, five or ten spring up saying, 'I'll get them back, the *compa* and the rifle!'

"We feel so angry when we lose a rifle, when the enemy takes it from us! And Victorino sold one! It's not what a rifle costs. It's the people who are behind that rifle. If weapons could be squeezed, ours would sweat the blood of many *compañeros* and *compañeras* who gave their lives for the people. How many of you here don't have a gun because we don't have enough to go around? How many will have to die because they don't even have a pistol with which to defend themselves? And Victorino sold his rifle!

"He told us that his mother was sick and he was desperate to buy her medicine, and that a man from Torola who likes to hunt deer offered him twenty pesos and Victorino didn't think twice before selling him his carbine. Our carbine! Here no weapon is private property. They all belong to everyone!

"Well, that's the problem. The commanders think we ought to punish him, and that the punishment should be severe. That's the opinion of the commanders. We've asked you here to this assembly so you could see someone like Roque, through whose hands thousands of *colones* pass each week to keep the kitchen running, a man who spends four, five days walking, day and night, without a complaint, to make sure we all eat. So you could see him and take heart in his example. And so you could see Victorino, and decide what to do with him. The floor is yours."

What followed was the most horrible, painful, leaden, and prolonged silence I've ever felt. Everyone, every last one, felt like me, like we'd been beaten. Beaten by Victorino's mistake and frightened by what we might decide. If someone raised his hand and said, "We'll have to execute him"... What would happen? But the silence went on, uninterrupted. I looked at Victorino, his chin stuck to his breast, white, pale, like a statue in a town plaza. I watched him and I'm certain that he felt the pain he was inflicting on the hundreds of his comrades standing in front of him.

"Since no one dares to speak," Jonás said, at last, "let's do something. The commanders have had time to reflect on this and it's only fair that you also have time. Take 15 minutes. Break ranks."

Each person sought out his most intimate friend. Santiago and I approached each other: "But that sonofabitch, why did he do that? He had no need to. Why didn't he tell Eduardo? Why didn't he ask any medic for the medicine? Who would have refused him anything for his mother?"

The 15 minutes went by. Attention. Everyone in line. The communications team over here, the logistics team here, the Venceremos team here...

"You've had time to reflect," Jonás says. "The floor is yours."

Again silence. An insufferable silence.

"If you don't dare to decide in a case like this, in which you yourselves are the victims, then we commanders will have to decide for you. The decision has been made and we expect you to embrace it as your own. Victorino, do you have anything to say first?"

Victorino could barely move his head to say no. He was destroyed. He was shame itself in a jar.

"Well," Jonás began, "the commanders' decision is that Victorino couldn't receive a greater punishment than that which he has already received. We believe that if a man has revolutionary qualities, even if he's committed an extremely grave error worthy of the death penalty, that he can make amends. We would rather err in Victorino's favour, because we believe he has those qualities. We give him a vote of confidence. Are you in agreement?"

"Yes!" we all breathed a sigh of relief.

"Revolution or death!"

"Break ranks."

That was the end of the story. Time passed and Victorino grew as a political and military cadre. Today he is a member of the party. He knows how to do everything and he does it well; he even writes poetry. Everything except selling arms. He doesn't even buy fireworks at Christmas. Once you've burned your tongue on hot milk, you even blow on yogurt.

Hiding in the Swamp

The commanders discovered a supposed CIA plot against Venceremos. They warned us the Yankees were planning a night-time commando raid. Was it true?

"A station that's always prepared is worth double," we said. "Let's take precautions."

So they split us up. All of us on the technical side, plus a security squad, went to a secret place known as El Pantano, the swamp. The Viking came with us, along with the aerial and the generator. We left the studios and the monitoring team back in El Zapotal. Neither Santiago nor Marvel nor anyone else who worked on the programme knew where we were hiding. They taped the cassette at night and in the morning one of us went down, picked it up from a little wooden mailbox, returned and at six o'clock we put it on air.

El Pantano belonged to the Perica family: Julito, Minchito, Payín, the most jealous guardians of Venceremos. For greater security, they decided to move the guards farther out, to broaden the defence perimeter. If anyone stumbled through they'd do their best to confuse him: "The path goes right over there, my friend."

"No, *hombre*, I know my way, it's over here."

"But you can't get through here."

No one ever found our hiding place.

Also hiding at El Pantano was Toni, the brother of Marcela, the one who had been elected mayor in Villa El Rosario. Mayor for only a few days, because when the enemy launched a counteroffensive, she decided to join the guerrillas. With her came Toni, her brother, and with Toni came Ricardo, his cousin. With them came Lolita, the one who raised them all. They were a family of farmers.

"So Toni," I ask him, "what can you do?"

"I'm an expert at de-worming cows."

"What else?"

"Medicinal plants. I know them all."

"And?"

"I plant henequen and oranges."

"And?"

"I'm captain of the Villa soccer team."

"Get ready, *compa*, because here we do radio. Are you up for it?"

You didn't have to get Toni excited, he was always ready to learn something new. Since we were under threat of attack from the CIA and all, we decided to give the equipment maximum protection. So we spent several days working with picks and shovels at the bottom of a gully to carve out a niche in the rocks for the Viking. The aerial up above could hardly be seen, because El Pantano is full of vegetation. At one side we set up the generator, a huge motor that weighs a ton. A single man couldn't carry it.

"Let's start with the motor. We've got to learn how to break it down as quickly as possible."

I started explaining to Toni how to take it apart: the rotor here, the stator there, the gas tank, this piece comes off this way, that one like that, each one wrapped up in its own plastic bag... That was it. And we put it back together.

"Now you try Toni."

I timed him. And that peasant who knew nothing about mechanics went at it with wrenches and screwdrivers, repeating everything he'd seen me do.

"Nearly an hour, Toni! Do you think the gringos are going to give us an hour to get under way with all these pieces?"

We put the steel puzzle together again and Toni tried once more.

"Thirty-eight minutes. That's a good time. But it can be done in less."

Since Toni never got tired, I let him work on it: put it together, take it apart, all by himself, timing himself and competing against himself. A few days later he called me: "Come here, Apolonio. Time me."

It looked as if he had been brought up in a garage. The rotor, the stator, the four bags, one in each...

"Fourteen minutes. A Guinness Record!"

Later he trained on the aerial. We'd do attack drills and his task was to bring down the aerial as fast as possible. No monkey could beat Toni climbing up those tall trees to unhook all the wires and cables.

In very short order, the cow specialist had become a radio expert. Toni learned to turn on the equipment, to control the broadcasts, to calibrate the Viking; for him nothing was difficult. I was delighted with the success of my "technology transfer". Richard, Toni's cousin, also learned quickly. Before long he became our point man on the FM signal.

"Now, let that CIA commando come if they like."

But what came was an unusually large army manoeuvre. Once we were all set up at El Pantano, we were called urgently back to El Zapotal. The soup was hot.

Hammer and Anvil

We heard this story about Monterrosa: It seems that at the Army High Command there was a meeting of the US advisers, Defence Minister General García, Vice-Minister Colonel Castillo, and the "gringo's man" Domingo Monterrosa, commander of the Atlacatl special forces battalion. Monterrosa ran the big operation against our guerrilla front on the ground.

"Well, Mingo," they told him, "you've got to make your name with the Atlacatl troops. It's time to wipe out those shit-eaters in Morazán."

"And Venceremos too," they say Monterrosa added. "As long as Venceremos exists, we'll have a scorpion up our ass."

In December 1981 the Salvadoran Army decided to wipe the Northeast Front's command post off the map, and the radio station along with it. From our camp at El Zapotal, we watched more and more helicopters go by on reconnaissance flights. They'd fly from south to north, return from north to south, and do it again. Of course, we had counterintelligence reports and knew what was coming, but we didn't know exactly where the shit would fly, so we used the radio to lay some Vietnamese traps. We broadcast that it was to be a big operation and explained how they could build bamboo traps to impede the enemy's advance.

We set up our defences on the southern flank, but then, according to new reports, we discovered that the helicopters had actually been moving troops and armament to the north, towards our rearguard, to attack us from behind like a hammer. In the south other battalions awaited, like the anvil to crush us. Damn! They were going to attack us from behind and here we were defending ourselves in front. And it wasn't just a couple of cats who were coming. They had concentrated nearly 4,000 troops against us! The panorama was getting very dark.

While we were redeploying our defences towards the north, the enemy was already advancing towards us. We had to stop them — the station's military squad would have to go into combat. It left us unprotected, with only the security squad of the command post, but there was no alternative. We had to start marching, and right away.

"What is the minimum, the absolute minimum, you need to transmit?" Jonás asked. "Take only that."

We hid the big motor, the big amplifier, everything that wasn't absolutely necessary and could be recovered later on.

"You, Pedrito, carry the Viking. This is the heart of the station, so handle with care, eh? You, Toni, carry the little motor. Richard, take care of the aerial. The other things distribute among the rest. Let's go!"

We headed up Pando Hill, trying to escape the big pincer that was closing in on us. The plan was to head up to the north of Morazán so that the operation would close in on nothing, leaving them as we had before to waste their ammunition on ghosts and abandoned trenches. But we moved too slowly, a damned error that cost us dearly, because when we reached the Black Road, it was already getting light.

"There are the *cuilios*! Look!"

There were the soldiers, shaking out their groundsheets, waking up. If we moved forward, we'd be an easy target, but the troops were also behind us. Now what? Jonás didn't hesitate, he gave the order to cross however we could, and we started running, running, running, trying to reach a ravine at the bottom, sticking to the hillside to stay out of their angle of fire. Everything was done in the utmost silence, praying that they wouldn't see us. But it was impossible. When half the column had passed, a tremendous gun battle began. They'd been waiting for us. For the first time, we fell into an ambush of theirs.

They would have made hamburger out of us. We owe our lives to our special forces, the Fourth Section, made up of the ten best fighters, trained by Jonás himself and Manolo.[7] With nothing but their balls to keep them going, they took control of one of the hills and engaged the soldiers on the other height. The rest of our people got across in the shadow of that infernal gunfight. Not all of them — Luisito, a kid, one of our best couriers, caught a bullet in the head and died instantly.

Just when we thought we were out of danger, helicopters attacked us from the air. We ran downhill, we ran uphill... We must have looked like mice in that hellish ravine. I thought: "If I get it today, well, I get it. If my number's up, well, that's it. I couldn't care less if I live or die."

You know, feeling so resigned gave me the courage to keep on running under the bullets. At last we found a natural drainage ditch and jumped in. One by one, waiting for each other, crawling along through tangled brush, moving ahead only when the helicopters were turning, we managed to escape from there without any further casualties. The escape took us the entire morning, but we made it. Then we headed off down another path and started marching. We marched until we were sick of marching, until we reached a well-protected coffee grove.

"Let's rest," Jonás said.

We all threw ourselves down to sleep, absolutely exhausted, but before two hours had passed they woke us up: "Get the column going, here they come again!"

The *cuilios* were right on our heels, so we stood up again, got into our column, a security squad in front, then the Venceremos team, then the communications group, then the command post and another security squad at the back. Everything seemed to be in order when they started shooting at us, sudden fire from close by. We'd fallen into a second ambush. Almost immediately Mauricio came to tell us that three of us had been hit, three wounded right there at the head of the column.

"Who is it?" we asked.

"They're all from Venceremos."

✳✳✳

We were in front and I remember going into a cornfield. There was a clearing there. In those days I wore a white hat and Toni had one like it, but bigger. When I went into the clearing, my first reflex was to squat down and take off my hat. I don't know why, but I wanted to tell Toni to take his hat off too. But right then shots rang out. We threw ourselves on the ground. After the first burst of fire, someone yelled: "Somebody's wounded!"

I raised my head and saw Dina and Evelin, running ahead. I looked back and I saw Toni.

"Who's wounded?" I ask him.

"I am," he says.

At that moment the shooting started again. We couldn't even crawl. When the *compas* answered the fire, I ran down towards a ravine. There I met up with Richard, Toni's cousin, who had banged his knee badly.

"Let's go get Toni," I tell him. "He's wounded."

"No way. I can't walk."

Pedrito was crouched behind a rock, his gun trained on the *cuilios*.

"Pedro, let's go."

"They're going to kill you Apolonio."

"What do you want me to do? I can't leave him there."

So I went back by myself. I crawled to where Toni sat leaning against a bush, with his eyes closed. Bullets were flying.

"Toni," I call him again and he looks up.

"Thanks Apo," he tells me, his voice very weak.

"Let's go."

"I can't..."

"Of course you can, you're strong. Remember how you climbed those trees to bring down the aerial. Let's go!"

On the ground nearby were the backpacks, the motor Toni had been carrying, the Viking, which had rolled off downhill. To tell you the truth, I'd forgotten all about it, about how important the station was. I put one of Toni's arms over my shoulder and tried to make him walk to the ravine. He had a horrible wound in his abdomen, an M-16 tracer bullet had gone through his stomach. After a few metres he started complaining again: "I can't, Apo, leave me here..."

We went under a fence at the edge of a canefield, and I saw Montalbo, the Venceremos logistics chief, walking alone.

"Help me carry Toni," I tell him.

"But I'm wounded too," he says, holding his belly with both hands.

Just then I saw Santiago run by with somebody else. I called to them, they came over, and between the three of us we managed to drag Toni to the edge of the ravine.

"Look, Apo," Santiago says, "the column got split up. We've got to go on."

"You go ahead. I'm staying."

"I'll go find a doctor."

"If he can come, tell him to hurry."

I lay him down, I put something under his head. I told him he was going to live. Toni opened his eyes, saw the red glow of the setting sun for the last time, and died in my arms.

Then I felt completely alone. I could hear gunfire but I couldn't see any *compas*. Montalbo had also died, he was stretched out above me. Javier, one of the security team, too. I panicked and started running down the ravine, following the footprints on the wet rocks.

***

Things got worse. They'd hit us from the front, at the head of the column, and now we started hearing another firefight at the back. We ran down a second ravine, while Sánchez and his squad covered our retreat. Run, run, run. Once we'd got out, the doctor went back to see to the wounded.

"The three are dead," he told Jonás.

"Are you sure?"

"There's nothing to be done."

"We've got to bury them," Jonás said.

"There's no time," Carmelo cut in.

"But..."

"They're going to kill us all." Carmelo's military realism prevailed over Jonás' moral stance. "Let's go."

It was already dark. We formed a column and started marching again. Sadness makes a march interminable, and we walked all night long, hour after hour, without a break.

"The radio!" Jonás suddenly remembered.

"We were carrying it," our group said.

He asked the entire column and no one had it. The equipment had been left behind, along with the dead. There lay Richard's pack with the instruments, the manuals, the diagrams, all the information the enemy wanted. There lay the aerial, the motor Toni was carrying, and worst of all, the Viking, our transmitter, which rolled downhill when Pedrito couldn't hang onto it during the gun battle. We'd lost Venceremos. Jonás, out of pure rage, thought of sending a security patrol back to try to recover it. But no, it would have been suicide. By now everything was in the hands of the army.

Nothing lay ahead of us but marching. We crossed the Torola River and reached the foot of the Cacahuatique Volcano. There we had a small camp, well hidden, very secure, but to reach it we had to keep on walking all day. We were beat, truly exhausted, and now the worst part began. We had to climb up the volcano. I couldn't figure out what to do with my FAL and ammunition. The cartridge boxes felt so heavy, as if someone's hand was pulling on the strap. What's more, my backpack was overflowing. Among other things, I was carrying about a dozen notebooks: my war diary, the notes I made during my first year in Morazán. I don't know how I managed to climb up to the camp on that volcano. We got there about four in the afternoon.

"We can stay here for a few days," they told us to ease the pain. "Lie down to sleep, food's already on the fire."

We'd been walking for two days and nights without so much as a bite to eat. We'll talk later! I didn't even spread out my groundsheet. I just took off my pack and fell down like a sack of rice. Before even half an hour had passed, they attacked us again: "Everybody wake up! Here come the *cuilios*! They're behind us!"

That was Domingo Monterrosa, quick and evil as a viper. While the rest of the army officers waged conventional war from their desks, Monterrosa would continually change his plans. When he figured out that we'd escaped from his hammer and anvil, he turned the operation around and started chasing us. There he was at our backs again, half an hour's march away, which is just a little jog.

"Move it! Move it!" they ordered us.

Packs on our backs, and in two seconds we were marching again, marching worried, climbing even higher on Cacahuatique, towards the north of San Miguel. When we reached the summit, at a house where our strategic radio operators worked, I saw they were burning papers. That gave me the idea. I could no longer lift myself, never mind the backpack, the munitions, the FAL and Evelin's orange radio, which I also had to carry. How could I lighten my load? I pulled out my twelve notebooks, my memoirs of the war, and threw them into the fire. Everything burned. To this day my friends reproach me for it. From then on, I never wrote another word.

Monterrosa didn't let up for a moment. From that house we headed off with the army at our heels. We were ordered to run to gain some distance. I can't make it, I thought, but running as it got dark, we reached a place called Piedra Luna. There they let us rest for a few minutes, but we weren't allowed to smoke, or to take off our boots, or to speak above a whisper.

"Listen to the *cuilios'* radio," a *compa* whispers to me.

"What the fuck are you talking about? What radio?"

"Come hear it."

It was true. Monterrosa's plan included a radio frequency and special programmes to accompany the operation. I tell you, that made us mad. There we were whipped, three *compañeros* dead, three nights without broadcasting, with Venceremos lost, and that bastard starts bullshitting over his "Radio Truth"! That's what they called it! And to really get to us, they called out our names!

We've got you surrounded, Jonás... We're going to wipe you out... Give up... Turn over your weapons... You've lost... Santiago, why don't you desert? What are you doing there?

They called me "the wolf of Morazán", maybe because I'm so hairy. They named our commanders, all of them. They made fun of us, and we had to admit, they had us by the balls.

On the rest of El Salvador's radio stations, General García was soon gleefully reporting the destruction of Radio Venceremos and the death of its announcers. It was contradictory, because the minister of defence himself had repeated a thousand and one times that our station transmitted from Nicaragua, and here they were capturing it in Morazán, but he was so thrilled, he didn't bother about such details. Domingo Monterrosa, meanwhile, was undoubtedly offering toasts over our Valiant Viking and telling his gringo adviser: "Now we've got that scorpion out of our ass."

Double Time to Jucuarán

Night fell and we continued marching. We hadn't slept in three days, we hadn't eaten, and we hadn't even fought. All we did was run. What were we? Delinquents? Wandering Jews? Hardly even wandering, because we couldn't even walk. Our column, weighed down with a hundred *compas* both trained and untrained, could barely crawl. When we reached the Seco River, Jonás made a decision:

"That's enough. We can't go on like this. You can't fight a war with a bunch of people who don't even have guns or know how to fight. All of you who aren't part of the military wing, get out of here. Those of you from Venceremos, go to Jucuarán. Ismael, you take charge of them."

We split up. The combatants headed north and we went south. Jonás's strategy was to act as a decoy, to draw the army back into Morazán, allowing us to escape towards Jucuarán.

Jucuarán! I knew where that was. I knew how many days and nights it would take to reach that town near the southern coast of the country. And in the shape we were in!

"Start marching," we were ordered. "And double time. Because when Monterrosa sniffs out that we split up, he'll split his troops up too to hunt us down."

Marvel, put yourself in the hands of Saint Christopher, patron saint of travellers. Before this new march began I was already exhausted, but what else could we do? We headed off, leaving the Seco River behind. Ahead of us a long road stretched off into the darkness. We had to walk by night because these zones were in dispute and our presence might be detected. Before dawn, we had to reach a hill way off in the distance. There we could rest. With that vision fixed in our minds, we set off towards our first goal. But the road stretched like elastic, and the hill never appeared. The hours ticked by, soon it was early morning and we still had a long way to go. Charrasca, the guide, who knew exactly how far we had left to go, told Ismael we'd better speed up. Daylight would catch us and that would be very risky.

"Double time!" Ismael ordered amid the silence. "Double time until we get there!"

After half an hour of trotting my calves were numb. I couldn't lift my feet and was tripping over every damned rock in the road. So to raise my spirits I began thinking of Santiago, because during all our training with Jonás, I had always shown greater physical endurance. If Santiago could do it, so could I. Santiago was about three or four *compas* ahead of me. I thought: any minute now he's going to slack off, the moment will come when Santiago's going to stop and say he can't go on. He can't stand it. But the minutes went by and I was the one who couldn't stand it. I was on my last legs. I couldn't even hold it up to pee. And everyone kept on trotting, trotting, thud, thud, thud... I was so amazed about how Santiago managed to do it that I decided to make a superhuman effort.

I pass the first one... I pass the second... I lift my head up over the third to look at Santiago... and I see... I see he's got Ismael on one side and Charrasca on the other, and each of those bulls have him by the belt and Santiago's feet aren't even touching the ground. They've got the bastard up in the air. Have you ever seen anything like it? When the fuck were we ever going to stop if they were carrying him like a saint in a procession? I had the longest face in the whole column. Since no one was going to carry me, I just kept on trotting in the moonlight.

We made it: we got there before dawn broke. We arrived, went into the brush, and without waiting for an order I was face up and snoring. This time, luckily, neither the Virgin nor the enemy turned up, and we were able to sleep and eat, massage our feet, and wait for another night, and another march.

When night fell, we started off again. Now we had to cross several immense cotton fields. We had to be extremely cautious because on those private farms there were guards, paramilitary guards. Any sound or delay could cost us bullets in the behind, or a new double-time order from Ismael. Let's give it our all, then, up to the Pan-American Highway. But coming down off the hill, the old proverb that "a sore finger always gets hit" came true. Only it was a toe in this case.

Before the cotton field there was a ravine that gave off a strange, rancid stench. I'd never smelled anything like it. Higher up was a factory that made rope out of cactus. When you scrape the cactus and wash it, you get that smell, and the factory sent all its waste into the stream. Crossing it was going to screw us, because the acid would burn our feet. Since we weren't a combat unit, we always used low leather boots, and the order came back "everyone take off your boots". That way we'd cross, dry off our feet on the other side, put on dry socks, dry shoes and that would be that. The order gets passed back in whispers, from one to the other:

"Take off your boots..."

"Take off your boots..."

"Don't take off your boots..."

"Don't take off your boots..."

I think we were so worn out that not even our tongues would work right. Of course, all this went on in total darkness and with the rush of the chase. The order got turned around; a few at the front took off their boots and the rest didn't. When we got to the other side, there was Ismael mad as hell: "Why didn't you take off your boots, dickhead? Now you're going to walk on blisters, sonofacorncob!"

For a leader, that was a serious problem, because people can't walk with their feet all blistered. In wartime, your feet are the most cherished part of your body, the part you pamper. A good leader is always thinking of his troops' feet: ointment for blisters, talcum for fungus... And we still had three days left to walk!

"We're fucked."

But we had to go on. With our boots dry or dripping, we had to get across that cotton field. Apolonio and some others picked some balls of cotton to put between their toes, which were already full of blisters. A full moon had come out, I remember, an enormous moon like a big medallion, and there you were staring out over that magic scenery of puffs of cotton like white bubbles floating in the night... The pain in your feet brought you back to reality, to the interminable hours of march ahead.

We crossed the Pan-American Highway and headed towards another volcano, Chaparrastique. On we went, marching in a great suffocating silence: marching at the same rhythm, without talking, without a flashlight, without a cigarette, just marching. Suddenly, thud! A faint crash. Dina, one of the monitoring team, had collapsed.

"Halt, halt, halt..." the order was passed back in low voices.

We stopped. They picked Dina up, gave her sugar water, gave her two pills. Once again, move those feet. Twenty minutes later, thud! Dina on the ground again.

"She fell, she fell, she fell..."

Several *compas* cut some bamboo and improvised a stretcher. Apolonio was one of the ones who had to carry her. Poor little Dina's body had finally rebelled.

We advanced, but by this time we were sleepwalkers. I'm not exaggerating, that's how it was. You can walk in your sleep. You wake up when the column stops and you bump into the backpack of whoever's in front of you. Then you continue, and soon you feel someone pull you back onto the path because you've headed off into the ditch. I think half the column that night was asleep. Suddenly, thud! This time it was Evelin, Mauricio's partner. She wandered off the track and fell right into the drainage pit from a pig farm. She woke up swimming in pure pigshit. From then on an incredible stench enveloped the entire column. It was so intense that it helped keep our eyes open, and it even worked as camouflage: that can't be people, it must be a gigantic piece of shit moving through the thicket.

When we reached the San Miguel River, she didn't wait for permission. She tore off her clothes and jumped in.

"Who's taking a bath?" Ismael was mad.

"Evelin," we told him.

"If it's her, okay, but tell her to scrub herself with evergreen oak!"

The shit was so encrusted she smelled like a pig for another two days until we reached Jucuarán. In all, I figure we must have walked about 120 kilometres.

The Saddest Christmas

At dawn, we arrived at Jucuarán, a village near El Jícaro where Commander Balta[8] had installed the command post of the South-east Front. While they prepared food, I sat down next to Roger Blandino, the column's political officer. He looked at me and joked "Now all we need is for them to say 'Get washed, we're going back.'"

"How could you say such a thing? I wouldn't go back even if Grandpa Jesus himself gave the order!"

"The leaders are the leaders," Roger insisted. "If they give the order, we've got to obey, right?"

"The leaders are the leaders because they know how to give orders. If they ordered us to go back now, it would be an absurd order, impossible to obey. The leader would have to be a jerk, so I wouldn't do it."

"Are you sure?"

"Absolutely. I'm not moving from here, understand?"

"Well, let's hope that order doesn't come and we — you and I and everyone — have to obey it."

As soon as we finished our philosophical discussion, Guandique, the best chef in the world, called us to eat — or rather to devour — fried fish, fresh out of the sea, crispy *tortillas* and a rice dish that could kill you.

"Hunger is the best sauce in the world," Guandique laughed.

After we stuffed ourselves, they gave us a whole saintly day to sleep. That night, they put on a welcoming fiesta for us. We couldn't dance because our feet were swollen like balloons, but there was Whitey César with his guitar playing the saddest *ranchera* tunes, which, curiously enough, are the ones that cheer you up. After the music, we went off to our beds once again.

At eight in the morning, they woke us up for a big breakfast. And there we were basking in tranquillity, when they handed me a message from Balta: "Jonás wants to speak to you". I can't deny it, a chill ran right down my spine to the dimples of my ass. I left Roger watching me like a warlock from the other side of the table, and I approached the communications radio where Jonás was on the line.

"Marvel, do you read me?"

"I read you, *comandante*."

"How is everybody?"

"Perfect, *comandante*."

"How is people's morale?"

"Perfect, *comandante*."

"How many days would it take you to get back here?" he tosses out that terrifying question.

I turn around and Balta holds up four fingers. It was 20 December.

"Four, *comandante*."

"Perfect, Marv. I'll expect you. Bust your balls because you've got to be here on the 24th. The radio has to go back on the air on 24 December!"

I think: What radio? Venceremos is in enemy hands! When I hang up, Balta tells me that right there in Jucuarán they have a reserve transmitter hidden.

"Venceremos is the people," he says. "The equipment can be replaced."

✳✳✳

Balta called me over to show me the cache. Was I ever surprised to find a new transmitter, another Viking, newer and more powerful than the one we lost in the ambush. It turned out that the organisation had bought it recently to set up a repeating station for Venceremos in the south. My brother Rafi had travelled to Jucuarán precisely to get that project going. We were saved! What's more, they'd got tape recorders, cable connections, all the spare parts we needed.

"We'll be able to go on air again," I told Balta.

"Soon is already late," he said. "Get going to Morazán."

Thanks to Isra, the strongest back Venceremos has ever had in all these years, we got our treasures out of their hiding place and brought them back to the camp, where the uproar over the return trip had already begun.

"Those who can't walk will stay," they told us. "Those who can should go. You've got to do in four days what took you eight before."

Dina, Evelin and Tita stayed behind to wait for a trip for normal people. Of the women, only Morena volunteered. She had more endurance than some of us men, I won't name names. They changed our packs, gave us all ammunition, and even though our feet were the same, they gave us new boots. Balta gave us a final gift: "Here, take this mule. I think he'll help you out with the transmitter, at least as far as the Torola River. Bon voyage!"

***

Like a movie in reverse, we retraced our steps: San Miguel River, Chaparrastique Volcano, Pan-American Highway, cotton fields... Every so often, Roger would come up to me just to rub it in: "What's up, Marv? So the leaders aren't leaders?"

"Enjoy the pretty scenery," I'd say.

The big news on the trip was the mule Balta gave us, the best burro and the least ass I've ever had the pleasure to meet. He didn't give us a single problem. Marching with an animal in a group of guerrillas, where security means silence, is no easy feat. But that mule walked in the column like just another guerrilla. When the column stopped, he stopped. When the mule felt the transmitter slipping to one side, he stopped. You couldn't make him walk until a *compa* who knew how to sort out the load fixed it. Once the harness broke and there he stood, steady as could be, until it was mended and in place once again. Another time, at the San Miguel coffee farm, he had to climb up a huge rock that had footholds carved into it only big enough for people's feet. Without so much as a snort, up he went with our transmitter on his back. He was just as sure-footed on the sides of the volcano and in the irrigation canals of the cotton fields. That animal was such a good collaborator that we started calling him "Compa Mule", and giving him all the consideration he was due.

"Let Compa Mule rest on this hill," Ismael would say and he'd take down the transmitter, that must have weighed a hundred pounds. He and Isra would then carry it up the steep hill so the mule could have a break.

Compa Mule came along for the first three nights of the trip. The third, from the Seco River to Cacahuatique, was the longest of all, longer than a buck and a half of tripe as they say around here: 14 hours without stopping! Your legs didn't belong to you any more; they walked on their own. The worst part was when we reached Cacahuatique on the 23rd. They decided to take away the mule because we had to pass very close to Osicala, right by the town, and the *cuilios* might hear us.

"Compa Mule stays here," they told us and reluctantly we bid him farewell.

I think Toni would have liked him. Toni was a specialist in loading cargo on animals, he had a whole ritual with the ropes and he knew how to balance it just right. They would have been good friends, the two of them, I'm sure. There are animals that are like people.

The fourth leg, the last, was a happier time, despite the extreme exhaustion and the heart-attack speed. We knew we were going to meet up with our *compañeros* after having lived through so much. We made it. We arrived at El Zapotal — which we had left when the hammer and anvil operation began — on the morning of 24 December. They had *tamales* and hot chocolate waiting for us. They also had some bad news, so bad it couldn't be true:

A thousand campesinos *murdered in El Mozote.*

What do you mean a thousand *campesinos*? Wasn't it just a typographical error? We brought with us the sorrow of three *compañeros* killed, and a thousand more sorrows awaited us. We didn't even have time to digest the information. We had to set up the new equipment to go on air that very afternoon. Luckily Mauricio, who had been placed in charge of the military squad, had already begun getting things ready. It was just a question of testing the new Viking we'd brought from Jucuarán. We plugged it in and it worked perfectly.

That very day, the evening of the 24th, we broadcast an announcement that Venceremos had not died. It was reborn just like the Baby Jesus that at that very moment was being feted by Salvadoran families across the country. We also broadcast the news that in El Mozote, very close by, the new Herods of the Atlacatl Battalion had just murdered a thousand innocent people.

It was a sad Christmas, the saddest of all.

Draining the Sea to Catch the Fish

I was born and grew up in La Joya. When the killings happened I was eleven. I lived with my parents, a little brother of mine who was about six, and a sister who was nine, still a kid.

I remember the soldiers coming up the Black Road at about three in the afternoon. My dad heard they were coming and said: "Let's go sleep in the woods."

But my mom didn't want to leave the house empty.

"You go," she said. "God won't abandon us."

"You've got to hide," my dad said.

"Go on ahead," she said. "I'll come along later with the girl."

The three of us went to a cactus field and my mom stayed behind hiding the pots and pans, the kitchen things. She stayed with my little sister, and said that if something happened the two of them would hide in the cornfield and they'd be all right. My mom always trusted in God.

My dad and I and my little brother climbed up a hill they call Brujo Hill. They say in the old days it was scary up there. From the hill we kept watch all night long. At about eight in the morning, we saw the soldiers come into town and start shooting. From up above we heard the noise of people screaming and gunshots. Then we saw a plume of smoke come out of our house, and heard the dog barking.

"They killed your mom," my dad said. "The dog ran out crying."

They spent the whole day shooting and killing and burning the houses. At about midnight we went down to the village to take a look. First we went to the home of a sister-in-law who lives a bit out of the way, thinking that maybe my mum had managed to hide with her.

"No, Petrona Chica isn't here."

That's what we called my mom. I started crying. My dad wanted to go to our house and all he saw were embers, a cloud of smoke and no one inside. In a nearby ditch he saw all the dead, piled up. He didn't see my mom, but he saw my little sister, squashed in among the other bodies, and his brothers, my uncles, all dead.

In the full moon you could see the bodies strewn about and all the destruction. We had to go back to Brujo Hill because the troops were still hunting down any survivors. We stayed on the hill for five days, still as could be, without eating anything, unable to come down. Then my other brothers came, who had been in the refugee camp at Colomoncagua in Honduras, and together we found the courage to walk through the entire village. The smell of death was strong. The men had been killed separately, one by one. The women had been taken off together and killed as a group. They dragged the prettiest ones into the pastures, where the soldiers raped them and then slit their throats. Then they brought them back to where the others had been killed. They didn't care if they were old or pregnant, everyone had to die just the same. They tossed the smallest children into the air and speared them with their bayonets. They hanged the old women and left them dangling from the branches of trees. They had no pity for any living thing. They even killed the animals, the pigs, the cows. Only the birds remained alive in that place. Especially the vultures.

Later, with my brothers, we went to El Mozote, about an hour's walk from La Joya. The *compas* had already been through and had found the church full of bodies. Since they couldn't bury so many, they knocked down the walls of the church to cover them up a bit, because the animals were eating everything. You could see bones that were already white. The rest of the dead were still in their burned-down homes, unburied.

"They are all guerrillas," the soldiers had said. "They must all be killed so there will be no more guerrillas."

Later I went to Colomoncagua. When I grew up, I joined the guerrillas. My dad and the youngest stayed there in the refugee camp. Of my two brothers, one died in '83 fighting in Ciudad Barrios. The other died in '87, I don't know where. Another cousin of mine also died. Only three of our family are still alive.

***

When we heard about the massacre we went out immediately to see if it was true and to tape an extensive report for Venceremos. As we approached El Mozote, we smelled that penetrating odour of rotting flesh. The town plaza was deserted, all we could see were pieces of bloody clothing and some abandoned toys. Everywhere there were spent cartridges from US rifles, the M-16s.

In the chapel of Santa Catarina everything was in ruins, the pews overturned, the saints on the floor, the walls peppered with bullets. At one side, in the vestry, was the most macabre sight I have ever seen: a mountain of rotting bodies, half-covered with the walls of the church.

They arrived in El Mozote at night, like bandits. Leading the troops was Colonel Domingo Monterrosa. He personally ordered the population to congregate in the chapel, promising them they would be evacuated by the Red Cross for the duration of the operation against the guerrillas. Instead, they divided them into several groups, the men on one side, the women on the other. The young girls were taken by the officers to Cruz Hill. There they kept them all night, raped them and in the early morning they murdered them. Then they went back to the chapel, set up M-60 machine guns at the entrance and sprayed everyone inside with bullets. They went crazy. They started chasing people down, shooting like hunters. They really vented their fury on the children. El Mozote was known for its bread. So the soldiers took the children and put them in the ovens, then forced the women to light the fire. No one would believe these things if there weren't photos and horrifying testimonies.

They weren't satisfied with only El Mozote. From there they went on to La Joya, to Los Toriles, Rancherías, La Chumpa... in all the villages of the region they repeated the same barbarity. Exactly 1,009 victims were counted, identified by their full names; most of them were old people or children.

On the radio we launched a war of information to denounce this genocide to the country and the world. The Voice of America said nothing about the crime. President Duarte went on television smiling and denying the massacre, saying it was all a trick by Venceremos to besmirch his government, which had always been so respectful of human rights — especially respectful since just then the US Congress was debating and approving new military aid for El Salvador.

Alas, it was no exaggeration, nor was it an aberration on the part of the soldiers. It had all been well thought out, planned with the advice of the gringos. These were their first experiments in the counterinsurgency tactic of annihilating the guerrillas' base of support. Draining the sea to catch the fish, they call it.

What got me madder than anything was that two nights before, I had warned the people over the radio that a big operation was coming. I told them to come with us. But in El Mozote there were a lot of evangelicals, who simply trust in providence. They don't understand that it's not enough to pray.

The day after my report, on 31 December, the last day of the year, Father Rogelio came to say mass in our guerrilla camp and to commend to God the lives of those thousand peasants absurdly sacrificed by Monterrosa, Duarte and Reagan. Who would have thought that the only station to broadcast a mass for the dead would be Venceremos?

***

This entire stage of worsening repression was preceded by discussions inside the Armed Forces High Command over what plan to follow. The debate turned on the number of dead needed to pacify the country and the political repercussions these deaths would have internationally. The thinking behind the plan was this: Once the popular movement was beheaded and a good part of its rank and file annihilated, a supposed democracy could be set up. They would hold elections and return a good part of the lands confiscated in the agrarian reform to their former owners. The armed forces' hold on power would be guaranteed, the economic and political dominion of the big families would be assured, and the United States would remove a source of tension in its sphere of influence.

The discussion of the need to annihilate the leadership and rank and file of the revolutionary movement was practically an open debate inside the army. Certain backers of D'Aubuisson even spoke of 100,000 or more dead, others spoke of 40,000 or 50,000. In the end, General García, supported by the United States, won the argument, and that explains this entire brutal process of repression — over 40,000 dead, half a million refugees, thousands of disappeared, hundreds of political prisoners, more than three years in a state of siege, unions and professional associations destroyed — which will conclude with elections in which Major Roberto D'Aubuisson, chief of the death squads and assassin of Monsignor Romero, will become president of the Constituent Assembly.

Commander Joaquín Villalobos
"Why Does the FMLN Fight?"
Morazán, September 1983

***

In the very first days of January, I went to La Joya. I went into a house, saw the plates on the table, the gourd of coffee, everything as it had been on the day of the massacre. Next to the stone walls of the yard I found the family that had lived in that house. There was an elderly couple, a woman who was probably their daughter with a small girl in her arms, a man who must have been her husband, and three more children in the middle. The bodies had been mummified by the sun, and were intact. Since animals had not eaten them, they had dried out right there, next to the wall, with their clothes on and their shoes, in the very position in which the soldiers had shot them. They were only skin and bones, but they looked alive. They seemed to be staring at me. The elderly man had his mouth open. What was his last word, his question before dying?

Later I went to El Mozote. Since the bodies hadn't been buried very well, the stench of rotting flesh was still strong. We had to dig out the rubble of the church which half-covered them and dig a large grave to avoid epidemics. As we pulled out, we saw the signs the army had painted:

The Atlacatl Battalion was here
The Angels of Hell

Since then, El Mozote has become a graveyard. Years later we had to go through there with a guerrilla column, and something very strange happened that I haven't told anyone about. It was a dark night and when we approached the abandoned village thousands of fireflies lit up at the same time. Thousands and thousands, the entire woods glowed. Then, as if by some mysterious order, they all went dark at the same moment. Then they all lit up again with that spectral light. Then they all went dark. I swear I've never seen anything like it in my life. I don't imagine anyone who was in the column that night has been able to forget the call of the fireflies.

Footnotes

[1] A reptile similar to a small iguana.

[2] Commander William Pascasio, member of the PRS central committee.

[3] General José Guillermo García, Minister of Defence and Public Security, the strongman of the Duarte regime.

[4] Commander Eleno Castro, member of the PRS political commission.

[5] A fruit with a rough brown skin and sweet orange flesh.

[6] Rafael Arce Zablah, founder of the PRS-ERP.

[7] Captain Francisco Emilio Mena Sandoval, who along with Captain Marcelo Cruz took over the barracks of the Second Infantry Brigade in Santa Ana on 10 January 1981. Later on, they both joined the guerrillas.

[8] Juan Ramón Medrano, member of the PRS political commission.

Section III
The Great Battles

The Voice of the Revolution

I admit it: I fell in love with Santiago's voice. I got into this whole mess because of it. From the first day they broadcast, on 10 January 1981, the day of the general offensive, I was bewitched by the conviction in that voice:

Fifty years of dictatorship are falling!
Join the ranks of the Farabundo Martí Front!

I don't know why, but I felt like he was talking to me, inviting me to join up. I wanted to take the first plane, grab a bus, even slog it on foot, and head right back to El Salvador. You see, I'm Salvadoran, but I was living in Nicaragua at the time.

I used to work in San Salvador at the newspaper *La Crónica*. My beat was stolen cars, stabbings, bottles thrown in fits of passion, that sort of thing. News, you could call it. One day just for fun, I wrote a political joke and showed it to the editor Jaime Suárez, who was a good friend of mine.

"Marvin, don't do any more news stories. If you bring me five jokes a day like this one, I'll double your salary."

With that stroke of luck I started writing a little column called "The Politics of Humour". Every day I came up with my five jokes making fun of politicians and members of the military junta. They hated it of course, but what really bothered the generals and colonels was the paper's critical stance. Not only our paper, but *El Independiente*, the YSAX radio station, the National University, the Human Rights Commission... It wasn't long before they assassinated Jaime, my editor. Then we started getting anonymous calls in the newsroom, that we're going to kill you all, that we'll teach you a lesson... Since I'm no hero, when they sprayed the building with bullets I made a decision: "I'm leaving. I don't want the death squads cutting off my tongue or sticking a screwdriver in my eyes."

I packed my bags and didn't stop until I got to Nicaragua. That was in 1980. I was still there in mid-'81 when I tuned in to Venceremos and heard that electrifying voice:

Transmitting its signal of freedom from El Salvador, territory in combat against oppression and imperialism!

Then the female announcer would come on, who wasn't bad, but she didn't make such an impression on me. I'd go nuts waiting for her to finish so the other one, someone called Santiago, would come on again. That guy's voice seduced me, I can't deny it.

All this time, without my knowing it, my younger brother was working for COMIN, the station's international publicity team in Nicaragua.

"Look Marvin, we need you," he tells me one day. "You know how to write. Come and give us a hand."

Can you imagine? They wanted me and I wanted to go. Who do I have to talk to? Talk to Carlos Argueta, the head of COMIN. Okay, let's talk. The next day I was sitting at my little desk in the COMIN office where the news team worked. My main job was to write cables based on what I heard on Venceremos, and distribute them to the news agencies. In other words, for my work I had to listen to the station from Morazán every day. I was happy. I remember as if it were yesterday the first story they asked me to write for Venceremos. My story on the radio! All excited, I tuned in way ahead of time, waiting for Santiago's voice to read what I had written. Such vanity! But that day a different announcer read it, someone called Marvel. Too bad.

In January '82 Carlos Argueta left Managua to work with Venceremos on the inside. Two weeks later I heard from him, a message in code: "Do you want to come to El Salvador?"

My feelings got all mixed up. I wanted to, but I had a three-year-old girl. I wanted to, but I was afraid. I wanted to but...

"Do you want to, or don't you?"

"I do."

So they set up the trip and in March '82 I was back in my own country. The *compas* sent me straight off to Morazán, to La Guacamaya, since the command post and the station were still at that camp then. I arrived at seven in the evening, just as they were finishing the broadcast. Marcela was at the mixer, Apolonio at the transmitter, Butterfly and Santiago announcing. Greetings all round.

"How's Managua?" Santiago asked. "And how's my girlfriend Lucía, have you seen her? What do you mean you don't know her? She's such a...! And Nidia Rosa, the captain? Don't tell me she married somebody else? And what about Claudia, the photographer, didn't she tell you to say hello?"

"Tell me about the last operation..." I asked him.

"And Ernesto Cardenal, is he still minister of culture?" He continued interrogating me, "What films have you seen there? Tell me, are the buses still bursting at the seams?"

"Tell me about the station..." I asked him.

No way. Who can withstand Santiago when he wants to talk? He peppered me with questions until exhaustion did me in and I went off to sleep.

The next day, without even saying "Here it comes", they put me in front of the microphone. Santiago introduced the news segment with a sound effect of gunfire.

And next, Radio Venceremos presents its programme... News Bullets!

That day the bullets flew fast, because I read at the pace of a machine gun. The truth is I'd never done radio before. Never in my whole damn life had I sat in front of a microphone. Written news I'd done, but that's a different hundred-peso bill, as the Nicas say.

I hadn't even recovered from my terror when the criticism rained down in the afternoon evaluation session:

"Inaudible."

"Unintelligible."

"Incomprehensible."

In sum, they thought my announcing was garbage, and they "suggested" that I write more and speak less. That didn't shake me up as much as what was going on in the camp. Imagine, the first day I arrived, just as they were showing me the radio's equipment, I saw them race by with about twenty people on stretchers, heading for the hospital. They'd just whipped us badly near Jocoaitique, nearly annihilated one of our squadrons. Sixteen of our people got killed, they told me. Then the next day the same thing. Our forces attacked Gotera and returned in bad shape, defeat written all over their faces.

What happened? During those days, on 28 March to be exact, elections were held. It was all a farce, a big fraud. The decision to remove Duarte and put in Alvaro Magaña as president was made by the army, not at the ballot box. The US ambassador helped divvy up congressional seats among the parties in the Constituent Assembly. General García, the one responsible for the massacres of recent years, was named to rule from the Ministry of Defence. It was the same old story; to disguise the repression and weaken the popular movement they tried to put a democratic facade on the military dictatorship.

The FMLN decided to boycott the farce, and called on people to rise up in an insurrection, but the people didn't respond as we expected. There was a lot of fear and not much political organising. We had a lot to learn about relating to the masses and waging war. Militarily they'd beaten us, and badly. The commanders were evaluating the experience and drawing up a new strategy, but many of us got terribly depressed, really demoralised. We couldn't hide it; the depression among the combatants was obvious. That's when Santiago arrived: "This is war, boys! Anybody can get whipped in a war!"

Then he grabbed the microphone with the same passion as every other day:

Victory is approaching, compañeros! *We're going to win!*

Listening to Venceremos at night lifted all the tension that had built up during the day. The same was true for very many people.

I believe a lot of people joined up because of Santiago's voice, and many others didn't desert when they were depressed because of the spirit he was able to convey. If things were going well or if they were going to shit, Santiago always sounded the same. Always tremblingly alive. Was it exaggerated optimism? I'd say it was more like the shot of enthusiasm you need to carry on through years and years of war, because in those dark days, when you haven't eaten, when you're covered with mud in a swamp, when you see your buddies get killed, you need something to restore your spirit.

That was his virtue. It's easy to sing when you're on top, but to keep on singing when you're the one getting kicked... That's why people love him so. His voice is a symbol, it's everyone's voice, the voice of the revolution. Even though several of us are announcers on Venceremos, Santiago is the one who always reads the official communiqué from the commanders, the one who curses the government, the one who orders highways to be opened and closed. Until he says it, it hasn't been said. That skinny guy speaks with such authority! He has so much faith in victory that it's contagious! You should see him when we start a new offensive, Santiago wakes up energised.

"We're going to win, today we're going to win!"

"Today, Santiago?" I ask, sceptically.

"Okay, maybe tomorrow."

A Battle in Episodes

Jonás called a meeting in El Mozote of all the forces in Morazán, including Venceremos. It still smelled like death where the village had been. Maybe a thousand guerrillas were there, most of them demoralised. We'd been crushed at Gotera, at La Planta, Commander Gonzalo[1] had been killed in Usulután, we'd just buried Ventura, a dearly loved squadron leader... From a distance I watched our leaders: María, Chico, Balta, Luisa, Carmelo, Licho, Memo, Manolo... All of them so young, I don't think any of them were over thirty. They looked serious too, weighed down by problems.

Jonás stood up in the middle of us.

"I'd like to ask you all a question," he started. "Are you demoralised?"

"No..." we all responded.

"Of course you are! It's written all over your faces. Discouraged and disappointed, that's what you are. It's to be expected, because they've whipped us badly in the past few months. Well, so what? That's how this shit works. You learn war by waging it, there's no other way. If you never climb up on a horse, you'll never fall off. But the story isn't over yet, no sir. Now is when the enemy's going to find out what the FMLN is made of!

"Demoralised? You ought to be mad as hell! And confident of our strength! Let's see, tell me, how many guns do you think we can recover in the next battle?"

"I'd say about fifteen, *comandante*."

"Fifteen! That's ridiculous! You, how many do you think?"

"Maybe thirty, *comandante*."

"Thirty! What are fifteen or thirty guns to us? We're going to get a hundred guns, do you hear? One hundred guns!" Jonás saw a few sceptical faces. "You don't believe we can? Of course not, neither do I! We won't get a hundred guns, no way! Because a hundred, look, is this," and Jonás angrily stabbed the air with one finger. "Two hundred guns is what we want!" and he raised two fingers, making a "V" for victory. "We won't be satisfied with a hundred little guns. We want two hundred!"

A tremendous roar ran through the crowd. Jonás's eyes gave off sparks, and all our eyes began to shine with the same anger and determination.

"The big battles are coming!" Jonás concluded, "and we're all going to be there! Journalists, radio operators, cooks, doctors, even the sick are going to fight! Everyone! Onward to victory!"

This happened at the end of May 1982. The following week we launched a big campaign called "Commander Gonzalo". The plan was to lay siege to Perquín to draw in the army's reinforcements and ambush them, but people left that meeting in El Mozote so fired up that we took the town wham-bam. The *cuilios* ran off scared to death and took refuge in San Fernando, about five kilometres away.

"Surround them and destroy them!" Licho ordered.

While our forces moved to surround the 250 troops ensconced in San Fernando, the army was up and on its way with 300 men to block us. The reinforcements came up the highway from Torola, and when they reached Moscarrón Hill they ran into one of our squadrons.

"Hold them there, we'll be right down!" Licho ordered by radio.

When they got there, a big battle ensued. Those of us from Venceremos were in the camp waiting for instructions.

"Get somebody ready to do a live report," they warned us. "We're making mincemeat of them!"

Without consulting anyone, Santiago grabbed his tape recorder and took off for Moscarrón. I stayed behind to announce with Butterfly and Rafi. A little while later, couriers started bringing us the first cassettes from the front lines:

At this very moment our guerrilla forces are advancing on the enemy's left flank. We can see several soldiers jumping from their trench. They're firing wildly, and they're being supported by machine guns and 90mm cannons. The compañeros *answer the fire... They've just set off a powerful contact bomb...*

Since the battle didn't end that first day, 9 June, our audience was left hanging. Who would win? The listeners wanted to hear more; they wanted to know what was happening, but for technical reasons we couldn't extend the programme. We announced that they should tune in again tomorrow to find out how the battle of Moscarrón developed — it was like a soap opera!

The next day, Santiago used a military radio to establish a direct line with us at La Guacamaya.

The helicopters are still flying low over the front lines. Three helicopters are firing... perhaps you can hear the guns... Our forces answer with a fusillade. We don't know if they've managed to hit one of those devils. Now they're turning around, flying off to the south...

Since the reporting was live from the front lines, all the sounds of gunfire, helicopters, A-37 planes, bombs going off, all the sounds most stations have on sound-effect records, went out on air, only here it was for real. The soap opera was real life!

The battle wasn't decided on the second day either. Our audience was left even more anxious, biting their nails to hear how the story would end. It was a battle told in episodes!

At last, on the third day, our *compas* stretched themselves to the limit and annihilated the enemy. The third episode of the soap opera of Moscarrón had a happy ending, and in thousands of Salvadoran homes Venceremos resounded reporting the victory:

El Moscarrón is now under guerrilla control. Perquín has been taken. San Fernando will soon fall. An arch of liberty is forming across the villages of Morazán!

It was an astounding victory. The enemy suffered badly — more than 200 casualties — young soldiers sent to fight by millionaire colonels who waged war from their desks. We captured some 40 prisoners, among them a lieutenant from the Belloso Battalion, trained in the United States.

"Your name?"

"William Reinaldo Sánchez Medina."

"Where were you trained?"

"Fort Bragg, Virginia."

"Who were the instructors?"

"North Americans."

"Do you know why the battalion is named after Ramón Belloso?"

"I don't know."

"Do you know that Ramón Belloso was the Salvadoran general who led the armies of Central America against William Walker² in the 19th century?"

"No, they didn't tell us that."

The battle of Moscarrón was a turning point. Suddenly our demoralisation was gone. A hundred guns? Two hundred guns? An entire artillery battery! Three 90 millimetre cannons! Heavy machine guns, military radios, piles of rifles, grenade-launchers, backpacks, thousands of rounds of ammunition! The *compas* were drunk with joy. I'll never forget what one of the combatants, a peasant, said when he returned to La Guacamaya: "My heart was bursting with joy! We had a volcano of guns!"

Despite the emotions, the victory was no flash in the pan, nor was it achieved by recklessness. It was a full-scale battle won by the side that fought better. Not long before, Jonás got hold of Clausewitz's black book, *On War*, and he spent every moment at the camp reading: about the inverted wedge, the pincer, about attacking on this flank and not the other — all about military strategy. It was strategy learned on the real stage of the soap opera, on the battle field, not at West Point or on the mahogany tables of the High Command. Jonás is someone who goes down to the front lines in the middle of a battle to say, "That isn't how you do it, sons of bitches", and he fires his shots and grabs some kid by the scruff of the neck who wants to run away and puts him back into the trench. Exuding confidence and energy, Jonás trained generations of combatants, including the ones who are leaders today.

After the battle of Moscarrón, a new stage in the war began: the time of the great battles. Our guerrilla army had reached maturity.

Convincing a Gringo

Fidel once spoke of the "Salvadoran guerrillas whose feats astonish the world". When I heard that speech on Radio Havana, my thoughts went to our *compañeros* and their assault on the bunkers of Jocoaitique. To knock off those fortified positions located on the bare hills surrounding the town was, militarily speaking, impossible. There was no way to do it, no way you could reach the big stone trenches where the guards sat with their boxes of munitions, receiving supplies and reinforcements directly by helicopter: totally unassailable.

Jocoaitique is a little town; its handsome plaza is lined with palm trees and benches, the church at one side. What's unusual is the way it's encircled by hills. One of them, the highest, is called La Planta, and it was the scene of a shitload of battles. There must have been an electrical substation there once, who knows when. What's for sure is that La Planta, with its big bunker on top, is the highest strategic point in town. Whoever controls it, controls Jocoaitique.

I went along on the assault on La Planta to report for *Venceremos*, and also to accompany Raymond Bonner, the *New York Times* correspondent we had invited to collect testimonies and photographs of the massacre at El Mozote. That guy Raymond is a fine journalist. He was in Vietnam as a lawyer and had some experience with war. He always carried his camera and his little notebook to write everything down.

Licho was leading our troops. He put Raymond and me at the command post for greater security.

"Don't tell me you want to get closer," Licho warned. "Suppose they kill this gringo right under my nose, what happens then?"

But we were journalists; we wanted to see our special forces take the bunkers from the *cuilios*. Our troops would have to turn into animals to sneak up those bare hills without being spotted. These *compas* are cats in the night. When it's dark as can be, they go out practically naked, wearing only underwear, camouflaged with dirt from the same terrain. They sneak up, sticking close to the ground, measuring every centimetre, making no more noise than a shadow. They toss a contact bomb or a grenade from a few metres away, and launch the assault. That's how they took emplacements that seemed impenetrable.

When they attacked the first bunkers at La Planta, the secret was out and the shit hit the fan. That's when Raymond got impatient.

"Ask permission," he says. "Let's get up to the line of fire."

I approach Licho and he goes bananas: "Stop bothering me. You're seeing the war. What more do you want? To see the enemy's finger on the trigger? You two are staying right here. As long as I don't move forward, neither will you."

After seven hours of combat, in the middle of an infernal gun battle, they tell us that the soldiers are abandoning their posts, they're giving up.

"Let's go," Licho tells us. "Now it's okay."

We walked over to the spot where twelve soldiers stood with their hands on their heads. They defended the town command post right up to the end. By now all of the bunkers had been taken and the summit of La Planta was under our control.

"Take down their names," Licho tells me, "their age, the battalion they belong to, all that. Then get that journalist out of here. The army's reinforcements are already on the way. The counter-attack is going to be a bitch."

"Couldn't I see just a bit of Jocoaitique?" asks Raymond. "Take a few pictures, do some interviews? Since I'm here..."

"Look Mr Raymond, we had a deal. You, Marvel, take him for a turn around the plaza. Then, back to camp. I don't want this guy here when we have to defend the town. He's seen enough. Get him out of here."

We had a few minutes to go into the town, look around a bit, and at least from a distance see those four unconquerable hills surrounding Jocoaitique that were now in the hands of the FMLN.

"It's one of two things," Raymond says, "either you have the best special forces army in the world, or the morale of the soldiers defending those heights is less than nothing. What do you think?"

"Both," I reply proudly.

We followed a stream that led to the soccer field, looking for the way into town, and on the way we saw the first bodies, two soldiers. We went on. A *compa's* body lay on a corner. While we walked, Raymond was writing everything down in his notebook and taking pictures of the empty streets. Not a soul was about. No dogs were barking, you didn't even hear a chicken, no pigs running about. Nothing. No one. Just the penetrating smell of gunpowder, which made it hard to breathe. We moved cautiously, because when you take over a town you can't just walk in admiring the clouds. There could be snipers anywhere.

In the palm-lined plaza, the local command post looked like it had been hit by a hurricane. The last soldiers held out so stubbornly that we were forced us to wreck the building. Piled up outside were military radios, two dozen rifles, helmets, uniforms, all the booty. Roque, with his team of mules, was already packing it all up to supply our camps.

We continued through the ghost town. Raymond wanted to talk to the residents, interview them. How could we? All the doors, all the windows were shuttered tight. There we were standing in the middle of the street, all alone.

"This is so strange," Raymond began. "You say you've got the support of the people, but you just took over this town and all I see are dead soldiers and prisoners of war. You've recovered weapons, but you don't have people in the streets. You're like the US Army when they went into a Vietcong hamlet. They'd take the hamlet, walk in like victors, but not even a dog would go out to greet them. What do you say to that?"

The question stuck in my craw. You're not going to believe it, but at that very moment the door of the house in front of us creaked open. A child's face peered through the crack, she put out a hand and waved at me to come. I approached and the door opened half-way.

"Come in *compas*," I heard in a whisper from inside.

I waved to the gringo and brought him to the house. Click, the door closed behind us. Inside, everything was dark. When our eyes adjusted, we saw two candles and two women, an older one and one who could be her daughter. Each was at a grinding stone, grinding corn. Next to them was the fire with a *comal* for cooking *tortillas*. Beside the fire, a man at a table. On the table was a box filled with ripe tomatoes and another filled with eggs. And there were three piles of *tortillas*, about thirty *tortillas* high. The man picked up a *tortilla*, put an egg in it and a tomato, and handed it to me: "Eat".

He made another with tomato and egg and gave it to Raymond: "Eat, you must be hungry. When you leave, tell another two *compas* to come and eat. When the shooting started early this morning we figured: 'Let's make *tortillas* because the boys are going to be hungry when they come in. We'll stay up all night.' So I told her, (she lives next door), and between her and my wife they made the *tortillas*. I brought in the tomatoes."

"But," the gringo spoke up.

"Shhhh!" the man said, "There are spies in town, you know, 'ears'. Here everybody's on your side, but there are a few frogs who sing when they shouldn't, understand? That's why nobody's outside. But knock on any door and they'll let you in. Everybody's watching through the cracks and there's food for you in every house. It's the middle of the night and you can hear people making *tortillas* and you can smell the fires!"

When we went out to the street, the woman, who had not said a word, said good-bye without a pause in her grinding: "Take care, boys".

We told the first *compas* who passed by. In twos, they went in and ate. Others knocked on other doors, and in every one, with less and less caution, they opened wide to let the guerrillas in.

Raymond sat down to take notes in his little book.

"Regarding your question..." I interrupted him.

"No, thanks," he said with a sheepish look.

The Bat Cave

After the battle of Moscarrón, when we got bombed by the A-37s, we couldn't carry on as if those planes didn't exist. We decided to remain at La Guacamaya, but the station had to have maximum security. The problem was how. Nolvo suggested a cave that he and his family used as a hideout when the army searched the villages.

"*Hombre*, I'm not going to say it's a first-class hotel, but it is well-protected. Not even Lucifer will find you there."

It was true. The cave Nolvo offered us was the safest spot on earth. It was hidden on a hillside with a good ten or fifteen metres of earth and rocks on top, so that any bombs that fell nearby wouldn't even scratch us. Getting in and out posed a few problems, though. First you had to walk along the edge of a path and then cross a fast-flowing stream on wooden two-by-fours that seemed to be made of soap in the rainy season. Incredibly dangerous. We ended up hanging ropes to keep from falling in head first. We also had to build some stairs on the last stretch leading to the mouth of the cave. To dive into that hole, which was about a metre wide by a metre high, you had to leap like a gymnast.

As soon as you got inside a disgusting mess of bats would start to fly about, so many of them and so annoying that Nolvo baptised the hideout "The Bat Cave". We set out to make ourselves comfortable there, which from then on was to be Venceremos' recording and transmission studio. Apolonio installed lights with a twelve-volt car battery. We all chipped away at the walls to make them straighter. We levelled the floor and even put down bricks. We got the tables and benches we needed from some abandoned houses. The biggest problem, though, was the damp, a steady drip drip drip. We had to set everything up inside a bamboo structure. We spread a big plastic sheet over this so the water would run off, like a transparent roof against the wet. But of course it was still damp, and the floor soon turned to mud. Pure muck, especially in the rainy season.

We hid the motor outside under good cover, and managed to hang the aerial from the branches of some tall trees nearby. Inside, everything was in its place. We set up one little table with the mixer, the recorders, and a pile of cassettes, another table held the two microphones for the announcers, and at the back was a third where we set up the transmitter, our Viking II.

That place was very secure, but it was a cave after all, and there was a lot of reverberation. Sometimes it seemed like an echo chamber or one of those booths they use for special effects. Other times the babbling of the stream flowing right outside carried over the air. When it rained a lot, it seemed like we were broadcasting from under water.

The worst thing was the rats. You'd be talking on air and you'd see these hairy beasts running around. Corn-fed rats, fat and huge. At one point Marvel wanted to stay and work nights in the cave, but he couldn't stand it because they would come out and run between his legs. Absolutely disgusting. The one who did work there late was Santiago. He'd be up all night with his editorials, and then, at five or so in the morning when it was cold as the devil, you'd see him come out of the cave wearing a black rubber poncho he'd got hold of, with the bats flying all around him. He looked just like Count Dracula in search of unsuspecting necks.

At six in the afternoon, all of us on the Venceremos staff would pile in with the rats and the vampires to put our programme on air. There would be the hosts, Butterfly and Santiago, Marcela at the mixer, Rafi with his "Workers in Struggle" piece, and me with my "News Bullets", Marvel the reporter, Morena helping everyone out, Mariana coordinating it all, Apolonio at the transmitter. We spent nearly all of 1982 in that cave. For a year the rats, the bats, and our production collective all lived together, and we produced a lot, even quarrels.

As it turned out, the Bat Cave became even more notorious as the Cave of Passion. I don't know if the place itself had a peculiar effect on us or if we — a few in particular — were already psychiatrists' fodder, but the fact is that this was the most emotionally confused time ever among the guerrillas. Everything revolved around Marcela. All the love was for Marcela. All the men's eyes followed Marcela. She was a very attractive woman, very sensual. She walked with her head held high, delicately balancing her body as if her feet never touched the ground. Imagine us stuck in that swamp and all of a sudden Miss Universe appears with these incredible hips, voluptuous, ravishing...

"If she stirs like she moves!"

"Oh mama, so many curves and me without brakes!"

In the camp compliments showered down on her, but she paid no heed. She'd go to her work and do it perfectly. Besides the mixer, they put her in charge of setting up the Venceremos archive. Nobody else could have done it better. Marcela was methodical, efficient, graceful, lovely, perfect. There were a lot of reasons for falling in love with her.

The first to succumb was Santiago. I think he had the hots for her ever since that day in Villa El Rosario when Marcela was elected mayor and he introduced her at the First of May rally. Afterwards, when the *cuilios* retook the town, Santiago brought her back to the camp. He trained her for the radio, taught her to run the equipment. Santiago, with his quixotic nature, started to see her as his Dulcinea.

Then Rafi joined in the race, and he employed a more realistic methodology: a love of fruits. While Santiago was writing her passionate poetry, Rafi was up early bringing her a ripe pineapple, a bunch of tiny bananas, a delicious sapodilla. Matter defeated spirit, and the mayor decided to hook up with Rafi. When Santiago found out, he nearly died. He got hold of a sword, I don't know where from, handed Rafi a lance and challenged him to a duel. Like errant knights, they jousted in front of Marcela, beating the shit out of each other. It was silly, but it was also serious. Marcela was really upset.

Just then Rafi got sent far away to carry out a mission in Jucuarán. Taking advantage of the empty seat, Marvel went into action. He's always been of the belief that in love and war any vacuum offers a bridgehead for combat. But his romance with Marcela didn't last, for a couple of reasons. First was Lolita, Marcela's grandma, who came to live with her when Villa El Rosario was taken back and who helped out in the Venceremos kitchen. Lolita's approval was crucial and Marvel was no saint of her devotion. The burned *tortillas* she sent him were an unequivocal sign. Marvel also had to travel — to Mexico to get fitted for a prosthesis and to do a few secret errands. Then, to the astonishment of Santiago who had not yet lost hope, Apolonio the engineer — Rafi's brother, to make things worse — proved he knew about more than adjusting the knobs on the transmitter.

***

After the hammer and anvil operation, I was very sad. Toni's death really affected me. When I got back to El Zapotal, I went to Lolita's house and found her crying. I asked for Marcela and she said, "Apolonio, she's out there looking for you."

Marcela was Toni's sister, and she loved her brother with all her heart. When she found out he died in my arms, she wanted to thank me. I also wanted to tell her of his last moments, but when we met on the soccer field, the only thing I could do was give her a hug and stand there. I've never been any good at consoling, the words don't come.

Later, in the Bat Cave, I had to do all the broadcasts. Toni wasn't there to help me out, so Marcela came religiously and brought me food, soup, whatever she had. Then she'd sit there on the steps to talk. Lolita spoiled me too, she'd send me hot crispy *tortillas*. In spite of all that, I couldn't be too careful around Lolita. All it took was one bad joke or some comment about Marcela, and Lolita wouldn't talk to you for a week. Having Lolita for an enemy was worse than fighting Monterrosa. Nothing beats the stubbornness of a peasant, and nothing could beat her affection for and dedication to Marcela and Toni. They were her children — she'd raised them since they were small. That's why she was so over-protective. So to have a good relationship with Marcela, first you had to win over Lolita. She was the door and she let me in, above all because of what happened with Toni.

***

When Rafi came back from Jucuarán, he faced a dramatic scene: Marcela, his mayor, shacked up with Apolonio, his brother. The jealousy! And to make the uproar complete, Marvel came back from Mexico and added his own passions to the stew.

At six in the afternoon, the bad feelings would reach a crescendo. All of us, the hopeful and the disappointed, had to shut ourselves up inside the same cave. Santiago, who faithfully nurtured his love, announced across from her; Rafi, his throat too dry to swallow, sat next to Apolonio. Even though at that time I was more preoccupied with airplanes than with boobs, I have to admit that her proximity set my insides flying too. With my mouth I said "Salvadoran people!" and with my mind I thought "What an ass!" But Marcela remained unperturbed, raising and lowering the mixer controls. Even the bamboo started to sprout leaves behind her chair, giving her the air of a Vietnamese goddess.

Weeks went by, months, and the situation, instead of easing up, got ever more complicated, like a soap opera. Marvel, seeking new fields to plough, fell in love with Mariana, but Mariana didn't love him. Santiago still drooled over Marcela. Marcela was with Apolonio. Rafi was angry with Apolonio. I was falling in love with Butterfly. Butterfly was falling in love with everyone. I think the only one who calmed things down was Morena.

"Wouldn't you like a little coffee, boys?" she'd say, gourd in hand.

At a meeting for criticism and self-criticism attended by the monitoring team, the security squad and the logistics team, we tried to reach the river of truth.

"Santiago's work is a mess," Apolonio complained. "He leaves things all over the place, the cables, the cassettes. You can't work like that."

"What about you?" Santiago jumped on him. "You're so full of yourself. Just because you're the engineer you think you're hot shit!"

They were off again and nothing could keep the rest of us from leaping into the fray.

"That's enough backbiting," Luisa interceded. "Let's get down to the real problem."

"The real problem is the marquise," said Marvel, raising Marcela's rank since she remained so remarkably clean amid the mud-slinging all around her.

"The real problem", said Apolonio in a burst of sincerity, "is that Santiago wants to screw Marcela. That's why he's mad at me."

"It's not true! That couldn't be the reason!" Tom blurted out suddenly. (Tom was a kid from San Salvador, a lumpen with dark glasses and a scar running the length of his cheek.)

"Why do you say that, Tom?"

"Because if that were the reason, we'd all be pissed off with the engineer. Who of you here doesn't want to screw Marcela, eh?"

Everyone laughed at his foul mouth, except the two contenders, and Marcela, who sat through the entire meeting without saying a word, shedding a few tears now and then. Blue tears, I'd say, because she was an aristocrat even when she cried.

"Get it together," Luisa concluded. "If you go on like this, it's not the enemy who's going to destroy the station, but yourselves."

The waters receded slowly later on. They transferred Marcela, because of her many talents, to another area — press and propaganda. At her going-away party there was a lot of crying. Santiago cried, she cried, we all cried. It brought out the poet in me and I wrote her a few high-tension verses. I still remember them, I've got them somewhere.

Marcela and War

To love Marcela in wartime
is to carry a set of pointy cufflinks in your pocket
to love Marcela in wartime
is to go six feet under
and let yourself be ambushed by wonder.

To love Marcela in wartime
is to manoeuvre under fire and advance towards the unknown
to love Marcela in wartime
is to force yourself to abandon your routine
and explore your wildest dreams
it's to sign off on a love-dispatch
and make an orderly unpoetic retreat
to tear your heart asunder with contact-kisses.
To love Marcela in wartime
is to hate clocks
the way you hate the *cuilios.*
The fragrance of Marcela's collar
is like homegrown coffee
at four in the morning.
Marcela's eyes
are like the moment the Dragonflies have left
after dropping 16 bombs
in Guarumas
without hurting anyone.
Marcela's lips
are like the 105mm artillery shells
that fall far off but send shivers up your spine.
To caress Marcela
is like drinking water during a retreat
knowing you have to keep on marching.
Marcela is a sign up in the sky
she's a silent black cat.
Marcela is a march down the hill to the Torola River
at full speed.
To love Marcela in wartime
is, sometimes,
another war.

Marvin

Fear is for Men

There were two things that scared me to death: winter and A-37 planes.

When those big winter rainstorms began, I'd get so nostalgic I'd sink into a funk I couldn't find my way out of. I couldn't get out of the rain because *everything* was wet. The tent was wet, the bat cave was wet, the paper where I'd write up the news was wet, my clothes were wet... and what bothered me most was knowing that tomorrow everything would still be wet. I don't know how many times I dreamt of a dry shirt, all ironed, like the ones I had at home! And the rains always reminded me of my daughter. I hadn't had news of her in months. I wasn't really afraid that something would happen to her, but that I would die without ever seeing her again.

The idea of death came from the air with the A-37s, the Dragonflies. In '82 I got obsessed with them, just as I had with the death squads when I worked at *La Crónica* in San Salvador. Just the sound of the motors far off, coming closer, would paralyse me. Then the roar when they'd dive, the pounding of the machine-guns, the thunder of the 500-pound bombs. I felt nothing but terror.

Perhaps driven by the intensity of my own fear, I used to go out after the bombings to survey the damage. After a bomb falls it's not only the destruction that gets to you, it's the feeling of death it leaves in its wake, the desolate landscape all around. The trees end up all twisted, bare, leaves on the ground. The rocks get blown out of place. In among the burned vegetation you see huge pieces of blackened shrapnel, razor sharp. Any one of them, just a bit closer, would have cut you up like a chicken.

Another thing that bugged me was the anonymity, though it was easier to take than the airplanes. In San Salvador I was part of a group of poets, artists, intellectuals, and in those circles names meant a lot. You'd sign an article or a painting. Here among the *compas* everything is "collective", all for one. Nobody worries about inanities like what's mine or yours. What counts is not who does things, but that things get done. I found that very hard.

Physical exercise? I've never been too bad at walking. What surprised me when I got to the camp was the physical strength of the peasants. Of course the people are malnourished, I know, I've written about it, but they've got legs like this! They're anaemic, it's true, but the world is all backwards. I had been eating three square meals a day, drinking milk, eating meat, yet after marching two hours I'd fall apart, my tongue down around my ankles, while the malnourished Indians with their muscles of steel were indefatigable! Once I got into shape, though, I got over my exhaustion on the marches.

What made my life bitter, as I said, were the airplanes — and missing my daughter. Marvel sensed I was going to break, so he came over and gave me some good advice, in his own way.

"What's the matter with you?" he said. "Get into the war. What do you want to be? A writer? A poet? If you leave here what kind of shit are you going to write? What are you going to write your poems about, you asshole, about the beauty of the sunrise? Open your eyes Marvin! This is where history is being made! If your number is up you're going to die anyway — in Managua or run over by a car in front of your house. Today you're afraid of the planes. Tomorrow you'll be afraid of cockroaches."

"But..." I began.

"But what?" Marvel lost patience.

"The planes scare the shit out of me, dammit!"

I was convinced the revolution was just, but let others make it, I told myself. As long as they fight wars with planes, count me out. I went to see Luisa.

"I'm leaving," I told her. "I'm not cut out for this."

"Fine," she said.

She accepted my decision, but some time went by before they could set things up for me to leave the front. Just then Alejandro Montenegro, a member of the leadership and commander of the forces in Guazapa, was captured. Alejandro cracked and started collaborating with the enemy. His betrayal really affected me, a lot, a real lot.

You can't call it anything but betrayal, the worst, because when a revolutionary gets caught, he knows what he's going to face. He knows perfectly well what's coming. There you are without a gun, without anything, alone with your beliefs. It's just you and your principles. Your friends, your memories of the organisation, your people, that's what you grab onto, not declarations or empty slogans. Your duty is to remain silent at all costs. If you say even half of something — experience has taught us — that's where they'll catch you and you'll end up singing like Pedro Infante.

Is it possible to withstand the worst tortures? Yes. Ana Guadalupe, Clelia, Chico, Galia — the bastards made their souls howl and yet they said nothing. Others have died and said nothing. You can always find an excuse: man, but they were breaking his finger, giving him electric shocks, sticking a mouse up her vagina, or who knows what other barbarity those psychopathic ogres come up with. I agree, anyone can have a moment of weakness.

Some *compañeros* talked and came out alive, and then they sent letters to the leadership criticising themselves, asking to be forgiven and to be let back in. Naturally, they were stripped of all their authority, but they came back. Mateo for example. But Alejandro Montenegro, a member of the organisation's central committee to make matters worse, not only broke down in front of the enemy, he stayed on to collaborate with them. He said things that cost the lives of several *compañeros*. He gave away positions. A well-paid Judas, that's what he was.

Montenegro betrayed us and the ERP put out a communiqué signed by Joaquín Villalobos. One phrase, above all, struck me: *One craven weakling will not hold back the revolution.* A craven weakling! I sat down under a tree in Agua Blanca and spent the entire night thinking about it. I thought about my daughter. What sort of expression will she have on her face when she finds out I took off?

"You ran away, Daddy," she'll say. When she learns the meaning of those words, that's what she'll call me: "a craven weakling". Cra-ven weakling. What do I want to do, go see my daughter, play with my daughter, watch her grow up so that one day she'll call me a craven weakling? How could I live the rest of my life labelled a coward? The next morning I went to look for Luisa: "I'm going to stay in this shit. No one's going to chase me out of here, not even with a stick! Until we win or until I die!"

"That's better," said Luisa, and she started to laugh, as she always does.

But I had to get over my fear of planes. If not, I wouldn't be worth an old rag. So I declared my war on the A-37s, a personal war against my fear. I started doing some strange things. The airplanes would come and everyone would dive into the shelters. I'd stay outside. I wouldn't go in because I just wouldn't. I'd hear the sound of the A-37 diving and my heart would start to bang away, thump-thump-thump... I'd grit my teeth and think of a poem by Almafuerte, the Argentine writer:

Don't feel defeated when you can't be saved,
even when you are, don't feel enslaved,
tremble with emotion, believe yourself brave
and leap to the attack when your wounds are grave.
Look to the strength of a rusty nail
which though old and ruined does not fail,
not to the craven bravery of the quail
who trims his plumage at first wail.
Go forth like God who never weeps,
or Lucifer who will not pray,
or like a grove of magnificent beech
that thirsts for water yet won't beseech.
Cry out your victory, scream and shout,
even as your head falls down and out.

How many times I recited that poem as I watched the Dragonflies race down at me! That's how I managed to get those A-37s out of me, with an overdose of stoicism. Of course, whenever they come over the horizon it gives me a shudder, like everyone else. Whoever denies that is a liar. Fear is for men, as Che used to say. But it stopped obsessing me. I could sleep and wake up and no longer be thinking only of the A-37s.

In my diary I wrote: *January '83: strategic defeat of the fear of planes.*

The Earth is a Football

No one invited me because I was just a crummy little Venceremos correspondent, and those meetings were for military officers. But I wanted to know. I'd taken part in battles, I'd broadcast the big gunfights, I'd seen plenty of the war, but I'd never seen them plan it out. How do they organise an assault? How do they choose one strategy over another? How do they deploy their troops? Jesus, my curiosity was eating me alive! I know the best way to kill a craving is to give in to it, so I went over to where they were planning the attack on Osicala and Delicias de Concepción.

The little house looked like a schoolroom; the only furniture was two school desks at the back donated by the Alliance for Progress. Around one, Licho and his squad leaders were discussing the next day's military operation. Beside them, at the other desk, Licho's radio operator was leafing through a book. Since it was already night-time, the room was lit by candles. Making like I wasn't interested in what was going on, I approached the radio operator and, though it was none of my business, I asked him what he was reading. Of course, shooting the breeze with him was a cover so I could eavesdrop on the others.

"Have you seen this?" the *compa* asks.

"Of course," I tell him. "I had it at school!"

It was Levi Marrero's book *The Earth and its Resources*, and it was true, I still remembered the illustrations because it's a good textbook. Now I had an excuse to sit down. The radio operator got excited and started asking me what this geography thing is all about. I was even more excited, and I started explaining how the earth is like a ball and it turns around the bigger ball, the sun, and that the moon turns around the earth, because of the law of gravity and the law of balls... I wasn't in any hurry. On the contrary, with my mouth I explained and with my ears I eavesdropped on the neighbouring desk.

Licho was my hero. I called him Commander Panther because in combat that's what he becomes. If you could only see him, he's a pure Pipil Indian: skin the colour of roasted coffee, eyes like almonds, flat nose, thick lips, clean-shaven, muscular, hands calloused from work. A genuine *campesino* from Morazán, one of those who joined Christian base communities and from there went on to the guerrillas. I never saw him unarmed, and he's got infallible aim, no *cuilio* ever gets away from him. His military training, the basics, he got from the enemy. On the orders of our organisation, he let himself be recruited and did his year's military service. Many have done that. It's a good idea because they learn everything there. The army teaches you to shoot, you use up a few rounds of ammunition, you see how the army is structured on the inside, how it works, and then you come out and fight against them. Licho did that in '77. From there he went on to become one of the guerrillas' best military officers, and a great political cadre as well.

So there I was playing dumb, blabbing on about the moon with the radio operator and listening to what Licho was explaining to the other officers: "We're in this ravine, right? Okay, there's a big boulder there, remember? Well that's where we've got to rendezvous. From there we'll advance in silence about 75 yards uphill to the mango tree by the first trench we're going to attack. Then the enemy's going to react from south to north, they won't have any choice. They'll retreat through the little gulch and come around this way, see? That's where we catch them. We ambush them in the little thicket on this side..."

I was fascinated by the way Licho explained it all, drawing lines on an improvised map. It was the first time I had a look at how they designed military strategy. What impressed me most was the absolute mastery these men had over the terrain. They talked about the battlefield as if it were their back yard. Inch by inch, they knew the potential of each spot, the difficulties of every path, and most important of all, they knew the relationship that the people — their's and the enemy's — would establish with that terrain. In war, such knowledge is half the battle.

"You take this height here. If there's any resistance, if it isn't over quickly, then all of you go off to the side and get your troops in order. They won't dare advance, they've got no protection there. This squadron will ask for heavier weaponry and they'll wait at the foot of the hill until it comes in from this flank here..."

They had photographic knowledge of the terrain, as if each stone and each tree had its own name! Licho knew where you could escape, where was the best place to lay an ambush, where you could find cover, where to carry out the wounded. All this information allowed him to put together an extremely rigorous, meticulous plan.

At about midnight, it was over. They finished up the last details and brought the meeting to a close. I said to myself: now I can go to bed. Now I know what's planned for tomorrow, and tomorrow I'll find out if they manage to pull off what they dreamed up here tonight. I started to get up from the desk, but Licho got up first and jumped on me like a panther.

"What's up with you?" he says.

"What do you mean?" I ask him.

"You were filling that kid's head with nothing but lies. What kind of garbage is this that the earth is round and it spins like a ball? Who said that?"

That's when I realised that the curiosity was mutual, that Licho was eavesdropping on me as much as I was on him. We'd spent the entire evening at the same party.

"What did you tell that monkey about the moon being cold? How do they know that? Sit down. Tell me."

Leaders don't beg. Licho is not a man to say, "Do me the favour." He leads 500, 800, 1,000 guerrillas, and if he says "Advance", they advance. What's more they will all have a blind faith that the order will take them to victory because it's been well thought out. Because it's an order from Licho. So, even though I was so sleepy I could barely sit up, I too had to advance. He launched into a scientific interrogation about the earth, the moon, the planets, lateral and rotating motion...

"What about the people who live in the south? How come they don't fall off if they're on their heads?"

Licho was fascinated listening to my explanations of geography and astronomy. We were at it until four in the morning. The supreme master of the terrain learned that night that the earth we stand on is round like a great big football!

It dawned. Our troops took Osicala and Delicias de Concepción, just as they had planned.

"María, Take Your Tit, Give Me Mine"

A shape appeared at the Sapo River. At first no one paid it any heed; later, several *compas* insisted. They said that when they passed by there at night, some animal would be making a noise in the water. At the slightest movement, it would run away to the other side.

"It's a sea dog," said the old folks.

This legend got tangled up with another one about a puma that was devouring the cattle on our front. Sure enough, we would sometimes find the remains of calves that had been killed and eaten, so they put together an operation to hunt the puma down. They set ambushes, even took radio operators along when the fighters went off to find it, a fully-fledged expedition. At last they cornered it and finished it off. A puma was a rare sight in Morazán, but there it was.

In high spirits from the hunt, the *compas* went off to find the sea dog. Since nobody found anything, they decided it must have been the puma that came out at night to drink at the river. But he who doesn't search can also find. Less than two weeks later, several *compas* came back to the camp white with fear. They'd seen the shape again. This time they saw its shadow clearly as it ran off through the thicket.

"It's a woman," one said.

"How do you know?"

"I saw her tits."

Some laughed, others got as serious as the ones who had seen it. This was nothing to joke about. Next to the river, at night, running and making men run: it could only be her.

"It's the Hag," concluded a member of the squadron.

"That's right," said an old man. "*La Ciguanaba* is around and we'd better keep our eyes peeled. She doesn't forgive."

"What can we do?"

"The only spell against her is this prayer: 'María, take your tit, give me mine'. You've got to repeat it many times, many times, until that damned woman disappears. It's the only thing that will make her flee."

"There's a better remedy," said a *compa* who'd had some experience. "Don't go near the river at night. Because when a man hears her laughter, he forgets the prayer. It happened to me. I froze like a stone, and that's the danger, because *La Ciguanaba* is cruel."

"What's this *Ciguanaba* you're on about?" mocked the sceptics. "That's bullshit, backward thinking. *La Ciguanaba* doesn't exist."

"But it does. I saw it."

"What did you see? Come on, tell us."

"A big black shape. It was horrible."

"It could be a *cuilio*. Or *El Cipitillo*."

"*El Cipitillo* is a dwarf, and besides he only goes after women."

"Well, come clean with us, if it's you she's after..."

"Don't kid around. Go to the river yourself. We can talk after that."

Some were crossing themselves and others were joking, but the legend soon spread throughout the guerrilla front. Believers and atheists alike broke into a cold sweat when it was dark and they had to stand guard or simply walk by that bend in the Sapo River.

Time went by, the BRAZ[3] was sworn in, Alvaro Magaña was inaugurated president of the country, '82 was over, '83 began, and the shadow was still an obligatory topic at evening bullshit sessions in the camps, because every once in a while, with faith or without it, someone would come in with the story that he'd seen it, or another that he'd caught a glimpse of it. One September night the boys of our squadron were doing exploratory exercises by the edge of the river.

"Look!" one whispered.

The shape took off like other times, but this time the *compas* summoned up their courage and followed it.

"María, take your tit, give me mine... María, take your tit, give me mine... María, take your tit, give me mine..." they all repeated down the line.

The shape ran off and they ran after it, until at last they caught up to it in the brambles. Sure enough, it was a woman, but a horrible woman. Her hair was all tangled and incredibly long, her face was caked with dirt, a few dirty rags barely covered that bag of bones.

"Are you from this life or the other?" they asked her.

She didn't say a word, just looked at them, her eyes out of orbit. The *compas*, still repeating the spell, took her and marched her back to the camp.

"We captured *La Ciguanaba*!"

In the uproar that ensued, someone had the sense to take her to the hospital. Eduardo, the doctor, examined her and checked her vital signs.

"This is a human woman," he told everyone.

"It's the Hag, doctor."

"She sure looks it, the poor thing. Give her a bath. Scrub her well."

"Any medicine, doctor?" a medic asked.

"Food," said Eduardo. "That's all."

They took the wretched woman to the washing hole, where they bathed her, dressed her and combed her hair. It was like a miracle: she became a pretty young girl, starving, but very pretty. They offered her coffee and beans. With the bath and the *compas'* good manners her tongue started working.

"What's your name, daughter?"

"Lucía."

"Where are you from?"

"From El Mozote, from before the killings."

This girl was one of the very few survivors of the massacre ordered by Colonel Domingo Monterrosa in El Mozote nearly two years before, in December '81. She managed to escape who knows how, while the soldiers of the Atlacatl Battalion machine-gunned everyone, and ran until she got to the Sapo River, which divides the region in two, separating El Zapotal from La Guacamaya. It's not very big, but in the winter it reaches up to some caves you can see along the banks. Lucía hid in one of those, and there she stayed, all by herself. The *cuilios* ended their operation, we set up the radio station again in El Zapotal, the front's life went on, and that girl, still terrified, only came out of her cave to go to the river. There she survived by eating leaves and a bit of fish. Nobody knew about her. Nobody looked for her because all her relatives, all from El Mozote, had died. She didn't know. New military operations were launched in the zone, the *cuilios* would bomb, then they'd leave. She said that when she heard the blasts she thought that they were still killing in El Mozote, that the *cuilios* hadn't left her town and never would.

She saw the face of the real monsters, the ones that do exist. She saw when they put children in the ovens and when they stabbed them with bayonets. She saw them rape the women and then cut their throats. She saw them shut her neighbours up in the church and machine-gun them. She saw so much horror that she didn't dare leave her hiding place. In the cave by the Sapo River she lost all notion of time and, being so alone, she even forgot how to speak.

"Now you can say all the things you've kept quiet these two years."

Santiago did a long interview with her for Venceremos. It was almost a series. We wanted everyone, every last person, to speak on the radio. Even *La Ciguanaba.*

Playing for Time

That year was one of great battles and spectacular victories. In the first few months of '83 we swept away the enemy's fixed positions north of the Torola River. In March we swore in the BRAZ and right from its first campaign it became the terror of the *cuilios*, gaining ground like a regular army. The truth is that in those days the only thing that made us guerrillas rather than a regular army was our audacity. The BRAZ had four battalions of 250 fighters apiece, and on top of that you'd have to add on the support personnel — cooks for a thousand mouths, corn grinders, *tortilla*-cooks, mule teams carrying bags upon bags of corn to front lines that advanced every day. It was an amazing organisation, difficult to imagine for anyone who didn't see it in action.

Despite Monterrosa's incessant attacks, the BRAZ continued advancing, victory after victory, towards San Miguel in the south, La Unión in the east, and Usulután in the west. By the middle of the year, around June, we were holding so much territory, so many zones were under our control, that we were getting bogged down. We had to change strategies, because once you've managed to deploy your troops over a broad area, penetrating enemy territory, how do you handle the logistics of maintaining so many far-flung operations? You've got a thousand details to pin down and a thousand new things to coordinate. For a couple of months we didn't take any offensive action and the enemy interpreted this as weakness, that we had run out of steam. They were wrong! We were preparing the great offensive of September, the one that did them the most damage of all.

According to our conception of regular war, we had to begin with an overwhelming assault. We wanted to launch the new campaign by attacking nothing less than the Third Infantry Brigade in San Miguel, the largest and most important base in the entire country, which housed some 2,000 troops and was led at the time by bigshot Colonel Jaime Flores, a fat sonofabitch as evil as he was obese. The plan was to crush the base with massive artillery fire. Since the Third Brigade is a bit outside the city, the risk that shells would fall on the civilian population was very small. The operation required tremendous military skill — and an incredible degree of coordination.

For example we had two 120mm cannons which we had taken from the army in the battle of San Felipe. Imagine what it meant to transport those huge heavy mortars from Morazán to San Miguel, drag them with tractors or mules, for hours and hours right by enemy positions until we could set them up just five kilometres from the base. It wasn't a question of shooting three times. We had forty 120mm grenades, which are papayas this big, and a battery of 81mm mortars. There were two groups of M-60 machine guns which we had to set up even closer to the base. From the south, we'd attack with 50mm machine-guns and a 75mm cannon, which is very destructive.

All in all, it was going to be a battle like we'd never seen, like the end of the world. I don't think any guerrilla force in Latin America has ever attempted an action like this one. Just to transport the artillery pieces, set them up in secret, then bring them out without losing them, would be an incredible exploit. But these military things merit their own book and aren't what we should talk about here. Let's talk about Venceremos, because it also cut in at the dance of the Third Brigade.

The shooting was to start at eleven o'clock at night. How could Venceremos, which did its programme at six, keep people's attention in order to broadcast the battle live? How could we keep our audience listening until eleven? Not only our audience but journalists from the other stations so the government couldn't deny the attack or censor the information the following day? It was pointless to win great battles if the media didn't cover it. The point was to cause a scandal in the papers, to make the propaganda impact as great as the military one.

This assault had a very special objective; to raise the morale of a people who had suffered genocide, to break the trauma of terror by defeating in their strongest fortress an enemy that claims to be invincible. But all this depended on everyone listening to us at eleven o'clock that Saturday night on 3 September.

The day before, on Friday, Atilio came over to the radio collective and told us: "Write a soap opera that lasts forty minutes."

"Forty minutes?"

"Yes, forty minutes, not one minute more or less."

"What about?"

"Any piece of shit, but make it funny, joke after joke. Let your imagination run wild. This soap is going to be crucial!"

We didn't know what they were cooking up. But in any case we had to make up forty minutes of kidding around. About what? The sex life of Reagan and Nancy? Monterrosa's intimate affairs? Since we didn't have a plot, we improvised a mix of all sorts of scenes, short dubbed-over commercials, a clown that would come on every so often to tell a dirty joke, things like that. We even had General Vides Casanova, the minister of defence, doing a Shakespearean monologue.

We spent the entire night recording; it seemed to go on forever. Laughing ourselves silly, we finally filled up forty minutes of jokes and skits. The mother of all of our "Subversive Guacamaya" pieces, nearly an hour long!

The next morning, still unaware of the plan, we went by truck to Ocote Seco, a hill from which you can see the city of San Miguel and the Third Infantry Brigade. Luisa, who along with Atilio had thought up the radio trick, came to tell us the news and to give us our instructions.

"Guys, we're going to assault that big fort you see over there. Get ready because it's going to be ugly. You've got to do this and this."

The idea, as I said, was to get the audience to stay tuned until eleven o'clock, zero hour, the precise moment of the attack. At six, as always, we put our usual programme on air. But throughout it we announced that during the second broadcast at eight — which was almost always just a repeat of the first — we would have big news.

Attention! All national media and all our listeners today, be advised that on our eight o'clock show tonight we will have an exclusive detailed report on the coup d'etat now being planned...

We made up the story about the coup to attract them and distract them at the same time. So they'd tune in, even if it was just out of curiosity to get the latest gossip, but they would never guess what was really on the way.

We started broadcasting again at eight, but only for a few minutes. Due to some technical problems, we said, we had to hold back the news until 9.30. But make sure you tune in, don't miss it, because the political scandal we're going to unveil is extremely serious. Oh yes, and we will also have an especially outrageous episode of the "Subversive Guacamaya"! Then we put on a few previews of the show, like the big stations do.

You'll hear this and much much more on our special broadcast at nine-thirty! A festival of fun on Venceremos!

When 9.30 came around we turned on the equipment once more and started our countdown.

In a few moments we will have the important news we've been promising. Don't miss it! It's urgent!

Some people from Perquín told us later that since the news didn't come on and neither did the Guacamaya, they put a chicken on to cook, invited over a few friends, and they all stayed up together waiting by the radio. Thousands of others in countryside and city were doing the same.

We ask you to please stay tuned, because in just a few short minutes...

We read a news brief, we repeated a commentary, gave another preview of the show, we broadcast whatever we could put our hands on. We had to burn up time.

At last, the clock crawled to 10.20. At that exact moment we put on our so well-announced and so quickly-slapped-together little show. Our tongues got a break. We had forty minutes to watch the cassette spin.

"Open your mouths!" Luisa turned up and shoved a no-doze pill in each of the broadcasters' mouths. Behind her came the gourd filled with coffee. We got so wired we plugged in another tape recorder and put on some music just for us, and there we were all dancing: Butterfly with Chiquito, Santiago with Luisa, me with the broom, everyone waiting for the show to finish so that the other one, the real spectacular, could start in San Miguel.

Two minutes left. Just as the clowns of the Guacamaya were signing off from their ever-faithful and ever-patient audience, we drowned them out with the Venceremos alarm. Ever since '81, everyone in El Salvador knows that when that siren goes off, something heavy is coming. Right then, at 11:00 p.m. sharp, the BRAZ started firing on the Third Brigade and Santiago opened his mouth:

People of El Salvador! At this very moment we have begun a ferocious artillery attack on the Third Brigade in San Miguel!

Jesus, that wasn't today's news, it was a simultaneous broadcast! Up-to-the-hour news? Up to the minute? This was up to the second! Atilio, who was directing the battle from the command post, came over with a big smile: "The base is burning! And Colonel Flores is screaming like an old woman in an earthquake!"

Atilio sat down in front of the microphone and began to read the first war dispatch, which had been written ahead of time. But by military radio we already had news that the situation was under control, that the mortars were crushing the enemy and the *cuilios*, scared to death, didn't know how to respond. So Santiago and I, with our tongues hanging out like neckties, started writing the next dispatch while Atilio finished reading the first.

We were in this rush five minutes after the shit hit the fan, when our monitors heard that KL in the capital had interrupted their dance music to sound the alarm.

Attention! Attention all listeners! At this very moment the clandestine Radio Venceremos in a special broadcast is announcing that... We have our first telephone contact with that city... Our mobile units are on their way to San Miguel to see for ourselves what is occurring there...

Just then a frenzied journalist began reporting from a provincial station in San Miguel:

...it's like the end of the world, ladies and gentlemen! This is the end! The roar is terrifying, we can barely broadcast!

We did it! We hit the base and the press! The rest was a chain reaction across all the news shows in the country. Meanwhile, we were broadcasting live and direct from our camp where we could see the lights of San Miguel and the cloud of smoke that was rising from the infamously impregnable fortress of the Third Infantry Brigade.

We wiped the enemy out: 300 killed or wounded. Colonel Flores himself got a good scratch. Seven thousand pounds of shells rained down on the fort, which was the operations base for the gringo advisers and supplied all the forces in the East. It was left in rubble. Not one shell fell outside the base, all those big papayas dropped right on target. The artillery attack, ten on a military scale of one to ten, was led by Manolo, Captain Mena Sandoval, one of the patriotic officers who joined the guerrillas during the offensive of '81. The entire operation was run by the BRAZ High Command, one of the most skilful and brilliant military units in the history of warfare. That's no exaggeration. You don't believe it? How much do you want to bet?

To the Cacahuatique Aerial

"From Cacahuatique you can see the world", a peasant from Morazán once told me. It's true. That volcano south of the Torola River is the highest spot around. From there you can see all the way to San Miguel and San Vicente and even to Honduras. Whoever controls Cacahuatique controls the entire province.

At the very peak of the enormous hill, the enemy had a base they called the Aerial where they had their communications centre, tracking equipment, television aerials, everything. Since the position was so vital, the US advisers had set up an incredibly sophisticated defence with fortified trenches, ditches, minefields. It was impregnable, but the BRAZ decided it was to be their next military objective.

To take the Cacahuatique Aerial was no piece of cake. Several days beforehand, in strict secrecy, we had to begin bringing in the support weaponry, the huge artillery batteries essential for such a large assault. The BRAZ columns left on a long march, skirting the usual access routes so the enemy wouldn't notice how many troops we were deploying. As on other occasions, I went along as correspondent for Venceremos. Marvin and Santiago stayed behind in the camp at El Pedrero to broadcast the attack live.

We arrived at the rendezvous point in the middle of the night. From there, on the side of the volcano, we were deployed to one flank or another. Luckily for me, I got to go up with Whitey Will's column, the one that was to take the base. Cacahuatique is a great big mountain of coffee groves. You should have seen us climbing past those coffee trees on tiptoe with all our gear, with mortars, even a 75mm cannon, the ones that have wheels! It took several men to push it uphill.

Before dawn broke, the secret was out, and the artillery fire began. Tape recorder in hand, I started reporting what I saw, live and direct. Since we expected the planes to show up right away, everyone carried a pick and a shovel. You'd get to a new position, dig yourself a trench and jump in before the bombs made mincemeat of you. A few minutes later, you'd head farther up the hill towards the Aerial.

The *compas* advanced quickly and soon we reached the base's first line of defence. It was a high point where several *cuilios*, dug in with a machine gun, kept us from even sticking our heads up.

"Just try and get us out of here, you shit-eating guerrillas! Come on up, sons of bitches, Pijirichi's here waiting for you!"

Rat-a-tat-tat, the stuttering gun kept us at bay. The *compas* tried to advance but we got nowhere. A political officer was cheering us on with a megaphone, and we were sent forward again to the tune of the National Anthem and slogans recorded from Venceremos, but again we'd hear that voice from the other side: "You dare, wimps! Pijirichi's here waiting for you!"

Rat-a-tat-tat again. Who was that damned Pijirichi? Our people would retreat. We'd get organised once more. Whitey Will: "You go that way, and you attack from here. I'll support you from this side. Send for our cannon... No, not yet. We haven't got this spot secured. We might lose it... I don't give a damn if we lose it! We've got to take that trench!"

"Come on up, *piricuacos*! Pijirichi's waiting for you!"

This was too much. The *compas* launched a mega-assault, they set up the 50mm cannon and a hellish gun-battle ensued. You'll think I'm kidding but a few minutes later I heard a *cuilio* yell out: "Duck down idiot or you'll end up like Pijirichi!"

At last we took the trench, along with our first prisoners, and we continued on up the side of the volcano.

***

From our camp in El Pedrero we could see Cacahuatique perfectly. There far off, up high on the nipple of that big stone tit, we could see the Aerial we wanted to take.

Marvel had gone along as correspondent while Santiago and I remained behind to run the programme. Although we still didn't have the cassettes with the first dispatches, we could measure the *compas'* advance by where the planes were bombing. At dawn they bombed down low on the sides. By 9am they were bombing halfway up, and that's how it went. Our forces would climb a little higher and the bombs would follow. Given the lack of other means, we got the news by eye. While Santiago was announcing, I'd go out and climb up on some rocks from where I could get a good view. I'd see where the bombs were falling and I'd run back to the shelter: "Santiago, they're already at La Campana! They've reached La Campana!"

And Santiago with all his passion would turn on the microphone:

"In these very moments, at such-and-such o'clock, our forces have reached La Campana and they continue their victorious march towards the Cacahuatique Aerial. More information shortly!"

Then he'd go off, leaving a musical bridge, and stick his head out from among the rocks. He'd go back on even more excited:

"Special bulletin! Special bulletin! Our troops are marching on the Aerial! They can't be stopped!"

I don't think any anchor ever had more first-hand — or first-sight — information. The news wasn't hot, it was boiling!

***

The first soldiers we took prisoner told us everything we needed to know about the base in return for being handed over to the Red Cross. These fields are mined, you can only get in by that path, the walled emplacements are here and there. Weighing the difficulties, our commanders decided to make a final assault by night. To make sure of the information, Whitey Will sent out scouts, four guys in pyjamas, their skin painted black, nocturnal cats, nothing but shadows, and on their return they filled in the gaps.

"This is a tough nut to crack but it'll be no sweat. Two grenades each, we slink along the wall, we wipe out this trench here, we take that machine gun there, and then we take on the other, then seven more guys can slip in, and then us. Once we're inside, the game's over. Okay?"

"All right," said Will. "In half an hour."

The commanders coordinated their plans and at ten o'clock that night so much shooting erupted that it even made the crater of the volcano tremble. We did it. We planted the FMLN flag on the Cacahuatique Aerial. The proud bastion that the gringos said could resist a siege for over two weeks fell to the BRAZ in less than 24 hours!

Along with their lieutenant, the *cuilios* who weren't killed or wounded scrambled to get away towards one corner of the heliport. They jumped off a cliff trying to escape, a leap which turned out to be pretty suicidal. The lieutenant hurt his spine in the fall, but even worse for them, they chose to escape exactly where we were waiting for them. All we had to do was open up our knapsacks and watch them fall in, one by one, as many as sixty prisoners.

I entered the Aerial with my tape recorder running, describing all I saw. I crossed the heliport and there, in front of one of the communications huts, they were piling up the captured materiel: a mountain of rifles, another mountain of backpacks, another of military clothes... All the *compas* were euphoric, trying things on, changing their boots. The political officers were trying to control things, to keep the euphoria from becoming banditry, because that's the psychology of war booty, of course. The insanity of combat and the smell of gunpowder gives you that urge to plunder. You should see how the smell of gunpowder makes you drunk! Real drunk! But like I was saying, the political officers made sure that everything was distributed fairly later on. It could well be that the unit that made the assault didn't get any of it because we had another unit in the military school that needed it more, who knows?

I went into the transmission room and found Licho talking to the technician who operated it. Licho invited him to work with us but the man said no, he didn't like war, he was just a technician, the army had recruited him forcibly and kept him against his will.

"So what do you want to do?"

"Go home."

"Fine. Go ahead. But first tell me which is the transmitter for such-and-such a band" — a radio-communications network which we were never able to penetrate and which was one of the principal objectives of taking the Aerial.

"This is it," the technician patted an enormous Motorola, taller than a man.

"Perfect. How do you run it?"

"Like this and this. There are the spare parts."

"Take it apart. We'll take it with us."

What a prize! We had in our hands nothing less than the National Guard's super-secret internal network!

In the kitchen I continued reporting. The *compas* had found a storeroom loaded with provisions: boxes of eggs, boxes of sugar, Maggi soups, instant coffee... We were hungry, and a brisk cold wind was blowing in the early morning, so we built a nice fire and started cooking. We were in the midst of this victory party, telling stories and stuffing our faces, when we spotted in a corner a soldier who had been shot in the abdomen. He was on the floor trying to keep his intestines from falling out.

"Finish that man off," one of our commanders said. "There's no way we can save him."

It's one thing to shoot in battle, but quite another to kill a man in cold blood. The political officer in charge of the zone went over to the soldier: "Do you want us to kill you?" he asked.

An expression of horror came over the man's face and he shook his head, so the political officer didn't kill him. Let him die on his own, then. But the man wouldn't die, and for the rest of the night he was like a spectre dragging himself about on the ground begging everyone: "Get me out of here. Take me to a doctor."

"What doctor?" they'd say. "There's no doctor here."

With all the tumult, the fighters didn't even notice him, but I kept tripping over this guy everywhere, and he'd look at me with that pleading expression. What could I do? I took my reporting and my tape recorder elsewhere. As soon as I'd get there I'd feel him behind me again. "Help me, please..."

He was really getting on my nerves. Finally, in the morning about four o'clock, Licho says to me: "Let's go see the prisoners so you can interview them. Let them make a statement on Venceremos."

We climbed over the precipice where the soldiers had jumped with their lieutenant. As we were going down the hillside I ran into the man again. There he was, falling down and pulling himself back up, heading downhill.

"Hey, where are you going?" an officer shouted.

"I'm going to find a doctor," I heard him say, his voice like a thread.

"Well, get as far as you can."

The wounded soldier went on down and several members of the BRAZ started arguing. These are the guys who a few hours earlier had been firing 50mm machine guns, 90mm cannons, the ones who attack like wild animals, who stop at nothing until they've taken their objective, and here they were getting all worked up over the dying man.

"I told you to kill him."

"But he's still alive. How can I kill him if he's still alive?"

"It's because he doesn't want to die. That's it."

"Worse for him. He's going to die anyway, but he'll suffer more."

"He'll probably make it, you know."

"No, *hombre*, make it? No way. The earth is already asking for him. Don't be cruel, man. Better do it with one shot so he won't die little by little."

"You kill him then."

But nobody could kill him. We went off to see the prisoners and I talked to all of them, one by one, including the lieutenant. After I'd been interviewing them for a while, a report came in that the Atlacatl Battalion was on the way from Osicala to take back the Aerial, and that the airforce were about to begin bombing again. This was about mid-morning, and then I saw our man go by again. He was still doing his thing, dragging himself down the volcano.

"Look," said one *compa*, "that soldier is escaping. Get him!"

"Let the man go," I said. "He's the only one who's going to survive this war. Some fucking will to live!"

We arranged with the Red Cross to hand over all the prisoners, including the lieutenant. It had to happen fast because Monterrosa's Atlacatl was already coming up the north flank.

"Marvel, write a full report of the battle," Licho said.

It was noon already. I sat down, left my rifle and knapsack beside a wall, pulled out my notebook, and started writing. I was leaning against a coffee tree. About ten metres away, Ada, Licho's radio operator, was also seated sending messages. In a few moments, Bravo came by dressed in camouflage and carrying a G-3 in his hands. Bravo was a very special *compa*, a great human being. He had been a soldier before and when we captured him, he said he'd like to join up. He took a course in our military school and soon became one of our best commanders. He was extremely well-liked and very brave, as if with the guerrillas he wanted to make up for time lost in the army. I saw him go by and I thought: let's ask Bravo something because an ex-soldier's opinion could give my report a nice touch.

There I was, interviewing Bravo, when bombs started to rain down right on the Aerial, which was close to the side of the volcano where we were standing.

"That plane!" Bravo yelled. "Run!"

I turned around and saw an A-37 diving right at us. I even saw it drop the bomb because you can see the little black ball falling, and you can tell if it's coming at you or not. It was coming right at us. Those were fractions of a second of course. Bravo squatted to pick up his gear, I ran a few metres downhill, jumped, and lay flat. As I hit the ground, the bomb went off. When I opened my eyes I couldn't see a thing. Everything was black smoke and the unbearable smell of gunpowder. My ears were buzzing like the howling of radio interference. I started touching myself to see what was missing. I've got my arms, both of them. I've got my legs, I moved them, they work. I checked myself all over and found no blood anywhere. When I sat up I heard Ada, the radio operator, shouting: "Marvel, are you there? They fucked me!"

I got up as best I could, got to her and she showed me her boot. There was a little hole in the heel and blood was pouring out of it like a spout.

"Don't take off that boot," I told her. "It's stopping you up like a cork."

"Take it off me. It hurts a lot. Look, here comes the plane again! Get me out of here!"

Again the A-37, which had turned around. I tried to pick her up but Ada was heavy.

"Hurry up, here it comes!"

I couldn't carry her. I dragged her, and since it was steep we ended up rolling downhill. Boom! the second bomb went off. That's when another fear gripped me, because the command post was in that coffee grove they were bombing. Licho was there, the political officers, everyone. Then I saw a medic coming.

"Sister, come here, help me! Ada's wounded!"

The medic cut her boot open with a pair of scissors and without any anaesthesia began to pull out the piece of shrapnel that had pierced her heel. Ada, crying from the pain, remembered: "Marv, I left my rifle up there. Please."

"I'll get it for you. I have to go anyway to get my pack and see what happened to the others."

I start climbing. When I get about halfway up, I get this horrible, uncontrollable urge to shit. I pull down my pants and since it was on a hillside I grab hold of a coffee tree. But when I start to shit I feel like throwing up, and I can't figure out which to do first. It must be the fumes from the bomb, I think. I empty myself out from both ends, clean myself off as best I can with some coffee leaves, and carry on up the hill.

When I got there, to the place where I had hit the ground with the first bomb, I started shaking. These are anti-personnel bombs. They don't make a crater, they destroy everything within a radius of twenty or thirty metres. There was nothing left, not a tree, nothing. Everything had been pulverised. I'd managed to throw myself down behind the dirt terracing that they build in coffee groves. There was the notebook I had in my hand when the bomb went off, and the distance between my notebook and the edge of the destruction was barely twenty centimetres. Since I fell onto a lower level, the shrapnel went over my head, and the destruction from the bomb ended twenty centimetres from where I had lain. I escaped death by that little bit of dirt! Oh, man!

A terrible fear gripped me and I got an icy feeling at the top of my stomach and an urge to shit that I can't describe. I pulled my pants down again and grabbed on to a coffee tree. When I was about to start, again the nausea. Vomiting and shitting at the same time. This time it isn't from any fumes, I thought. I pulled up my pants, grabbed Ada's gun, and since I didn't see anyone about I started back down the hill. Halfway there, again that sick feeling in my stomach, insufferable cramps, but this third time when I squat down I feel cold on my back. Cold? I touch it and look at my hand and it's soaked in blood. I'm dying and I didn't even know! Holy shit! What is this?

I take off my shirt to see the size of the hole. Sure enough, the shirt's all stained with blood, but when I look through it at the light I can't find any bullet hole. Then I remember the little hole in Ada's heel. It's a fucking piece of shrapnel. Where did it get me? Did it puncture my lung? I breathed deeply, remembering the awful noise other *compañeros* who had been wounded in the lungs made. Of course, I thought, the vomiting and shitting is because I'm torn to shreds inside. Now I get it! My thoughts filled with all the garbage you think when you're wounded, and holding my bloody shirt in my hand, I ran down to find the medic.

"Buddy, what's the matter?"

"Look me over quick. I think I'm dying"

"Take it easy, *hombre*."

"Hurry up, I'm bleeding."

"It's nothing, *hombre*. Just a little shrapnel."

"In my lung?"

"In your skin, *hombre*. It's nothing."

"Are you sure it's nothing?"

"You've got to be kidding. You won't hang up your sneakers on account of this one."

"Thank God and all the blessed souls in purgatory I don't have to join them yet!"

I calmed down and put my bloody shirt back on. Ada was still there, holding the foot the shrapnel had pierced.

"Ada can't walk," the medic says. "We've got to find some *compas* who can make her a stretcher. Go back up and let them know."

I climbed up again, panting. I found Licho back where the bomb fell, looking very serious. It was like a scene from a horror movie. In one hand he held the twisted barrel of a G-3. In the other, a mangled arm with the camouflage uniform still on it.

"Bravo died. The bomb tore him to pieces."

Who knows what expression I must have had on my face to make Licho speak me so sternly: "Marvel! What's wrong with you?"

"Nothing's wrong with me..."

"THEN WAKE UP, SONOFABITCH!"

When Licho yells, Licho yells. That must have been heard all the way to the enemy's command centre on the other side of the volcano. It worked because it knocked me out of my state of shock.

"War is war," he told me. "Come on, help me pick up Bravo. Are you all right?"

"I'm all right, but don't make me pick him up. I was right next to him when the bomb went off. It would be like picking up myself."

"You were here?"

"Here."

"Don't lie to me. If you'd been here, you wouldn't be here now to tell the story."

"Well I was here and I'm going to tell this story over the radio. I've got my report here still unfinished, with Bravo's last words."

"Put in your commentary that... that this is why we're fighting. So that this should never happen to Bravo or even Pijirichi or anyone. Put that in."

"Anything else?"

"Nothing. Oh, yes. We got word from the *compas* who were with the Red Cross. They say that at mid-afternoon a wounded soldier showed up."

"A soldier?"

"One with his intestines falling out. He's going to be okay."

The Devil's Always Ready

We began transmitting on FM in 1982, in September I think. We set up a low-wattage repeating station in Guazapa, and since it's only 25 kilometres from Guazapa to San Salvador, the signal entered the capital like a bullet. We started to get a big audience in the city, especially among the youth.

The technique was simple. From Morazán we'd send a signal on the two-metre band to Guazapa, about 120 kilometres as the crow flies. The *compas* there would receive it clear as could be and bounce it towards San Salvador, and that was that.

In June '83, when Monterrosa came up the Torola River with the Atlacatl Battalion, we had to move to Colorado Hill. We set up a new link to send the signal from there to Guazapa, but at that height the enemy was able to zero in on us right away and they started interfering with both the short wave and the two-metre link. Since the signal they received in Guazapa was fuzzy, they couldn't send it on to the capital. Damn! They screwed us! As Lenin would say, what was to be done? Or rather, what was to be done with Lenin? Because "Lenin" was the code name for the big station that sent the signal from Morazán.

We thought of a trick: broadcast on two different frequencies, one to ring the bells and the other to send off the procession. We continued broadcasting on the two-metre band to Guazapa at six o'clock, the hour of Venceremos's usual programme, but that was only a ghost signal to catch their interference. Before that, at an agreed-upon time, we'd broadcast the same programme on the six-metre band. They'd record it on cassette and then carefully synchronise with us at six o'clock to play it as if they were just bouncing our two-metre signal at that very moment. The *cuilios* were dumbfounded, they went nuts. They interfered here but it still came out clean as a whistle over there, and in the capital people tuned in as if none of this were happening!

We needed a trick like that when we were in the camp at El Pedrero. The September offensive, the BRAZ's tremendous advance, gave us a stable rearguard, so much so that we were no longer satisfied with only having FM in Guazapa. We set up another in Torola to cover the middle of the country, another in Joateca to cover La Unión and the city of San Miguel, and one more in Usulután that sent the signal over to Santiago de María and all along the Chinameca Mountains. The three new repeating stations and the one in Guazapa, right under the enemy's nose, were small, under a hundred watts. With a simple aerial and two *compas* to guard it, you've got a repeating station.

The four little FM stations linked up with the big station known as Lenin in Morazán. Each of them also had a code-name. The one in Guazapa, for example, was "Hurricane", the one in Usulután was "Star". I don't remember what we called the ones in Torola and Joateca. Coordinating them was a lot of fun, because they all had to go on air simultaneously with us. If they didn't, it simply wouldn't work. This came on top of the normal pickle of having to keep the whole shebang running in the middle of a war, never knowing which front was going to be attacked. When six o'clock came around, you'd see the entire Venceremos broadcast team at their places, on the tottering tables at El Pedrero, amid the rocks fit only for *garrobos*. Marvel would be at the mixer and now, besides the technician, we needed five more *compas*, each with watch in hand, for the FM repeating stations.

Three minutes before broadcast, you could hear the internal communications: "Lenin ready!"

"Hurricane ready!"

"Star ready!"

And the other ready and the other ready. In the central studio we had our own code-name which was "Devil". So when all the FM's were connected up, the final question would come: "And the Devil?"

"The Devil's always ready, *hombre!*"

The countdown would begin: five, four, three, two, one... zero! The national anthem would ring out, and with all the buttons that were clicking you'd think you were in the Challenger.

"Radio Venceremos transmitting..." Santiago's voice would begin.

Suddenly a station would report: "Overmodulating!"

And another: "Overmodulating! Way overmodulating!"

"¡*Coño!* Chico, wait a minute," his Venezuelanness would come out. "You're going to give me a heart attack!"

That was really an exciting time. Our little network was taking off, reaching a larger and larger audience.

"Get down, brothers, we read you loud and clear!" the lads in the city would tell us.

You could hear us in the markets in San Miguel, where they put us on loudspeakers. You see, FM has a certain class. With FM you can put it on and start cooking. It's not like short wave where you have to struggle to tune in and it always sounds awful. Besides, by that time they were interfering with the short wave, but they never managed to disrupt the FM, I don't know why. Maybe because we broadcast right next to the frequencies of the commercial stations and it might have messed them up.

It was a great time, but it didn't last long. The station always developed in accordance with the military struggle, right? When we had the FM, we were busting the *cuilios'* ass in the great offensive of '83. I'm talking about the BRAZ and the Felipe Peña group of battalions, and the Julio Clímaco Battalion, the PRTC[4] troops... Large units made up of all the forces of the FMLN were crushing the enemy. In those days to capture thirty rifles was chickenfeed. These were the great battles of '83, with the enemy cowering in their barracks! It gave us the stability to be able to do what no insurrectional movement had ever done before: set up a network of guerrilla radio stations!

Later on, the military situation changed, and the window that allowed us to develop our network to such heights closed again. The gringos introduced a fleet of helicopters, expanded the army, brought in elite battalions... an avalanche of counterinsurgency activity that forced us to change our tactics radically. We could no longer sustain such an extended radio network. What is to be done, Lenin? What is to be done? Well, we boosted the signal of our own Lenin up to 400 watts, and tried to cover with one strong signal what we previously covered with several little ones. It was never the same, but by the end of '84 we managed to reach several areas of the capital and much of the central and eastern part of the country with our FM from Morazán.

Today we want to increase the power of our transmitter even more, and we have incredible plans for FM, very ambitious. But we'll talk about them some other time, okay?

The Eagle Misses His Prey

Domingo Monterrosa Barrios. Lieutenant Colonel Domingo Monterrosa Barrios. He was the commander of the armed forces' first elite battalion, the Atlacatl. In December '81, when the station accused him of direct responsibility for the thousand murders in El Mozote and other hamlets in Morazán, he swore to get Venceremos. Destroying Radio Venceremos was one obsession. The other was winning the war against Villalobos. The enemy always personifies everything: Joaquín Villalobos was the genius, the inventor of the BRAZ. They will never understand that things are collective, that the BRAZ represents the efforts and the contributions of thousands of *compas*.

Monterrosa also had a personal grudge against Joaquín Villalobos. He didn't like one bit the secret document in which the gringos called Atilio the best field commander in the country: what about me? Nor did he like how they described Venceremos as a master of psychological warfare which the army ought to learn from. We laughed when we read that, because no one on the team had ever studied a single line of psychological warfare. They made Santiago out to be Machiavelli, a monster capable of making the army collapse. Santiago doesn't know a damned thing about psychological warfare, he just speaks from the heart. If that shakes them up, if it worries them while it gives morale to the *compas*, well that's another story.

Monterrosa was obsessed with the competition. In May of '83, acting on a tip, he launched a surprise attack on Agua Blanca. He knew the station was near the command post, so he reckoned he could kill both tormentors with one stone: Venceremos and Villalobos. Under cover of darkness, his Atlacatl brigade reached our camp. Unfortunately for him — not because we knew he was coming, but because we had launched our own operation in Santa Rosa de Lima — the command post and the station had been transferred to Colorado Hill. We'd been gone a week.

Monterrosa didn't hesitate. He knew we had to be nearby and he was ready to march.

"Set up a line of fire," Atilio ordered. "The colonel won't get past Agua Blanca."

At six in the afternoon, I don't remember what day in May, the shit started. The entire BRAZ was in that zone, so it was a battle between the BRAZ and the Atlacatl. Monterrosa didn't even request much air support. He wanted a personal confrontation, like a duel between medieval knights: him and Villalobos.

"If that's the way he wants it," said Atilio. "Fire!"

We had never been able to capture weapons from the Atlacatl. From other battalions, yes, but not from the Atlacatl. In that brutal firefight we took one of their positions, grabbed three of their rifles and captured two prisoners. The BRAZ couldn't match the Atlacatl in logistics, so what Monterrosa wanted was to draw us into a conventional battle where they would have the advantage. We taught them a lesson and that was that, or so we thought. The BRAZ pulled back.

The Venceremos team was on Colorado Hill, 45 minutes from the battlefield. Since the fight started at six in the afternoon, it provided sound effects for the programme. From the camp we could hear everything, we saw the tracer bullets, our microphone picked up the "boom" of mortar-fire. We were in the middle of broadcasting when a member of the security squad came running.

"We've got to get out of here," he shouts. "Just sign off and let's go."

Santiago, who was only halfway through his speech, finished up as best he could:

...and for all these reasons, compañeros, *for all these reasons... we have reached the end of our broadcast. Revolution or death!*

Quick, take everything apart. Quick, they're coming. Monterrosa faked a retreat, only to turn around and march on us. We packed everything up in seconds. We were trained to pack the equipment in plastic bags — this was winter, the rainy season — stick them in backpacks, take down the aerial, burn papers, don't leave a trace, and start marching. We took off like a bottle thrown by a whore.

Monterrosa reached the spot where we'd been. We heard him on his radio: "I've found the house of *the man*."

Our camp was empty. The BRAZ, the command post and Venceremos were all far away by then, but there on Colorado Hill, Monterrosa found a model built by an American architect who had worked with us and was later killed in combat. It was a scale model of Cacahuatique volcano which the BRAZ High Command had used to plan the assault on the Aerial. The model had little flags at different heights marking the access routes, the enemy positions, the entire battle plan. We didn't have time to destroy it before we left.

"Look how prepared these bastards are!" Monterrosa said. "Not even the army does this!"

He took the model to his office at the Atlacatl Battalion headquarters, which at that time was still in San Salvador. He was building a collection: earlier, he'd found several videos and other things belonging to the BRAZ, and he took them too. They were his little war trophies.

Before June was over, Monterrosa had launched yet another operation with his tireless Atlacatl. No question, under his leadership the Atlacatl pushed hard. All the other battalions were greenhorns — they stuck to little skirmishes, while Monterrosa stepped on the heels of the command post and Venceremos. His dream was to capture us. One operation followed another, and we saw we were pushing our luck.

"This guy is really obstinate," Atilio said. He got up, paced back and forth, went out and came back into the tarpaulin tent that held the command post. "We've got no choice but to kill him. I don't know how, but we've got to get rid of that big-nosed bastard. It's vital. If he lives, after we win he'll be the chief of the Salvadoran contras and he'll still cause trouble."

From the moment he took the reins of the eastern front, Atilio recognised the enemy's true nature. One thing is fundamental: you can't underestimate your enemy. You have to know his strengths if you're going to beat him. If you think he's stupid, you're the one who'll take a beating. Monterrosa was renowned for his military expertise, above all because he was one of the few officers who actually went to the battlefield. Apart from those he trained, Salvadoran Army commanders are all desk officers: a well polished table and a pointer on the map. Monterrosa wasn't like that; he was a trooper, a field strategist. He'd be on the front lines just like the guerrilla commanders. The fact that he was a son of a bitch doesn't mean he wasn't brave.

We drew up a plan to kill Monterrosa. We found out he had a girlfriend in Chinameca, so we laid an ambush there, but that day he didn't visit her. We mined the field where his helicopter was to land, but that time he didn't land. We pulled back from one failed plan, tried it again, made several attempts, but the guy seemed to smell it coming and he never fell into our traps.

We got a report that he was with his unit on Miracapa de Carolina Hill. Atilio coordinated the entire approach, we had them surrounded, and somehow he got away. Barely, but he got away. Then the *compas* from the BRAZ cornered him in San Luis, but he escaped once again. Now we were the ones stepping on his heels, but we couldn't get him either. By this time 1983 was over.

The '84 elections were approaching. With the gringos' help, José Napoleón Duarte was about to get back the presidential sash he had handed over to Alvaro Magaña a couple of years before. To analyse the situation, a meeting of all the BRAZ commanders was called on 19 February in San Gerardo, a little town in San Miguel. At that time the Salvadoran Army still hadn't picked up the gringo tactic of ferrying in troops by helicopter, at least not on our front. By then, Monterrosa wasn't only the head of Atlacatl, but of the Third Brigade and of all the infantry troops in the eastern part of the country. Somehow he found out that all our commanders were at the meeting and in the blink of an eye he set up a helicopter assault on San Gerardo.

The *compas* who were there say that it started at six in the morning when almost everyone was asleep. No combat force was present, only the commanders, their bodyguards and their radio operators. As dawn broke, we could hear an observation plane overhead. Let's get ready, perhaps it's a routine bombing run. Sure enough, a few minutes later two Dragonfly A-37s came roaring overhead. Are they going to bomb the town? Suddenly the sound of helicopters reached us. We'd seen two or three, but this time a dozen choppers in a row were circling the hamlet. It was an excellent air command operation. The planes started bombing on the outskirts of town, while troops disembarked on the hills that lie on both sides of San Gerardo. We saw the first parachutists jump and the firefight started right there, on the streets of the town.

Jesus! How could we break out with the bombs falling and with that herd of choppers ferrying in more and more troops? The situation was absolutely critical. They were going to burn us to a crisp in a matter of minutes. Just then, the Virgin of the Rosary, or Tetecu, or who knows who, kissed the hand of one of our *compas* and he managed to hit a helicopter's propeller with a bullet from his AK. The blade broke apart and that beast swerved to one side, hit the propeller of another chopper, and the two of them went crashing down. Thirty killed, because when a helicopter really crashes everyone dies, and these were full of soldiers: Thirty parachutists! A parachutist is worth a lot, he's not just any soldier. From that moment on, their operation was out of control. Things fell apart in the air. They left holes through which we could escape. The *compas* took advantage of them and vanished into the hills like smoke.

We lost four people. None of the commanders were killed or wounded. Before leaving we had to execute seven spies we'd captured from Monterrosa's network of informants. We couldn't take them with us, in case they escaped and ratted on us again.

The *cuilios* occupied San Gerardo and soon the last helicopter arrived, Monterrosa's.

"Where are the dead?" he asks as soon as he gets out.

"There they are *mi coronel*," a *cuilio* tells him.

Monterrosa starts turning the bodies over with his boot.

"But, what shit is this? This is so-and-so, this is the other...!"

They were the seven spies, his collaborators.

"The others are over there, *mi coronel*."

"Four grunts!" Monterrosa screams. "Where are the *comandantes*? Where is Villalobos? Where is Jonás? The AKs! I want to see the AKs!"

We hadn't lost a single AK rifle. His operation, his golden opportunity, had left thirty army dead, plus seven informants lost and two helicopters downed.

We did a report on the story of San Gerardo and played it over Venceremos to celebrate. Later, when they told us this was a new tactic the army was going to start using, we sobered up. It's a Yankee tactic, they used it in Vietnam and it's called "The eagle catches its prey". This was the beginning of the terrifying helicopter assaults.

The Trojan Transmitter

After what happened at San Gerardo, we were more determined than ever to kill Monterrosa. The bitch was how. The people in the electronics workshop came up with some ideas; so did others.

"How about a letter with plastic explosives?"

"No, *hombre*," said Atilio. "You're going to be the ones who get killed. You've got to have special training to do that."

"A car bomb? Another mortar attack on the Third Brigade?"

"More guile and less force. We need to study the guy's psychology. What's he like?"

"An exhibitionist," said Luisa. "Being such a show-off could get him into trouble."

"Exactly," Atilio continued. "What has Monterrosa done since he came here? Who has he been after? The command post and Venceremos. What does he do when he leaves? He takes trophies. He took the model of Cacahuatique. He took the videos. Okay, he wants Venceremos? He'll get Venceremos. We're going to give it to him. What better souvenir of Morazán could he ask for?"

From that moment on, Atilio became a frequent visitor to Mauricio's workshop. They were cooking up something big. Besides repairing the thousand components of the radio-communications network and the station, the workshop began experimenting with integrated circuits for explosives, radio-activated time detonators, radio triggers for mines, all that sort of thing. One afternoon, Mauricio came over with a damaged transmitter, a Kenwood from the old days.

"What's this?" I asked. "Are we going to add another short wave signal?"

"We're going to add eight sticks of dynamite, dummy."

One day a C-47, one of those enormous reconnaissance planes, flew over our zone and dropped several white boxes swinging from little toy parachutes as they drifted down to earth. We were suspicious, since we had no idea what they were. Could they be placing microphones in our territory? Could it be bacteriological warfare? Mauricio sent for the plastic boxes and opened one. Inside, he found a tiny atmospheric laboratory for flight information, with a little gadget that measured wind velocity, another for humidity, and an altimeter.

"We've got to thank those gringos," said Mauricio. "They run a good home delivery service."

The altimeter was a flexible disk that moved up or down according to atmospheric pressure. It had a needle that marked the altitude.

"We'll use this to set up a secondary mechanism for the bomb."

The bomb was to go inside the transmitter. It would be triggered by a remote control device like the ones you use to turn on a television set, except this one was more complicated. It worked on radio frequency. If the radio trigger failed for any reason, then the altimeter's little needle would complete the circuit when the transmitter was taken to a height of 300 metres, and the bomb would go off by itself.

"And who is going to carry the transmitter up three hundred metres?"

"Monterrosa in his helicopter."

That was the plan: leave the booby-trapped transmitter in a hiding place so that it would look like we didn't want it to be seen, but not so well hidden that he wouldn't find it. Then pray that the exhibitionist would arrive, discover it, and take the fake Venceremos with him. He takes off in his helicopter with the trophy and gets blown out of the air.

"Isn't eight sticks of dynamite a bit much, Mauricio?"

"The rocks have to match the toad."

"That's enough to knock down a three-storey building!"

"Better too much than not enough," Mauricio insisted.

"Okay," said Atilio. "Now we just have to wait for an opportunity."

18 October arrived. We were on one of the ridges of Pericón Hill, near Perquín, where we had been peacefully encamped for several months, but we could smell an operation coming. Suddenly at about ten in the morning, we started seeing helicopters pass overhead: one, two, three, four, five, six... sonofathousandbitches! This time it was for real! Twenty helicopters: the first big airborne assault on our front!

"Pack everything up, but fast!" shouted Ismael, the head of security.

"They've got us pinpointed, right on such-and-such coordinates!" the radio operators said.

"Let's get the fuck out of here!" we added. "They're going to fry us on this hill!"

"Wait," Atilio ordered. "Now is our chance. Let's leave the 'Venceremos' here and since they know where we are, they'll think we left it behind in the rush to escape. Abel, get it ready!"

Mauricio wasn't there, he'd gone off to repair our FM repeater in Joateca. He and Jonás's brother Abel, who was also a technician, were the only ones who knew how to connect up the charges and get the bomb ready, but the troops were already on the ground in Llano del Muerto, right nearby.

The bombs were already falling. We had only seconds. Abel raced to the workshop where he kept the transmitter open with the eight dynamite sticks ready to be put in place. One *compa* stayed outside to warn him if the *cuilios* turned up. Abel started making electrical connections and, nervous as he was, he let two wires touch and boom! They set off an explosion: not the TNT, but the ones that activate the main charge. When we heard the bang we ran over and found Abel with his midriff sliced open still trying to connect up the wires.

They carried Abel off in a hammock with his belly all bloody, amid the roar of helicopters and pandemonium as everyone tried to pull out.

"El Cheje!" Abel screams, "Tell El Cheje!"

El Cheje, the third technician, comes running over and Abel gives him the final instructions on how to activate the bomb: "Look, this is the frequency that it has to register, understand?"

He said the number that only he knew, and then he passed out. Just like in the movies when the hero reveals where the treasure is buried just before he kicks the bucket. Abel didn't kick it, but he told El Cheje what he needed to know to take charge.

"Now what?" he asks Atilio.

"Now nothing. First we have to take care of Abel. Let's go."

"What about the device?"

"Take it with us. It'll work next time."

It was almost noon when we started marching. We reached the road that runs from Joateca to Arambala and crossed it in groups of five, crouched over, our guns on automatic. It started to rain. We crossed the Sapo River in a downpour. In front of me was the mule carrying the infamous transmitter with the eight sticks of dynamite, the present we didn't get to give the colonel. We marched for hours and hours until we reached a place they call Volcancillo.

"We'll stay here," Atilio told us. "Go on air and tell Monterrosa his operation has been a total failure."

It was 5:45 p.m. We had 15 minutes to set up the radio, the real one. Open up the packs, take out the mixer, set up the recorder, align the link-up, the generator and the gasoline, who has the cassette?, find a bit of table and a bit of roof because the downpour continued. El Cheje took the controls and we did the announcing, all of us huddled together against the cold, soaked to the skin, not having eaten, absolutely exhausted, but at six o'clock our tongues were lashing out at the army. We did an hour-long programme. It was more shouting than anything else, for sure — well, it wasn't quite the moment for a pedagogical discourse, was it? What we wanted to do was insult them and to rub it in that they hadn't caught us. To maintain our good radio manners we put on a musical bridge between swearing at them and cussing them out. Afterwards, we packed everything up again because we didn't know what fate held in store for us, then we crashed out under the mango trees.

The next morning Atilio said: "We can't go on carrying that bomb around. Let's hide it here. What can we do? Our plans got messed up. If we leave it now as bait, they won't bite. Back in Pericón they would have, since we had to leave in such a hurry. But that we just left it by the side of the path, no one will swallow that one."

We hid the bomb-transmitter in Volcancillo and continued the march towards Garrobo Hill, which is more or less five kilometres towards Joateca as the crow flies. It forms a triangle with El Mozote which is also about five kilometres away. From the heights where we set up camp, you couldn't see Joateca, though you could see the hollow where the town lies and the church belfry. The command post, the Venceremos team and the radio communications team set up shop.

Another day went by, the third one of the operation. In the early morning of 21 October, Chiquito comes over and shakes me.

"Wake up!"

"What's wrong?"

"Write commentaries for Venceremos."

"Commentaries in the middle of the night?"

"That's right, start writing."

"About what?"

"Anything at all, but it's got to be in your handwriting." (On other occasions the *cuilios* had found notebooks of ours and they knew our handwriting.)

"What for?"

"Stop whining! Write and don't ask questions."

I was lying propped up on my elbow in my tent, filling up pages by flashlight, when I heard noises outside. It was Mauricio, just coming back from somewhere, and Atilio, in a big hurry: "Look Mauricio, you go to Volcancillo and bring that thing back. We're going ahead with it. It's now or never!"

Later, I heard him speaking with Nolvo, the guide who was with our unit. Nolvo is a *campesino* who looks a lot like Farabundo Martí [5], brown-skinned, moustachioed, with a big pistol and a rifle.

"Look Nolvo, Monterrosa's time is up. He's going to pay for all he's done."

"God willing."

As dawn broke, Atilio brought together the little team that would carry out the plan.

"We're going to fake a battle where someone gets wounded and we have to abandon the transmitter. Simple as that. Julito Perica, you lead the security squad and carry the device. It's got a bomb inside. It's a booby-trap. Get into a shooting match with a squadron of *cuilios* and then shout out: 'Leave that shit behind! Get the wounded out!' Come on, let's hear it."

"Leave that shit behind! Get the wounded out!" Julito Perica rehearsed.

"Perfect, but you've got to make sure the *cuilios* hear you. Get close enough to them before you scream."

"Then what?"

"Take a rooster with you. Slit its throat and leave a trail of blood. Let them see the blood of the 'wounded'."

"And then?"

"Then, right then, and only when you're sure the *cuilios* are on your heels, get a little stick and push up this switch. Look. Inside this little grate you turn on the whole system. Make sure it's up, that it's on. Then leave the device on the path. Got it?"

"Got it, chief."

"Adilia, come over here. You're going with them too. When you run out of there send this message over the radio: 'We've got trouble. We lost the package. What do we do?' Repeat it."

"We've got trouble. We lost the package. What do we do?" rehearsed the green-eyed radio operator.

"Send the message clean, without any code. The operator at the other station will be ready. He'll answer: 'Don't talk to me here. Go on such-and-such a frequency.' So you go to that frequency and give him the same message, this time in code, understand?"

"But they know that code."

"That's why we're using it. The *cuilios'* computer will decipher the message right away. That's what we want. You send the message and then add: 'We've got a wounded man'. The other operator will respond: 'Forget about the package and pull out with the wounded'."

Everything was meticulously planned so as not to arouse suspicion. Immediately, a report would be sent to the commanders over a more secret internal network, also in a code in use for a long time. Atilio would communicate with María outside the country. He'd give the "bad news" and say that we'd have to figure out how to buy another transmitter and get it into the country. The point was to make the enemy's entire intelligence service absolutely convinced that they had captured Venceremos.

"Mauricio," Atilio concluded, "you take charge."

The word he used was *garantizar*. It's a sacred word for us. The only excuse for failing to *garantizar* is to be dead. Everyone knew what they had to do, and Mauricio knew what everyone had to do. He took charge of the entire plan.

Mauricio, Julito Perica, Adilia and the security squad headed off. They reached the point where the *cuilios* were supposed to have been and found no one. That's not unusual for them: they report to their superiors that they're where they're supposed to be, but they don't really go that far, because they're afraid. Anyhow, our team had to go in closer to Joateca. At about five in the afternoon they found the *cuilios* and the show began. They shot back and forth a few times and then came the shout, the rooster, the switch and the message.

From up on the hill, we could hear the gunfight. A minute later Adilia's voice came over the communications radio: *Xylophone, potato, tango, charlie, whisky, delta, stripes.*

"That's the message in code. Everything's going well."

Now the green radios, to hear what the enemy would say. Atilio was pacing back and forth like a caged lion, and we were all chewing our nails. At long last they were capturing us, capturing Venceremos!

It came an hour later, without code and with a euphoria we'd never heard from them before:

"Witches Company of Fonseca Battalion reports... that we've captured Venceremos!"

"What? Repeat."

"We captured Venceremos's equipment! There were 200 of them, but we beat the pants off them!"

Half a minute later:

"Fonseca Battalion commander calling Charlie Carlos.[6]*"*

"Go ahead, go ahead," Monterrosa answers. "I hear you. Over."

"We have captured Radio Venceremos on a ridge of Tizate Hill, in the jurisdiction of Joateca, at such-and-such coordinates."

"Wonderful! Congratulations! Look, take that to Joateca and wait for orders. I'll be right there."

They had it. We figured that they spent what was left of the afternoon comparing intelligence reports to see if it all checked out. Those of us who worked on the broadcasts were told we wouldn't go on air that day. Never, in four years of war had such a decision been taken: today there will be no programme!

That night went on for ever. The entire monitoring team spent it going back and forth over the dial, waiting for the news. At last it came:

News flash! The army just reported that the clandestine Radio Venceremos was captured a few hours ago in Tizate, Joateca, after fierce combat. More details from our correspondent in San Miguel!

We sat in a circle in the big canvas military tent where we all slept. Atilio was bursting, more excited than ever. He wasn't sleepy, so he started telling stories about when he was a student, about the boys in his *barrio*, Santa Anita in the capital, about when they'd watch the girls on the corner in high school, about the student struggles in 1970, about the first urban guerrilla cells, about Rafael Arce Zablah, the ERP's first leader who was killed in combat in '75.

"If Lito had lived...!"

It was late. People deserted him one by one. Eventually I gave in too and went off to sleep. I can't remember what other stories Atilio told that night.

The next morning the Voice of America, after its usual and unpleasant *the following programme is in Spanish*, announced its top story:

After so many days of uninterrupted broadcast, Radio Venceremos has stopped transmitting. The Salvadoran Army reports that the clandestine station was captured in...

In San Salvador all the stations —YSU, KL, Sonora — were giving the story big play, and of course we were getting coded messages from the other organisations, from alarmed friends.

"We'll explain later," was our only response.

Licho, who was on another mission, called up immediately: "What the fuck! What do you mean we lost the station?"

"We'll explain later."

The uproar was growing; the story became more and more triumphant. One station even put out a news flash that the Venceremos announcers had been captured.

"Did you hear?" said Butterfly, dumbstruck by the news, as she came up to Santiago, Marvel and me.

"What, Butterfly?"

"The announcers!"

"But we're the announcers, shrimp! You are Venceremos' announcer! Monterrosa's the one who's going to get it!"

But Monterrosa didn't show. He gave no sign of life. Abraham's beetles, the boys of the intelligence team, who hadn't slept a wink all night, continued on alert in case there was a report of a helicopter coming to pick up the captured transmitter. Nothing. All afternoon, nothing. "We'll explain later" was becoming an awful lot later, and the situation was turning against us. The fighters, demoralised, were sitting by the radio, fixed on our frequency, hearing nothing, hoping that we'd come on the air to tell them this disaster wasn't true. Their station! Their station captured! That's when I realised how much Venceremos meant to them and what's meant by the audience empathy you read about. Messages were pouring in, not only from the war fronts, but from journalists, allies, people overseas. Jesus! That second night of silence nearly drove us mad!

23 October. We awoke to the same news and the same tension. Atilio paced back and forth. He carried a stick and kept slapping it on the palm of his hand. He stopped next to Abraham.

"What do you think? Where have they got it?"

"They've got it in the town hall in Joateca. Where else?"

"What would happen if we set it off right now?"

"Well..."

"Will it work in the helicopter?"

"Let's hope so, *hombre*. It'll work."

"If it doesn't, we're the biggest jerks in the world. We're handing them the victory they didn't get in Pericón! Even if what they picked up isn't the real thing, who's going to believe it when they show off the device and we've stopped broadcasting? Who is going to explain that it was all a misunderstanding, a booby trap that trapped us?"

Just then, a helicopter appears. We pick up a helicopter's radio. It's nine in the morning.

"Who is it?" Atilio asks.

"I don't know," says Abraham. "He hasn't identified himself."

"Then it must be Monterrosa, because he's the only one of them who is careful never to identify himself."

"No, it's not him," a young radio operator butts in.

"Why not?" says Atilio impatiently.

"It isn't him," the kid insists. "I know the voice of Monterrosa's pilot. That's not him."

"Do you have it recorded?"

"Yup, listen."

They sit down and listen to the tape, and agree that it isn't him.

"But, suppose it is? Let's go up above!"

Atilio, the commanders and all the rest of us climbed uphill a few metres to the highest point, where the radio operators were set up for strategic communications. From there we had a panoramic view of the valley, with Joateca in the distance. Mauricio carried the remote control, the radio-detonator, and El Cheje had the aerial, a directional aerial that the technicians built just for this operation.

The helicopter comes into view, lands in Joateca, stays there a few minutes. It takes off and, when it starts back towards San Miguel, the arguments begin.

"Suppose we fire and that isn't it?"

"And if we don't fire and it is?"

Since the kid insisted that it wasn't him, they believed him and didn't shoot. The little guy was right, because later on we learned that the helicopter was carrying medical personnel who had gone in to pick up a wounded man.

At noon, Radio Sonora in the capital announced an interview with Lieutenant Colonel Domingo Monterrosa Barrios. We leapt from our posts and surrounded the radio.

Journalist: How is the operation north of the Torola River going, Colonel Monterrosa?

Monterrosa: Well, what we're doing is not just any old operation. It's a region-wide action. It's going well.

Journalist: How long do you think the operation will last?

Monterrosa: We're going in to stay. As I said, this time it's different. We're not going to leave like the other times.

Journalist: What's the story on Venceremos?

Monterrosa: It's true, we've captured Radio Venceremos. I'd like to say that the myth of Morazán is over. We've given the Witches of the

Fonseca Battalion who achieved this feat a well-deserved one-month furlough. This afternoon at four o'clock I've asked the national press and foreign correspondents to come to the Third Infantry Brigade in San Miguel. I will show them the radio personally.

He was coming! He had to come to pick up his trophy! Or would he send someone else to Joateca to get it? Damn! We were in an agony of enthusiasm and nerves. The whole camp was counting the minutes on their fingers, counting the seconds. No one could even think about eating. Everyone was watching the sky, the clouds, just waiting to catch sight of him.

At about two o'clock we picked up a helicopter approaching.

"Now that one is Monterrosa's pilot," said the same kid as before.

"Did he actually say so?" Atilio asked.

"No, he didn't say so, but it's his voice."

"The kid's right," Abraham interrupted. "I'll put my balls on an anvil that's him."

The helicopter was on its way. From our hill we watched it all like on a big movie screen. We saw as the helicopter approached, hovered, settled down and disappeared into the town. Of Joateca, as I said, we could only see the church belfry.

The helicopter flew up over Joateca.

"Is Monterrosa on it?" Atilio asked.

"I don't know," the radio operator answered. "They haven't said so. But it's his pilot."

"Where the dog goes, so goes the master. Get everything ready."

There was El Cheje with his aerial lined up, Mauricio looking ten years younger, Atilio truly thrilled, Chiquito flushed with tension. Everyone feverish with the excitement of that decisive moment. The helicopter came towards us.

"Fire, Mauricio!" Atilio orders. "Fire!"

Mauricio pushes the button of the radio-detonator, he pushes it again, and nothing happens.

"Fire, I tell you!" Atilio screams. "Cheje, aim it right!"

El Cheje, holding his aerial as if it were a rocket launcher, following that point in the sky. Mauricio pushing the button so hard he nearly breaks the switch. But the helicopter peacefully continues its course.

The silence that followed was a sonofabitch. Mauricio aged a thousand years. El Cheje wanted to hang himself from the highest tree. It was Chiquito who said: "We blew it."

Mauricio started checking the remote control, to see if it was the circuit or the connection to the aerial or what it was that failed. His hands were shaking.

"Wait, Mauricio," Atilio said. "Isn't there a failsafe?"

"Yes."

"How high is that bird now?"

"Over three hundred metres."

"And the altimeter?"

"I don't know. It didn't work either."

"*¡¡Puta!!*" was the last thing Atilio said, and he stalked off.

Chiquito, demoralised, slumped down in some tall grass. Julito Perica buried his face in his hands. I remember old Germán, our political officer, going off towards the kitchen: "At wakes they serve coffee. Anybody want any?"

Right then Atilio jumps up as if he had springs in his butt.

"Mauricio, come here!"

The aged, ruined technician comes over, dragging his feet.

"Mauricio, what would happen if we had a radio operator in Joateca now and we wanted to talk to him? Could we establish communications with him?"

"It would be possible from a height. If he climbed up in the church belfry, because the town is down in that hollow, boxed in, and radio waves travel in a straight line..."

"It's difficult?"

"Yes."

"The transmitter is still in Joateca!" Atilio shouts. "That's the problem! They haven't taken it out of Joateca!"

"Then they must have discovered the bomb."

"No *hombre*, how could they have discovered it? They would have reported that over the radio."

"So why didn't it blow up on the ground?" asks Julito.

"That's why, because it can't. There's no direct line. Monterrosa is still in Joateca!"

Atilio goes over and shakes Chiquito.

"Chiquito, it didn't work because the device is still there."

"And I'm still here."

"Don't be a crybaby. Come on, get up!"

While Atilio is explaining and arguing, we hear the sound of another helicopter approaching from San Miguel. It's quarter to four.

"You see? There he is! Let's go Mauricio, get moving, check the cables! Cheje!"

Everyone on their feet again, and the excitement begins all over again. When the helicopter calls in, our operator confirms it: "That's Monterrosa's bird. Same pilot."

The speculation begins. Didn't he come on the first flight? Or did he come and not go? Where is he, on the ground or in the air? One thing for sure, his helicopter was making its approach. It landed again in Joateca. Those minutes while the helicopter was down and we couldn't see it...!

Atilio is a very tall man and Chiquito is like his name, tiny. There were the two chiefs, big and small, each with his eyes on Joateca. Atilio didn't lower his binoculars even for a second.

Another kid comes over, another of Abraham's radio operators who are busy scanning everything with the seven communications radios we captured from the enemy.

"From the Third Brigade they're telling Monterrosa that the press is all waiting for him."

"So he *is* in Joateca!" Atilio screams. "Now his time has come!"

The helicopter starts climbing into that blue sky. It starts moving horizontally. When we have it in front of us, exactly in front of us, Atilio orders:

"Mauricio... fire!"

As soon as he says it I see a ball of fire, a huge ball of fire that sends showers of flames out the sides.

Have you ever heard the Brazilian soccer team score a goal in Maracaná stadium? That's what the yelling was like! Chiquito wrapped his arms around Atilio. Mauricio and El Cheje were hugging each other. The radio operators, the kids, everyone in the command post in one big cheer, hugging and kissing each other like at a wedding!

"Long live Morazán! Long live the FMLN!"

Germán climbed downhill to tell the rest of the camp waiting in the kitchen, since everyone couldn't fit up above, and from the kitchen another uproar arose.

"Silence!" says Abraham. "Shut up!"

"Have they said it yet?" Atilio asks.

"They haven't said anything."

You see, with all this cheering all we knew was that a helicopter had been downed. We had to confirm that Monterrosa was on board. We were all sure. But the devil has his devilish ways.

Once again it was quiet, as everyone waited by the green radios to hear what the enemy would say. About twenty minutes later, the voice of the head of the battalion in Joateca requested communication with the Third Brigade in San Miguel.

"Send me a bird immediately."

"We just sent one. What happened?"

"Look, this is an emergency. Send me a bird immediately."

"What sort of emergency?"

"We've had problems with the bird you just sent."

"Where... where was Charlie Carlos travelling?"

"Affirmative. Affirmative. Hurry."

Again we started yelling and screaming! A goal scored in the stadium of the world! Our guerrilla camp went wild! Atilio then called Leti, who was in charge of communications on the front.

"Send a message to all the stations that we just got Domingo Monterrosa, the murderer."

His helicopter fell right between Joateca and El Mozote, where he had committed one of his worst crimes. He and his "Angels of Death", as he liked to call his Atlacatl Battalion, went to El Mozote. He gave the order to machine-gun the very people he had asked to congregate in the church. He authorised the rapes, he laughed at the children stuck with bayonets and thrown into the ovens alive. He did all that. In December of '81 alone, a thousand innocent people were murdered very close to where he had just been blown to pieces in his helicopter, at 4:15 in the afternoon of that judgement day, 23 October, 1984.

Atilio ran over to the strategic communications centre to talk with María overseas.

"We got Monterrosa!"

"Are you serious?"

"Absolutely. You've got to telephone the stations here and tell them that Venceremos will go on air right now, at six o'clock. Tell them we have a surprise for the journalists who are still waiting for Monterrosa at the Third Brigade in San Miguel!"

"Is it confirmed?"

"Absolutely confirmed."

"So the colonel didn't read the story of the Trojan horse in time."

That's right, the Trojan horse. Never had an ancient legend of war seemed on target. In a few minutes we learned that it wasn't only Monterrosa. Other Trojans were with him.

"So Charlie Carlos was there?"

"Affirmative. That's right."

"Listen, and my Charlie too?" asks the one from the Atlacatl Battalion.

"Affirmative. Your Charlie was there."

On board the helicopter was Major Armando Azmitia, Domingo Monterrosa's assistant and successor, who took over the Atlacatl Battalion when his boss was promoted! Azmitia, the best hope of the Salvadoran Army, considered by many to be just like Monterrosa only better!

"Listen, was my Charlie there too?" asks the one from Gotera.

"Affirmative."

What? Calito too? Lieutenant Colonel Herson Calito, well-known bastard, commander of Military Detachment Number Four!

"And my Charlie?"

Another asks, and then another. All the strategic commanders of the Torola IV operation were dead! The six heads of battalions, Monterrosa's entire high command, the ones he had trained, his key men in that crazy operation he and the gringos had designed! He'd called them all to come to Joateca to witness the unveiling of the captured Venceremos! He'd also invited a military priest to congratulate the soldiers and bless their victory. He'd brought along a journalist from COPREFA[7], a cameraman and a soundman to film the moment when Monterrosa personally helped carry the transmitter-bomb into the helicopter. They and their lieutenant colonel, the gringos' Rambo in El Salvador, were all dead. The only one who missed the appointment was James Steele, head of the US advisers, who ran the Torola IV operation along with Monterrosa. Not even the devil wanted to have him.

"Set up Venceremos, we've got to go on air at six on the dot!"

I will never forget that broadcast. Even though it was October and the rainy season, the sky in Morazán was choked with stars. A thousand of them had names.

We declare this day 23 October a day of vindication for the patriotic martyrs murdered in El Mozote, La Joya, Los Toriles, Poza Honda and all the hamlets and villages of Morazán where this executioner massacred so many innocent lives. This is Radio Venceremos, indestructible like our people!

When the programme was over, Atilio called us all together: "Now, get the band and let's have a big party! We aren't going to celebrate the death of a man, we're going to celebrate the people who'll live now that he's gone!"

Footnotes

[1] Francisco Martínez, killed in combat on 28 March 1982 in Usulután.

[2] An American adventurer who invaded Central America in 1855 with an army of mercenaries.

[3] Rafael Arce Zablah Brigade, the elite fighting force of the ERP.

[4] The Revolutionary Workers Party of Central America, one of the five member organisations of the FMLN.

[5] Salvadoran revolutionary of the 1920s and 30s, after whom the FMLN is named

[6] Monterrosa's nom de guerre.

[7] The press office of the Salvadoran Armed Forces.

Section IV
Back to Basics

We Live to Fight, We Fight to Win

When the Rafael Arce Zablah Brigade was at the height of its power, when all the FMLN's brigades were at their strongest, and the Salvadoran Army was approaching the breaking point, the commanders decided to disperse our forces.

We had brigades! Che Guevara would have been shaking in his boots. These weren't mere guerrilla columns, they were brigades of thousands of troops that took on the enemy face to face! We moved 120mm cannons to assault the big bases, the impregnable ones, breaking through all their lines of defence. We travelled up the Pan-American Highway, no less, in a caravan of 18 buses filled with guerrillas to take over Nuevo Edén de San Juan. You wouldn't believe it. At six in the afternoon, the BRAZ finished knocking off a position near El Semillero and at six the next morning they were getting off those buses to capture a far-off town near the Honduran border as well! Such well-planned insanity confounded all the enemy's expectations.

The end of '83, beginning of '84, was the moment when the army — even the Yankee advisers admit it — was on the point of collapse. In just one year, the Armed Forces lost 3,104 men in combat, equivalent to over four battalions wiped out by the FMLN. Add on the wounded and those we took prisoner and we're talking about 8,000 casualties. Then add on the casualties of the two previous years and it's practically all the troops the Salvadoran Army had when the war began.

At that peak moment of victory after victory, the FMLN General Command met and evaluated the situation: "If we go on like this, we'll lose, because we aren't made for a regular war. That's where the enemy wants to take us: into a conventional war that they'll end up winning for sure, or rather, that they'll never completely lose."

Our struggle became an indirect confrontation with the Yankees, since they took over the strategic direction of the war. They supplied the army with great quantities of materiel; they dictated the political strategy. They made Duarte and the High Command look like puppets. Their financing grew to over a million and a half dollars a day, and we had to face high-tech weaponry and the escalation of low-altitude air war using helicopters.

> *In '82 the Salvadoran Army had about 12,000 men. By '84 they had 45,000. Where before they attacked with two battalions, now they sent in three with air support.*
>
> Commander Leonel González, The Long Road to Victory

What army in history has survived a beating like the one we gave the Salvadoran Army that year? Yet they didn't lose the war. Why? Because the United States kept them on their feet. Three billion crushing dollars is what they've sent down over the years, the largest slice of the US military aid budget for the smallest country in Latin America! We'd knock down a helicopter and they'd send down ten. We'd recover ten rifles and they'd send a thousand. We'd cause thousands of casualties and they'd just pressgang more people and fit them out with gringo equipment. There was no way to beat that.

It wasn't only a question of weapons and armies. It was the people, the masses. If in '83 there had been a popular explosion to accompany our great military achievements, we would have won the war that year. Out of sync, right? In '79, the people were overflowing the streets and we had no military strength to speak of. Later it was just the opposite. Even though we'd developed our popular army and were beating the enemy, the people were still terrorised by the horrible repression of '80 and '81. Without the people we couldn't ever win!

Without the people you can't win a people's war. Take for example, the smashing, spectacular blows meted out by our special forces against army bases. Those were key operations, part of an integrated strategy, but they could never decide the war. If you show up, attack a police post, and then take off, how many people can you win over? There's a National Guard post in the *barrio* of Mejicanos. It's not enough to wipe it out — you've got to go to Mejicanos and stay there so the youth, the people who sympathise, the ones who want you to win, will get to know you and take on the revolution as their own. They'll see the guerrillas' faces and chat with them, and in the end some will join up and all will collaborate. But for all that political work, you've got to stay in the *barrio* two, three, four days — the longer the better.

What's an insurrection? An insurrection is when in a question of minutes, of hours, a force of dozens becomes one of thousands. That sudden flood of people over to your side is what wipes out the enemy. Let's imagine that you're the enemy and you're fighting 50 guerrillas. Because of their mobility and capacity for surprise, you need a battalion of a thousand men to keep that handful of guerrillas at bay. If you maintain a relationship of ten to one throughout the country, you can stop them winning. Those fifty and then fifty more attack your battalion? You just send in another battalion for reinforcement and you're in control again. Even fighting badly, you can keep the war going that way.

But what would you do if those fifty, in a very short time, became five hundred or five thousand? How would you respond? You'd be thrown off balance and fall flat on your face. That's why the people, the people's participation — with weapons, I mean — is decisive in winning this sort of war, which isn't a war between two armies, but between the people and the army.

We, those of us from Venceremos, were invited to the meeting of the Central Committee in the eastern part of the country where the decision was taken to transform the war with a fundamental change in tactics. That was in the middle of '84 on Pericón Hill.

"We're going to disperse our troops," Atilio announced. "We've been taking the war where the enemy wants us to, towards a regular war. Since they get a million and a half dollars a day from the gringos, that's no problem for them. War is their business. But we don't have the logistics to keep this up. We'll get bogged down, or even worn out, so we're going to turn the tables on them. We're going to wage a war of attrition, and we'll see who gets tired first. What do they want? A prolonged war, a hundred-year war? Who gives a shit? We can spend our whole lives in this struggle. Do they think they can defeat us with their helicopters and special battalions? They're wrong. Because sooner or later this struggle will end in victory. There is no other option, and that will be the slogan for this new stage: *We live to fight, we fight to win!*"

What was the plan? To get close to the masses. To make use of all the terrain we conquered in '83 and work on grassroots organising. To develop ourselves as individuals and become capable of doing everything. That was the end of separate military and political officers; the military officer would be a political officer as well, and the combatant would be someone who not only shot at the enemy, but worked with his neighbours, with families and grassroots groups to strengthen popular organising.

The BRAZ would be dispersed: instead of battalions and companies and platoons, we'd go back to fighting in squads. Each unit of five or seven would have to create its own base of support. Each combatant would have to win over ten or twenty new recruits, not by dragging them into the guerrilla war, but by raising their political consciousness. The winner of this war — so they told us — would be the side that grew fastest.

For the military struggle, we had to develop new home-made weapons and guerrilla tactics. Achieving a lot with a little. Our principal weapon from now on would be explosives — we'd wear the enemy down with mines. We'd destabilise them with sabotage, close the highways, blow up electrical poles, harass them, ambush them, make their lives miserable and the economy impossible. In a phrase: we'd wage guerrilla warfare.

It sounds sensible enough, but you should have seen the cataclysm it caused in our ranks. Quite a few members of the BRAZ were used to war as war, and they didn't understand the notion of dispersal. If we aren't capturing a hundred rifles a week then we're losing the war, some of them thought, and if we're losing the war, what's the point of staying in this mess?

"Anyone who wants to go should go," the leadership said. "Those who stay are the ones truly willing to spend their whole lives in this struggle. This war is going to last a long time."

Many deserted. Others, older people, including some founders of the guerrilla struggle in Morazán, had to be sent to the refuge in Honduras. Guerrilla tactics demand a lot of energy and constant mobility, and a 55-year-old man, no matter how robust he may seem, can't take it. Some of them cried when they left, a bit resentful at being half forced out.

There were executions. Some people had fallen apart completely and gone over to the enemy. We had a very sad experience with an excellent artillery unit from the BRAZ which had lost a lot of its members in combat. The survivors didn't understand the change and couldn't accept it. They had been artillery men in a large military unit, and from one day to the next, they had to bury their 81mm mortars and head off like monkeys, in groups of three or five, planting a little bomb here, shooting a couple of bullets there, giving talks to the peasants. They couldn't outgrow their militarism and went to pieces.

The crisis was so deep that even two cadres from the Central Committee ran away. They left a letter: good-bye, nice knowing you. In all, '84 was a really tough year, perhaps the year in which the FMLN could have lost the war. Add it up: in Morazán alone, between deserters, those who retired, volunteers who wanted to leave, those who had to be expelled, and several executions, we lost 800 men.

Morazán was the least serious case, perhaps because we had relatively stable control over our terrain and, above all, because on the fifth day of the infamous Torola IV operation we did away with Monterrosa and all his commanding officers. That gave us a bit of relief and raised our morale. But Guazapa was a sorry sight — Chico was in charge there, and he says that every day he'd lose four, five, six people. The Paracentral Front practically disappeared. The enemy infiltrated it and there were an average of 17 desertions a day.

Maybe it was for the better. Many fled, but the ones who stayed behind were the best. Those who stayed on in '84, from the chef to the commander, believed in our cause body and soul.

Pols and Listeners' Circles

So where did Venceremos end up in all this? What role would the station that had accompanied the BRAZ in the great battles play during the stage of dispersal? How could we adjust the station's work to fit the new tactics?

The essence of the new strategy lay in turning each guerrilla into a political organiser, and developing all the skills of our fighters. To do grassroots organising you had to have your own head organised first, so Venceremos concentrated on contributing to that objective by broadcasting political debate.

"The idea", Atilio said, "is to arm our people with arguments. Just like you have to train to have good aim with a rifle, you have to sharpen your political judgement to be an organiser. The station has to provide a lot of information, and analysis for digesting that information. That's the bottom line."

We'd painted it ourselves on a wall in Ciudad Barrios:

To be uninformed is like being unarmed.
Listen to Radio Venceremos!

How is a group of four or five guerrillas dispersed about the country, working alone in a zone, going to stay informed? Suppose they show up at a house and an old man invites them in for coffee: "Come on in, *hombre.* Come in and let's talk. Isn't it something that Duarte's going to the United Nations to propose a dialogue with the FMLN? Or don't you folks want to dialogue?"

The combatants lived in what was perhaps a very small world, very local, with some national vision and not much awareness beyond that. So here was a man kicking the ball at us and if we didn't get into the net fast, he'd score a goal. What reliable source could they count on? Where could they find out about things and be sure they weren't being tricked? The other media twisted the news; they made Duarte out to be the last bottle of Coca-Cola in the desert. Our men knew that wasn't the truth, but they needed arguments both to explain it to themselves and to convince that old man.

"The first priority is radios!" the commanders declared. "Every guerrilla unit needs a radio receiver right away, no matter what the cost."

The organisation made the effort, and the political officers of every guerrilla unit were given a radio as an indispensable piece of their equipment. They were little Phillips radios, sealed up in brown plastic. Besides being good and cheap, they withstand storms, dust, thumps — they were made for guerrillas. All the political officers — all the pols as we called them in guerrilla lingo — have those radios hanging around their necks. If you go to Perquín and meet up with a group of guerrillas, and you want to know who the political officer is, all you have to do is see who has the radio. That's him. For a political officer, that little radio with the Venceremos frequency is an umbilical cord linking him to the entire organisation and its political line. It's also a very practical tool for working with people.

"Hello!" a pol arrives at a little house he's never visited.

"Hello," the peasant woman tells him, "come on in where it's swept clean."

"How is it going, señora? How are the kids?"

That's how you start up a conversation, asking about the kids, about the firewood getting wet from so much rain, whatever. Pretty soon the pol, who always makes sure he shows up more or less in time for the Venceremos broadcast, says casually: "Gee, you haven't heard Venceremos today? It must be on already."

"No, we don't have a radio."

"Ah, but look at this little radio I've got, it's really good."

He starts talking and they turn to the station, and then they talk about what they hear.

The image of the pol with his radio says a lot about the role the station played during this decisive stage. Making sure of communications with our listeners was vital in keeping the organisation together. How could you disperse hundreds and hundreds of units throughout the country without ensuring you had a way of guiding their approach to the work, without some channel for direct communication? From then on, to this very day, Venceremos has been the means of communication and political education for the entire FMLN family dispersed across the country.

We also used the pol's radio to encourage people to set up listeners' circles. In part this was a practical response to the lack of both radios and batteries, but we were also interested in getting people into the habit of listening to the station in groups, so that after the show they could debate the issues we raised and understand them better. We encouraged these circles not only among guerrilla units, but among friends in unions, among the lads in the street, among neighbours, among the women of a *barrio*. Listen to the editorial, we'd say, and then discuss it. Listen to the editorial and you'll find the elements you need to analyse society correctly. During this stage we considered the editorials to be more important than ever. The trouble was we were so meticulous about saying everything clearly that we ended up confusing it even more. In the end, what were we saying? Could anyone understand our oh-so-brainy editorials?

Listen to what happened to me once. On Venceremos we were always talking about the listeners' circles: form them, meet together, but I'd never been able to take part in one. When I got hepatitis and had to be taken to Tancredo, I got the chance. Tancredo is where the sick and anaemic guerrillas go for a rest: rest and eat, sleep and eat. Of course, the schedule includes a Venceremos listeners' circle, so at six o'clock, yellow or not, there I was running the discussion and getting a new shock every day.

"What was the most important thing on today's programme?" I'd begin.

"Well, they laid an ambush in..."

"Not the military news. The important political message."

"Ummmm..."

"What was the issue they took up today?"

"Gee, I don't remember."

"Damn! So you weren't paying attention."

"No, well, yes I was paying attention, but I can't remember now."

"You can't remember anything?"

"Of course I do. They laid an ambush in El Semillero that..."

"Forget about the ambush. What was the editorial about?"

"Sorry pal, it's that... I've got this disease that makes me forget what I've heard."

"Does everybody have the same disease?"

The experience cured my vocabulary as much as my liver. That's where I realised we had to change the way we did editorials. People didn't understand them. If during the editorial I said "Open your ears! Today's message is important!" then you could see them concentrating, listening carefully, overcoming whatever technical problems or interference we had, and above all trying to overcome the worst interference of all: language. That's right, we'd act like college boys and use some sociological jargon, far-out abstractions that even when understandable, were never very pleasant to listen to. Of course, people's commitment and militancy were serious enough to overcome the tedium. People knew they needed to grow politically in order to improve their organising. When you haven't got fresh bread, you eat stale old loaves, and despite everything, those editorials that were so inappropriate for radio ended up feeding the pols and everybody else.

That's where the other side of the problem lay. What do you do if you have a lot of saints, but only one candle? Which one do you light up? We had only the one radio station, one station and one programme to reach very different audiences. In the editorials we had to give orientation to our fighters, but the same editorials were an arena for debating with the enemy. Even though you have the pols as a captive audience, you can rest assured that the enemy officers are listening too. Not the soldiers, they're not allowed to, but the officers, following the basic principle of know thy enemy, all have to tune in. How could you waste such an opportunity to argue with them? The buzz words, the language had to be very different for them.

The language had to be different again for influential personalities like Father Ignacio Ellacuría, for example. The rector of the UCA[1] was a man whose opinion mattered, not only to his students but to the guerrillas as well. He always deserved our respect, even though we didn't agree on a lot of things — and we agreed on many others — we had excellent relations with him. At times debating with Ellacuría was important, and you couldn't debate with him using some *campesino* fable; you had to use more academic language. That day we'd have to plan: "This editorial is for Ellacuría". He couldn't listen to the station, but he read transcripts of Venceremos, and the next day he'd respond, giving his opinion on the issue.

In other words, on our one and only programme we had to speak to the pol and the peasant woman he was organising, and Ellacuría, and the shameless colonel — and they were all priorities. If we'd had a weekly magazine or a big daily newspaper, we could have done some pieces with more depth, others with less, but Venceremos had to be a station for both the masses and the elite, for the organised and the unorganised. It was the only media we had, though that's no excuse for the yawns we provoked with our notoriously boring editorials.

Closing The Highways

Attention! Attention all truckers! The General Command of the Farabundo Martí National Liberation Front has ordered transport on all of the nation's highways to cease as of Monday at six in the afternoon. We call on all combatants to enforce this order and keep it enforced until the General Command gives the order to allow traffic to circulate once again.

Radio Venceremos, 8 July, 1984

Perhaps they supported us, or maybe they were afraid of sabotage or didn't want to go to work, or maybe it was just the novelty, but on that Monday the highways of the eastern part of the country were empty. You could have taken a nap in the middle of the Coastal Highway or the Pan-American. Nothing, private or public, moved. In San Miguel, the capital of the East, there was a bit more activity, but since no provisions were coming in, the city seemed to be under siege. The week wore on: Monday, Tuesday, Wednesday, Thursday... By Friday, San Miguel was screaming: no gasoline, no food, no nothing.

"A military convoy is coming from San Salvador to supply the city."

"They shall not pass," we said, as revolutionarily as we could.

"How are we going to stop them? With missiles? It's a shitload of trucks, helicopters, planes — it looks like they're invading another country."

"So what do we do?"

Jesus, we were worried. It was a question of honour. They were going to make a mockery of our order! No minefield could stop a convoy that big, so we found out what time they left San Salvador, and worked out they would enter the East at about one in the afternoon.

"Let's lift the ban at twelve!" Atilio said. "That way they'll pee outside the bowl. Santiago, get going and announce it fast."

We turned on Venceremos at noon and Santiago went on air:

Since our goals have been achieved, we advise all truckers and all of our people that today, as of right now... all the highways are open!

A few minutes later, when the convoy entered the East with all its clatter of armoured trucks and air support, there was no longer any ban on transport. If we achieved nothing else, at least we made them look ridiculous.

The bans on transport spread from east to west. On our front we could paralyse everything, even the flies took a break. Then the paracentral region took up the tactic, then the centre of the country. In the cities, where it wasn't so easy to sabotage those who refused to obey, traffic, especially public transport, functioned more or less normally. But little by little, ban after ban, people began to get used to the idea and obeyed the order given over Venceremos.

Where we weren't able to achieve much of anything was in the West. In '87, I don't remember just when, Santiago turned on the microphone and spoke with such authority he sounded like the Big Daddy himself announcing the flood:

All transport is hereby banned as of tomorrow at 6am, this time with special emphasis on the western part of the country! We call on our combatants, our militia columns, urban commandos, clandestine militia, encamped militia... [he mentioned about seven categories of forces, some of which I don't think even existed] *...to enforce this order with maximum rigour in the western part of the country!*

The next day, even the city of Santa Ana was like a cemetery. The city buses stayed in their lots. I don't think we ever paralysed the East as completely as we did the West that time. It was because of the strength we'd built up in the West that year, but it was also because an order given over Venceremos was like a knockout punch. It hit so hard that even the commercial stations underlined the part about "special emphasis" and "maximum rigour" in the West.

The enemy tried a few times to break the transport bans with fake calls to stations in the capital. They had a miserable jerk in COPREFA who tried to pass himself off as our representative.

"This is Commander Mario speaking, the spokesperson of the FMLN, to inform you that the transport ban has just been lifted."

"But has Venceremos said so?" the announcer asked disingenuously.

"I'm telling you that I'm the official spokesman of the FMLN."

"Okay, thanks."

The announcer at KL hung up the phone, turned on his microphone and said:

Well friends, we just got a call — someone named Commander Mario, who claims to be a spokesman for the FMLN. We don't want to cast doubt on anyone's word, but let's wait for the Radio Venceremos afternoon broadcast and see what they say. In the meantime, we hope there will be no civilian victims on the highways...

That's how it is: until Venceremos announces it, no one believes it. That's why when we decree a transport ban our audience rockets. Everyone, friends and enemies alike, turn up the volume on the not-so-clandestine Venceremos, waiting for the moment when they can go back out on four wheels. It's not in the rulebook, but it's a great way to boost your ratings.

Santiago has a unique style for the transport bans. He doesn't say "The ban is over". He raises his voice and proclaims as if from the balcony of the presidential palace:

Throughout the country, the highways are open!

As soon as he says the word "highways", the alarm sounds on KL and all the others:

At this very moment the clandestine Radio Venceremos...

Armed with Imagination

The victory over Monterrosa was guerrilla tactics pure and simple: do a lot with a little, sharpen your wits, use trickery before force. That's what it's about, that's how we had to confront the new situation where the balance of military power had become so enormously unequal. How could we fashion a slingshot to defeat an army that the gringos had turned into a Goliath?

This was the stage of the mines. The enemy expected established lines of fire, but their battalions would arrive and find no one. Suddenly we'd fire a few shots. Logically, the soldiers would look for a place to take cover; they'd run for the nearest tree. Boom! A mine would be waiting for them. A casualty. A foot. Two more soldiers who had to carry him would be put out of commission, and they'd all be demoralised, because the wounded man would be screaming, crying out in pain. So a mine could stop an entire battalion. Who would take the first step? Who would march into a minefield?

Say the Atlacatl takes up a position near a spring. At night a few of us sneak in and leave a mine between the camp and the spring. The next morning a soldier gets up and goes to fill his canteen. Boom! Another casualty. The army goes go to San Fernando. *Viva el FMLN* it says on a wall. A sergeant approaches to tear down the poster. Boom! A mine blows off his face. Another casualty. One soldier finds an abandoned rifle. Two more come over to check it out. Boom! Three more casualties. The worst of it for them is that they never see us. They don't know how many we are or where we're shooting from. What are we doing in these hills? the officers wonder, and they leave. The Torola IV operation, which the late Monterrosa said would "stay put", didn't even last two months — he's the only one who really stayed put. After 48 days, to be exact, the battalions left Morazán. They never found anyone to fight, but they had a shitload of casualties. They kept tripping mines the whole way. In Osicala, when they stopped to drink before crossing the river, boom! the last mine went off.

The results of the new guerrilla tactic managed to convince the remaining doubters. It proved that five kids with a handful of bullets and a mine could tear the enemy to shreds. Some people, when they hear about this, are horrified: that's terrorism! Yes, it's horrible, it's cruel. We wish we didn't have to do it, and it certainly doesn't make us happy to see anybody get mutilated. But it was the army that set the logic of this war, a war which we would have won long ago if they hadn't had US support. What else were we to do? Give up? Let the 14 coffee families continue running this country as if it were their private *hacienda*?

We didn't have the weaponry to face US support for the Salvadoran colonels indefinitely. Forget Russia or Cuba or Nicaragua! We had to make use of our own resources: get explosives from the mines at Montecristi here in Morazán, in the mines of San Sebastián in La Unión, find out where they sell explosives, make TNT ourselves in our own workshops. Who would suspect the lady on her way to Gotera to buy Palmolive soap? That soap is the basis for making the guerrilla napalm we put in the RPG-7. Who would suspect the little rich kid who buys a few flashbulbs for his camera? Flashbulbs can be used to set off explosives.

Everything was so homemade that we had quite a few accidents learning how to make bombs and experimenting with where and how to set them up. If you don't do it right, it'll blow up in your face. Nor can you just leave it somewhere and take off, because a *campesino* might come by and get hurt. So you've got to bury the mine and sit where you can see the *cuilios* when they show up, then shoot a few times so they'll take cover behind the tree where you left the mine, and wait for it to explode.

At Venceremos we also had to fire ourselves up about the new tactic. Before we used to brag about huge victories: sixty casualties, so many mortars recovered, so many rifles, so many rifle cartridges! Now it was just one little electrical pole. An electrical pole dynamited, and a greeting to the unit there at kilometre 44 who carried out that great little attack. Whatever the combatants did, no matter how small, Venceremos announced it and congratulated them. That did a lot to strengthen morale.

We started a new item on the use of home-made weaponry. Undoubtedly it's a risky business, the most risky of all, because teaching people how to handle explosives over the radio — you could kill your listeners! A few too many drops in the soup and bye-bye, we'll see you on the other side. That's why they say an explosives expert only makes two mistakes in his life: the first is getting involved with explosives, and the other is the one that sends him upstairs. On the radio, however, we were extremely careful. Rather than ask the audience to do crazy things, we invited them to use their imagination. Think of things, suggest them, and we'll check them out here in our workshops. It worked. People came up with things you'd never imagine!

We tested people's ideas in the Nivo workshop. When our combatants became explosives experts, they started suggesting loads of new ideas. On Venceremos we did a lot of publicity for the "atonal" mine which scared the *cuilios* as much as they scared us by bragging about their ultra-modern aircraft. The atonal works like this: a soldier steps on the charge, but instead of going off on the ground the mine jumps about a metre into the air before it blows up, filling everyone within reach with shrapnel. Then there's the "Yankee-hunter" mine, which doesn't get tripped — instead you hide nearby until a patrol walks past, touch two wires and good-bye patrol. There's the "fan" mine. It's used for ambushes on the highway and has about thirty pounds of explosives, which is a respectable amount. The combatant hides about a hundred metres away, sees the military convoy coming, knows just when to touch the wires, and blows the truck to shit.

On Venceremos we announced the innovations and their results. We got word from another front that they'd invented the "Manuel José Arce" mine, an improvement on the fan. With the fan it was hard to gauge the velocity of the truck to know exactly when to set it off. The new one had a double charge, spaced out, so that if you didn't get it with the first, you squashed it with the second. From another front we got word that they'd made one with three charges to be absolutely sure. Out on the highway you'd hear those terrible triple blasts! There's also one called the "booby-hunter", which comes in several forms. There's the "jumper" which can knock down helicopters, and there's the "rampla", which can destroy the house next door if you aren't careful when you aim the piece of wood that catapults the ball of explosives.

People got so creative with home-made weapons that they even sent us suggestions on how to poison *cuilios* at the top of the hill above the Torola River. The soldiers, the listeners wrote, are going to be tired when they get there. The first thing they'll do is stop for a drink. Suppose we leave them a bucket of oranges injected with cyanide? When they see them, they're going to eat them, and that's that. Unfortunately it would be incredibly dangerous — imagine, a civilian might come along and find the bucket. So we left the oranges idea to rot, but the important thing was that people were developing their creativity and Venceremos was encouraging them. It was always the same principle: do a lot with the little you have at hand.

We combined the mines with propaganda to break the army's morale. In particular, we wanted to drive a wedge between the troops and their officers. Signs would appear on trees:

Soldier: let your officer go first. The mines are for him!

One morning painted all over town:

Soldier, you're poor. Don't defend the rich!

On another wall:

Don't be a fool, soldier, you're poor like us!

They even painted a cow, and that cow wandered all over with a motto on its back:

Soldier, desert!

There was so much graffiti that you'd get debates on the walls between the *cuilios* and our combatants:

Soldier, you're poor!
   Poor your ass!
Soldier, give up!
   Your grandmother first!
We'll take your grandmother too if she knows how to shoot!

What didn't we do that year? We even used advances by the *cuilios* to train our people. Suppose they landed their troops somewhere in Morazán.

"Great," our officer says. "This is our turkey of the week. Get all of the militia units together and we'll run a workshop for them."

All the novice guerrillas would meet the officer for their first lesson.

"Today we're going to learn to be good snipers. To shoot like a sniper you do this and this... The positions are like this and that..."

During the day they got the theory; at night they practiced on the soldiers encamped nearby. Like field training.

"Today we're going to learn about harassing the enemy. Not just that, we're going to learn how to use an RPG-2. This is how you use it, this is its range... Now go out and practice!"

Since the workshop had different levels and a lot of *compas* had to practice, the *cuilios*, who didn't move an inch because they didn't know where to move or whom to attack, were perfect targets. In the morning two militia would do their sniper homework. Bang! Bang! At noon, a guerrilla unit would practice a fire and manoeuvre exercise. In the afternoon, a special commando would practice a camouflaged approach. At night, they'd often ask Venceremos to help out. We'd record cassettes so the soldiers couldn't sleep. Those poor *cuilios*, harassed since five in the morning by our little school, would cap off the day with a special serenade. Several *compas* would take big speakers and set them up as close as possible to the soldiers' camp. They'd turn on the battery and Santiago and Marvin would go on at full blast:

Soldier, right now you're here, but have you wondered where your officer is? Your officer is sitting pretty in San Salvador, drinking whisky with the whores, and you're here enduring this shit with nothing to drink but water. This morning we got two of you. Did you notice that we got two of you right inside your camp? That's a piece of cake, right? So come on, get a few of us. What, you don't know where we are? Well, find out... But nobody's going to tell you. You know why? Because the people don't like you. They tell us all about you. It's the people, soldier, the people which is you too...

After this big paragraph, we'd put on loud music, FMLN slogans, and then the show would continue:

Talk to your grandma, soldier. We've already talked to her. Because it's easier to talk to your grandma than to talk to you. You think we're your enemy because the officers told you so. The officers got you to believe it. If you could only talk to us. After all, we're just as poor as you. Think about it. This is Radio Venceremos. We're watching you soldier, and we'd like you to think about it...

We had to place the speakers where they had some protection, because as soon as the yakking started, it would be bullets and more bullets until they got tired of it. Then they'd have to listen. Our purpose was to break their morale and more than a few realised the idiocy of wasting their lives fighting against the people, but the real point was to ruin their sleep. That was easy for us, all it took was three *compas* staying up with the speakers. The army, on the other hand, had a whole battalion, 800, 1,000 men, unable to shut their eyes. The guards because they had to guard and the rest because of the lecture — no one got any sleep!

Hey, soldier, what's new? How are you? We know you're in bad shape now. You haven't even been able to take a shit because the latrine is too far away. You're shitting like a cat, right? Well, you asked for it. Plenty of others have deserted, but you're still there defending the rich. And your grandma — what would she say about all this?

All night long listening to that sermon. They'd get fed up, shoot a bit, send out a patrol. We couldn't just stay in one place. We'd put the speakers here for a while, then over there. Later on, we figured out a better way. While one of us set up the equipment and another stood guard, a third went and planted a few mines that would blow off their feet. So in the middle of the programme, boom! You'd hear a bang, then nothing.

Before dawn the three giving the serenade would gather up their things and, until tomorrow, same time, same channel!

I'm Líber's Marv!

I lost my girlfriend in that fucking COP². How could it be otherwise? At the school for revolutionaries there was nothing but screaming, dancing, running, someone putting on a play over here, others climbing up a hill over there, still others playing brainteasers, hand games, any kind of game... But it wasn't just fun for fun's sake. It had an educational basis and a clear objective: to rid peasants of their inhibitions. Everybody knows that because of their living conditions *campesinos* are very reserved. A political activist has to be just the opposite: he's got to be the guy who stands up on a rock and runs a meeting, grabs a megaphone and mobilises the village, carries the child, talks to everyone. Shyness isn't allowed.

For the new guerrilla tactic we needed combatants who had ideas and knew how to express them, so losing your inhibitions was very important. Balta and Marisol, I remember, had a book on group dynamics filled with all sorts of games. They studied the games, made a few modifications to adapt them to our situation, and then the party began: everybody was doing body movement, making up slogans, inventing skits with costumes, all that stuff. Sometimes they used these techniques to explain things people found hard to understand because of their cultural level. But basically they were looking to develop self-confidence.

The results were obvious. Too obvious. As I said, I lost my girlfriend in the COP. Meeting so many people and becoming so uninhibited, she dumped her shyness and ended up dumping me too. The truth is our relationship had been in crisis before she even went to school. From living so far apart? Maybe. She was a medic and there was always too much work. I was in Venceremos, which for security reasons is a very closed organisation. We only saw each other every thousand years and even then it was too rushed. The relationship had become more of a formality.

When the dispersal of our forces began, it was decided that the first COP should be for the best cadres on the front, who would then become catalysts. So Libertad — I called her Líber — went to take the course in Arambala. That's when she let down her hair.

"Marv, you told me our relationship had to be different, right?"

"That's right."

"And if it's just a habit it's no good. Isn't that right?"

"That's right."

"And that love is kind of crazy."

"That's right."

"Well, Marv..."

Libertad was a peasant with all the traditions and customs of a peasant. Marisol, the one from the school, told me once — and I'll never forget it — that it's dangerous to put "strange ideas" in the head of a peasant woman, because later on she'll take you to hell and back. You'll never find a way to stop her. That's just what happened. When Libertad grasped a new idea, she took hold of it for dear life, as if she'd never thought any other way. If she understood that something — not to kiss in public, for example — was simply a social convention, or the fruit of a repressive upbringing, right away she'd start smothering you with kisses in front of the Pope. The peasants of Morazán, the peasant women of Morazán, have always seemed to me to possess an incredible mental agility that allows them to question backward ideas passed on from grandparents to parents, and to modify them just by understanding their error.

"I agree," I said, "our relationship is bullshit. I come here and we're both bored. Right now you'd rather be playing around with that bunch of lunatics, right Líber?"

"Look Marv, I think we've reached the end. Let's do something: Let's separate for a while. You make your life, you find a new relationship, and let's see what happens."

"What about you?"

"The same thing, of course."

"In other words, each parrot to his own perch."

"Yup, because we aren't getting any pleasure out of this. It's a sad excuse for a relationship. Let's separate and then we'll see how each of us feels. Okay?"

"Okay."

I agreed to the pact a bit reluctantly. She was right, but I loved her. I enjoyed her, and I still had the hots for her, but what could I do? I accepted my defeat. I returned to our camp in Pericón and she continued with her damned uninhibitions course.

A day went by and I felt terrible. The second day went by and I fell totally to pieces. The third day, and I couldn't stand it any more, but a deal is a deal. On the fourth day I was putting together a huge poster of Che Guevara, like a jigsaw puzzle, for a Guerrilla Day celebration. I was there on the ground putting the pieces together when Marvin walked over. I could see he was up to no good. He sat down and gave me a cigarette.

"So Marvel, have you met your competition?"

"What do you mean, my competition?"

"Yeah, they say Libertad's moved in with somebody."

I felt a chill in the pit of my stomach. I stood up, pushed Che aside and even though it was late at night I took off like a bean fart downhill. I ran half an hour until I got to Arambala. At the entrance, the guard shouted at me: "Halt! Who goes there?"

"Marv!"

"Which Marv?"

"Líber's Marv!"

You see in Morazán you're not you. You're somebody's or you're from something. You're from the Nivo organisation. You're one of Abraham's radio operators. Men who have a partner are "so-and-so's so-and-so". You belong to that woman. That's the way things are.

I got past the entrance to the camp. I went two blocks. When I got to the door of her house I ran into a mutual friend who was also in the COP.

"Hi, how are you?" I asked nervously. "Is Líber in?"

"Look, I think she's at a meeting..." she said, even more nervous than me.

"Oh! I'll wait for her."

"Well I think..."

"What?"

"I think they won't be back until late."

I took a deep breath and went in. The few people there stopped talking when they saw me. I crossed the floor and went to the room where Libertad had her bed. There were two lumps in her bed. Two and neither of them was me! Two and I was looking at them with this pair of eyes that the worms are going to eat! I turned on my heels and left. I didn't even say good-bye to anyone and couldn't have cared less if I lived or died. There I was heading back, gored and beaten, when the guard stopped me again at the edge of Arambala.

"Halt! Who goes there?"

"It's Marv!"

"Which Marv?"

"Marv, sonofabitch!"

I got to Pericón, looked discouragedly at Che, lay down alone and dreamed about Líber's great-grandparents.

Time went by. In the end there's no soup that won't grow cold. About five months later I moved in with a girl who worked in layout with the press and propaganda collective. (It was all within the union since Libertad's boyfriend was a radio operator.) As it turned out I caught a bad case of hepatitis and got put in the hospital at Tancredo, the rest and rehabilitation spot we have on the front. I'm there in Tancredo and one fine night Libertad shows up. Since the day of the two lumps we hadn't even said hello to each other.

"Can I see Marv?" she asks Eduardo the doctor.

"You can see him," Eduardo says with a smile, "but nothing else, understand? The man is on a diet."

Libertad turned the colour of a sapodilla, because here when they say diet they don't mean food.

"Hi," Líber says. "How are you?"

"Fucked but happy."

"Can we talk?"

"Sure. Sit down."

"Well. And... How's it going with the layout artist?"

"Great! And how about you? How's everything with the radio operator?"

"Bad. It's bad for me."

"Really bad?"

"Worse. I made a mistake."

"So?"

"We made a deal, right? Well I've come to fulfil my end of it, and to tell you that this separation didn't work out for me."

"You just came to tell me that?"

"And that I want to be your woman again. Marv's Líber."

"But..."

"I'm not saying anything else. You figure out what you're going to do."

That medic walked right out and left me with my head more mixed up than my liver. In the end, when I left Tancredo I went back to Libertad, and we lived happily ever after — at least for a while. And that's the end of the story.

Three Kernels of Corn

In our camp, when we lined up in military formation, someone at the back would shout:

"We live to struggle!"

And everyone would shout back:

"We struggle to win!"

That voice at the back always resounded with so much conviction, with such beautiful enthusiasm, that Atilio wanted it on the radio. One day he popped the question.

"Who was it that first asked me to yell?" she said.

Her name was Leti, and she was in charge of communications on the front. She'd helped out with codes and monitoring, she'd done skits, but speaking on the radio? Never. As to getting involved with radio people — God forbid. We were bearded, crazy city-folk who liked to spend all day in an interminable ideological bullshit session. Leti was just the opposite, a peasant from Morazán who sold clothes before joining up, one of those women who carry baskets on their heads and travel down to Usulután.

"Well, now's the time. Here's the microphone."

Against her will, very much against her will, they put Leti on the Venceremos staff.

"Marvel," they tell me, "teach her how to broadcast."

We started out by reading *Nobody Writes to the Colonel* out loud. I don't know where I came up with that technique, but I figured the problem was comprehension.

"Look Leti, the trick is to understand what you're reading. Don't read the words, read the ideas, understand?"

"No."

"It's really simple. You read a couple of words with your eyes before saying them with your mouth. Your eyes stay ahead of your tongue, okay? That way you get the meaning of what you're going to read. Once you learn to do it that way, you can rest, stop after a phrase, breathe at the right time, change a word as you go if it's not right. Ready?"

"Forget it. I can't do that."

"Of course you can, it's a breeze."

"No I can't," she said nearly crying. "I can't because I can't. You guys made a mistake."

"So?" I felt discouraged.

"So let's start."

Leti had a strong sense of duty. If they chose her for this job, the earth would quit before she did, so we began our broadcasting classes.

"You're going to do two kinds of reading. First, the most important, is to read to yourself, without opening your mouth. Without moving your lips either. You're going to read just with your eyes.

We took a paragraph, just one paragraph. After Leti read it, I asked her: "Are there any words you don't understand?"

"This one: 'peritoneum', and this one: 'eccentric'."

"Well, that means this and that. Now read the paragraph again."

She read it again, to herself.

"Do you understand what it says there?"

"I think so."

"Now let's read it again, this time out loud."

Leti read it, but the words all ran together, as she rushed along to get it over with as soon as possible.

"Patience girl, the night is young! Now *you* understand but the audience has to understand too. Read it again, but don't skip the commas. Pause at the periods. Pay attention to all those little things that give each phrase meaning."

After she managed a more or less acceptable reading, it was time to analyse the content. There's always a main idea and secondary ones. There are always protagonists and others who play a supporting role.

"What is the main idea, the essence of this paragraph?"

"I don't know."

"Well, let's figure it out."

That's how we spent our lunch hours, paragraph by paragraph, until the final one when the colonel won't eat the rooster.

***

Doing the broadcasting was the least of it. They sent Leti here to be head of the station, to take charge of our political direction. Our team was a bit bohemian, very undisciplined, so the commanders wanted to send in a cadre who could put an end to what they called our petit bourgeois habits. The purpose wasn't to purge us or screw us, but to consolidate the team. The Venceremos team was good, but sometimes we rubbed out with our elbows what we'd written with our hands.

At first Leti was very rigid. She questioned our jealousies, our ambitions, she questioned everything.

"You're just a real square," I told her.

"Right, and you're too round," she answered.

Her task wasn't easy. Butterfly was on her way out, and then she became the only woman: a peasant with no experience in radio, coordinating three old foxes, Santiago, Marvel and me. When she first arrived she put her foot down, then bit by bit she gained authority, since the authority you get just from pointing your finger is somewhat relative, don't you think? Real authority gets built little by little.

How could Leti lead a radio collective if she knew nothing about radio? That's the question that set off the confrontations. Some of us felt that since she wasn't up to scratch on the technical side, she wasn't the best person to be in charge. But technique is a lot easier to pick up than community values or revolutionary attitudes, and Leti had such an enormous capacity for learning that even if she wasn't doing what she liked, she started liking what she was doing. She put her heart into the station. She had never broadcast before, but she learned to broadcast. She had never written an article or a commentary but she learned to write well. She edits news, processes it, debates it, monitors the BBC of London, keeps up on world events. She's become a great journalist, and to this day she coordinates and runs the station team.

I think that Leti's work, her presence, is a good indicator of the values that drive the party. At Venceremos the highest authority isn't the most intellectual of a group of intellectuals, or the best technician in a highly technical medium, or the man in a team that's mostly male. It's run by a peasant, a woman, and she's in charge because she is, without doubt, the person who can best ensure that it runs well.

***

It's one thing to talk about it now, but it was something else to live through it day by day. Imagine, an engineer like Apolonio, educated in Germany, who could have been earning good money in any big company, or a crazy poet like Santiago, who had to struggle constantly not to get swept away by his moods, or a journalist like Marvin who was always hungry for knowledge and even hungrier for a chance to show it off, or a filmmaker like me, with a degree from England, arrogant in my ways and hungry for stardom. In the same stew we had Morena, a peasant from San Fernando who'd spent ten years fighting the war, who had accumulated a history of jail cells, clandestine life, arms trafficking, bombs in cathedrals, but had barely had the time to learn how to read and write, and hadn't the least desire to be famous. Someone like Rafi, humble, with a reverence for work, who respected people for the callouses on their hands, while the rest of us loved to read — an activity no *campesino* would consider work — and weren't able to shake that vague feeling that physical effort wasn't for intellectuals. Some, like Isra, were born and raised around here and could catch rabbits by the ears without wasting a shot, while we couldn't tell coriander from parsley. It was a difficult mixture, a very complex meeting of cultures and ideologies, because those of us from the city had a tendency to compete, to feel superior because we worked closely with the commanders, to swell up like peacocks if Joaquín Villalobos asked our opinion. Such all-knowing individualism went against the grain of the whole project, didn't it?

Here's an example to clarify the conflict and it has to do with the way we took care of things, like the tape recorders. Do you know what it cost to get a tape recorder to Morazán? I'm not talking about dollars. On top of the money you've got to add the hours, the risks, the people who got killed, the years it took to build up a network of hundreds of hands to pass that tape recorder along from one to the other, a logistical chain made up of thousands of men and women who could bring a tape recorder from New York to Morazán, from Panama to Morazán, from Munich to Morazán... Then you don't take good care of these tools you need to make the revolution! It's not a question of being utilitarian or finicky, it's an attitude towards that damned tape recorder that must have cost, say, sixty dollars. What's sixty dollars in a war that lasts ten years? It's not the price, it's the value of the little stone that together with all the other stones forms a great wall to block the designs of the empire.

That's the communal mentality that we lack, especially those of us from the city. Like when you're grinding corn and you drop three kernels in the mud, Germán's never going to leave them there. He'll bend over, pick them up, go to the stream, wash them off, and put them back in the grinder. Three kernels of corn! But not Marvel. After I've spent two hours turning that handle and my kidneys feel like steel wool, I'll see those three little kernels and I'll leave them where they fell, because I'll be thinking only of my back. What's three kernels anyway? But three here, three there, three more somewhere else... Why not bend over and pick them up if you can? They were lost for no other reason but your laziness. That attitude just doesn't fit with the programme, it doesn't correspond to the type of person who could create a different sort of economic system, a person who wouldn't end up wanting to be rich, who couldn't end up bought by the Medellín Cartel. It's all there in the simple act of bending over or not. For the tape recorder to work you've got to clean the heads every day. It's not a question of buying another, even if we had the money. That's not it. What's sad is to see it ruined because you didn't do something you could have done.

Similar things happen in combat. When someone gets wounded, do you risk your life to get him out? You could leave him there and go on living, or you could try to get him out and maybe both of you would die. What should you do? Another death among seventy thousand, three little kernels in a million — that's the big difference you discover in small things!

One day I went to do some monitoring on our portable television and it was missing the aerial. Where the devil could they have put it? It had already been broken in an accident, so you had to treat it delicately. If you pulled it out hard, it would come apart in your hand. One detail in a million, that's all.

"Who was monitoring last night?" I started my investigation.

It was Marvin or Santiago, the last two to watch television. Marvin said that when he saw it the aerial was already gone and Santiago said he really didn't remember if it had one or not. Leti walked in, got angry, said it couldn't be left like that. For her the problem wasn't the aerial, but rather that Marvin had seen it didn't have one and hadn't bothered to search for it, and Santiago hadn't even noticed.

"If you broke it, what could we do?" Leti asked. "That could happen to anyone. If you lost it, well, you fucked up. That can happen too. But what should never happen is that it was you and you won't admit it, or it got lost and you didn't even notice. That's something else."

"What something?" Marvin screamed. "I take no responsibility for that fucking aerial!"

"That's just what I can't accept," Leti continued. "That you two don't admit there's been a mistake. It's your attitude Marvin! The way you relate to the equipment!"

"What a crock of shit!" Santiago entered the fray. "You're making a storm in a teacup. Just put on another aerial and forget about it!"

"We can't forget about it because tomorrow it'll be the same story with a cable or a cassette."

"In other words, you don't trust me," Marvin was really pissed off. "I'm not going to put up with this!"

The tone of the argument grew sharper as the words cut deeper: Did the organisation have the right to doubt his word? Was his attitude so irresponsible that he couldn't even tell what was irresponsible and what wasn't? And so on. By chance, Luisa came by and asked if she could join the meeting. Marvin continued to say he was offended by the lack of trust, he was committed to the cause, and that...

"The television doesn't have an aerial," Luisa cut him off. "That's the issue. The rest is bullshit, and those little-rich-kid attitudes don't suit you."

"What little rich kid?"

"You. The one who's out of line, declaring how offended he feels because someone asks him about something that belongs to everyone."

"It wasn't me!"

"Forget about the 'me' and think in the plural, *hombre!*"

Leti got up and went to ask Mauricio to fix up an old aerial for the old television set.

***

We're made of flesh and bone. You join the guerrillas and you take your baggage of existential conflicts with you: your solitude, your hang-ups. For me, getting used to winter and sleeping with the noise of the airplanes was tough, but the anonymity was harder still. When I joined Venceremos I was 24 years old. I came from the art world where even a fart carries a signature. I came from an environment that was cannibalistic, where everyone tried to get ahead by biting or stepping on the head of whoever was in the way. Suddenly I had to adjust to collective things, to work without a name and without competition. Fights like this: Which job is more important on air, reading the editorial or doing the agitation to encourage soldiers to desert? Which task is the real one and which is a filler?

We fought a lot, it's true. I was a spoilt kid, I admit it. But we're still here. The Venceremos team survived, it became established. Leti had a lot to do with it, by always asking us where we were heading. She was always more concerned about direction than speed, concerned with not losing sight of the alternative society we were attempting to build, and not forgetting that it had to emerge within the Venceremos team. It wasn't enough to talk about it over the air and to publicise it in debates. In us you can see, at the very least, the beginnings of the new man!

***

We have come a long way. I think that over the years and through all the fights, the people on the team have changed in fundamental ways. On what do I base this? First, on the fact that we stayed. You've got to see how we live and sleep and roll in the mud in a guerrilla camp. Yearning for adventure or just plain stubbornness won't get you through nine or ten years under those conditions. It might you through at first, but the struggle itself makes the difference later on. You experience the process, and you change. You change inside and out, your life, your hands, your toenails, the way you view the world, what you love and what you hate. Your spirit changes.

Then there's the big change, the change in the country, the one we're sure to achieve. We're going to win! The Salvadoran people risked everything and they'll win! In '81 we only dreamed about it, but now we have forged a real alternative, we're on the home stretch towards victory. The road has been travelled by many of us together, it has been a battle of thousands of hours, innumerable written notes, interminable night-time marches, countless gunshots, endless political debate, inexhaustible people like Germán or Leti — of many kernels of corn picked up from the ground.

One Tortilla for Three Soldiers

Miguel was legendary. An ambush on the road to Santa Rosa? It was Miguel. A soldier killed at El Divisadero? Miguel. Slogans painted on the walls of Jocoro? It was always Miguel, a phantom for the *cuilios* and a beloved *compa* for the people of southern Morazán.

Miguel was the political officer for the zone we expanded into, far away on the other side of the Torola River, near where Morazán meets La Unión. Everyone knew him and he knew everyone. He'd show up at a house, shoot the breeze with the *campesinos*, laugh with them, eat with them, make friends with the grandfather and the baby. He often went to the village of Flamenco, where a very poor woman put him up at her house. It was one of those little peasant houses made of cornstalks tied together, a thatch roof, dirt floor and in the middle of the only room a pole with a Bristol almanac hanging from it. On one side, the cooking pots; on the other, rough-hewn beds for sleeping.

Miguel would go to that woman's house to rest or hold meetings. They almost caught him there once, along with another *compa*. They were inside eating, when there was a loud knocking at the door.

"Get under there!" the woman told them under her breath, pointing towards the bed.

Miguel managed to peek under the door and saw the jungle boots the *cuilios* wear.

"Open up!" they shouted. "It's the authorities!"

Miguel and the other *compa* nervously grabbed their rifles and hid under the bed. The woman, calm as could be, opened the door.

"Good evening. What can I do for you?"

"Tell us, señora, have the guerrillas passed by here?"

"They sure have. A little while ago, they went down that road over there, about eighty of them."

"Eighty?" The *cuilios* were surprised.

"Well, I didn't count them, but the dogs barked the whole night as they were going past."

When the soldiers heard there were so many, they did an about-face without so much as a look inside.

The *campesinos* of Morazán are very astute. They're not the dumb peasants some people imagine. Even the stupidest will get to be a bishop if

Rome doesn't watch out. There was a guy from Torola who was planting his crops one morning when five *cuilios* from a PRAL[3] turned up.

"Hey you, have the guerrillas come by here?"

"Sure. They just went by."

"No kidding. How many of them?"

"Only a few. Actually, they were wearing underwear and little caps and they were carrying funny bags, but I'm sure they were guerrillas."

The ERP's special forces dressed like that. Unlike the regular caps, theirs have short visors and earflaps. That way when they are advancing or crawling, they can feel the tiniest branch and recognise the path. They go barefoot, wearing only underwear and carrying the absolute minimum: a bag with explosives, pliers for cutting triggers in mine fields and a sawn-off shotgun. When they attack they paint themselves black, camouflaging themselves like cats. The enemy is scared shitless of these guys because they're invisible. They'll jump you and put a contact bomb up your ass, before you can even see them.

"And were they painted?"

"Yes, all painted up. You'll be able to see them around that curve, look."

"Thanks a lot!"

"Hey, wait! Don't you even want a drink of water?"

Laughing, the *campesino* held up his gourd, but the *cuilios* were already running in the opposite direction from the one he'd pointed out, their shirts billowing behind them and their feet kicking up the dust from the road.

Let's get back to the woman in Flamenco. She'd been given an urgent message for Miguel.

"If any *compas* come by," other *compas* told her, "tell them to give this to Miguel. Be careful, it's really important."

When people are given tasks like that, they get anxious, they want to get it over with, to pass on the piece of paper right away. That's how the woman felt as she waited for the boys or Miguel himself. But who showed up? The *cuilios*. They knew something was up with her house. If they hadn't come before, it was because they wanted to catch Miguel when he was there. They'd been after him for days, but he was a first-class fox and always smelled them coming, so the *cuilios* decided to check out the old lady.

"Hello, is Miguel here?"

It was a corporal and two soldiers, but the three of them were dressed up as guerrillas. The woman was caught off guard. Should she give them the message for Miguel? She looked at them with their worn-out packs, their beat-up rifles, their muddy boots, dressed just like us: Dear God, how can I tell if these men are *compas* or *cuilios*?

"Is Miguel here?" the one who was a corporal asked again.

"Come in please," she said softly. "Would you like a *tortilla*?"

"Sure."

The woman went to the kitchen, picked up a single *tortilla*, put in a little bit of cheese and offered it to the one who had spoken.

"You'll have to forgive me, but I only have one. We're poor, you know."

The corporal took the *tortilla*, folded it over twice and swallowed it in one bite. This one is a *cuilio*, the women knew right away. If he doesn't share, then they must be *cuilios*. The *compas* aren't selfish like that.

We taped a lot of anecdotes like this one, and then broadcast them over Venceremos. The *campesinos* split their sides laughing when they hear them, and by laughing at the enemy, they lose their fear.

The Bridge on the Torola River

They started quoting Venceremos in the mainstream media. They've always quoted us, but in '85 it was like an echo chamber. No matter what garbage we put in our editorials, the news agencies, the rest of the stations, even the television picked it up. All the time you'd hear: "The measures implemented by the Christian Democratic government won't work, Radio Venceremos said today in its morning broadcast... 14 casualties in Guazapa, according to a report from the clandestine Radio Venceremos..."

That gave Rey Prendes, who was minister of culture then, a pain in the butt: "Why the fuck do we bother jamming their signal if it's getting repeated everywhere else, and with TV images to boot?" Rey Prendes shouted at the press. He couldn't impose a gagging order, but he told them they were aiding and abetting the enemy because the guerrillas would never let the government talk on Venceremos.

"Why not?" said Atilio. "We'd be delighted!"

Atilio called us right away and told us to put out a communiqué that very day with a proposal for the minister:

Venceremos is willing to give the government two full days of airtime. We will only identify the station at the beginning, and at the end state that the ideas put forth were not our own. Besides that, you can say whatever you please to our combatants. Send us the programmes on cassette, since we don't work with reel-to-reel recorders. In exchange for two full days, we ask for just twenty minutes on a national television and radio hook-up. May the one who has the better arguments win.

When they realised we were serious they got scared and clammed up. A few days later a journalist asked Rey Prendes: "What do you think of the proposal made by Radio Venceremos?"

To this day we are still waiting for his reply. Even though we didn't get our national hook-up, we did get a few of the news shows to continue giving our proposals broad coverage. We even swapped programmes with some of them, like Sorto, the famous reporter from Radio Chaparrastique in San Miguel.

Sorto is unique, as sensationalist as he is egocentric, and he has always been plugged into the brass at the Third Brigade. So plugged in, in fact, that he ignored us completely. On his news show the FMLN didn't exist, which is why on many occasions we had to take over the station, and on others we had to tie him up in order to get our communiqués on air. In the end, we reached a gentleman's agreement with him.

"This is a spokesperson for the FMLN," an urban commando told him by telephone.

"What do you want now?" Sorto answered.

"We'd appreciate it if you'd broadcast this communiqué of ours, since you broadcast the ones from the Third Brigade every day."

"Friends, don't think you're the same thing. The military is the military."

"And the guerrillas are the guerrillas. Look Sorto, we aren't asking you to speak ill of the army. Everybody takes sides and supports whoever he wants, but you're a journalist. We insist you broadcast the official communiqués of the FMLN. If not, you'd better be prepared for the consequences. So, yes or no?"

"That seems reasonable. Start reading your communiqué and I'll record it and put it on air right away."

He did it that time. He still does it when we need him to, and he introduces the communiqués with that apocalyptic tone he does so well and people like so much:

Attention everyone! We have a special news bulletin! We have here a communiqué from the General Command of the FMLN, a special broadcast only on Radio Chaparrastique, first in the news!

Once our text had been read out, an announcer would advertise Gillette razor blades, poplin at ten colones the yard, just like a marketplace, and then Sorto would be back kissing the military's ass. But that's him, number one in San Miguel, as he's always boasting. Everyone tunes in because the reporting he puts together is an amazing blend of exaggeration and fact, and no one can deny that Sorto is always on the spot wherever the shit hits the fan.

That was when the Army High Command decided to launch a new operation against us. This one was to be called Torola V, as if predicting a failure similar to Torola IV. Thirty-six truckloads of troops, four entire battalions, were on the way, expecting to march into Morazán. No way!

That was too daring, too disrespectful of the territory we controlled. As soon as he found out, Jonás gave the order to blow up the bridge that links San Miguel to Morazán. The convoy would have to stop there.

We blew it up at night and the next morning, at first light, Colonel Méndez, Monterrosa's successor, was there inspecting the site. A large number of soldiers went with him, as did Sorto, number one, the colonel's special guest. As soon as he got there, Sorto started reporting live and direct:

> *Here we are, friends of Radio Chaparrastique, seeing with our own eyes how the terrorist guerrillas of the FMLN destroy our roads, destroy everything, dynamiting the very bridge the civilian population uses to travel peacefully to market. Here with us by the ruins of the bridge is Colonel Méndez, head of the Third Infantry Brigade of San Miguel...*

Sorto was laying on the rhetoric, with Colonel Méndez at his side, when rat-a-tat-tat came the bursts of machine-gun fire. Our *compas*, who were on the other side of the river expecting the *cuilios* to show up, were all set to harass them. It wasn't much fire, just a three-man unit, but three gunners hidden from view up on a height with a bunch of soldiers in their sights can cause mayhem. How they ran! Sorto, who never dropped his microphone, narrated it all, and you could hear him shouting:

> *This is Vietnam! This is Vietnam itself! Listen to the gunfire! Colonel Méndez isn't here, I can't find him right now... Where are you, Colonel?*

"Méndez the Doll" they called that colonel. Always polished, every hair in place, he never left his office. The one time he did, it was just to run like hell. Sorto couldn't find him anywhere near the bridge, and had to end his broadcast without the words of the brave leader of the Third Brigade.

Back at Venceremos we were recording Sorto's report. We recorded it all, even the gunfire, and put it on air, and repeated it with pleasure. It was our way of returning the favour for all the communiqués he'd broadcast for us.

The Battle of Arambala

15 September, 1985. We woke up happy. First, because the day before, the *cuilios* had abandoned the zone after another failed operation. Second, because it was independence day in El Salvador and all of Central America, and to celebrate we had planned a big soccer game with players from different parts of the guerrilla organisation. To make our happiness complete, somebody had caught a *tepezcuintle*[4] and they were cooking it up in the kitchen.

We were in Arambala, a ghost town only two kilometres from El Mozote. After the massacres in '80 and '81, all the surrounding villages were abandoned. Whoever survived, emigrated — and far away. But that day Arambala came to life. Now that the army was gone, we took over the empty houses, relaxed, and started kicking around a soccer ball amid applause, betting, and general revelry. At noon we stuffed ourselves, and in the afternoon we went back to scoring goals. Long live 15 September!

16 September. Several *compas* got up early to do their washing. White sheets, red pants, black underwear: full dripping clothes-lines in the backyards, awaiting the sunrise. From the abandoned houses rose the unmistakable smell of freshly made *tortillas*.

Schafik Hándal[5] also got up early. He'd spent a few days with us and now he was in a hurry to negotiate over Duarte's daughter.[6] He climbed up on a horse that could barely hold him, bade a heartfelt farewell to our camp, and headed off. The rest of us lazybones continued having breakfast and telling stories. Unfortunately, like every other day, the Venceremos staff had a monitoring meeting. Every day of every year, we had our 9am monitoring meeting. We had no choice.

Leti took off her shoes, her feet swollen from the beating they had taken the day before. Santiago told Marvin about Duarte's latest speech, when he cried for his poor little girl, kidnapped and in the hands of the FMLN terrorists. The whole collective was in good humour, with our packs open and all our things spread out, enjoying our second day free of the Third Brigade's battalions, who by then had crossed the Torola River on their way back to the barracks.

As the meeting began, we heard the sound of helicopters. Usually, we couldn't have given a shit about just another more helicopter. In our shelter, we survived their daily machine-gun blasts and then went about our business. Of course we had heard about helicopter troop landings and they'd trained us for such an emergency. We did drills at all hours: a gunshot was the helicopter alarm, then in three minutes we had to pack up the entire station and get out of the camp. We had also heard about what was happening on other fronts, how they'd captured Nidia Díaz, how extremely dangerous and surprising the new gringo tactic was. But it hadn't happened to us. Maybe nobody really learns from the experience of others.

"The bitch!" screamed Julito Perica of the station security squad.

The gunshot rang out. Helicopters were approaching by the fleet. They weren't the UH-1H; they were the UH-1M rocket-launchers equipped with electronic machine-guns that shoot thousands of rounds per minute.

"Into the ditches, quick!"

We managed to grab all our stuff, pull out the tangled cables, put in the tape recorders, put away papers, pick up the packs, our hearts pounding boom-boom-boom, our balls up here in the rush to get away undetected. But our presence was all too evident. The pilots saw the smoke, the clothes

drying, people running. To make things worse, the sun was brilliant, not a cloud in the sky. The plains of Arambala at the foot of Pericón Hill are like a big billiard table, perfect for an aerial troop landing.

Within seconds, the helicopters began shooting. Never in my life could I have imagined the hellish roar of that barrage. They flew low, right over us, and shot point blank. The General Command was all there! Atilio, Mariana, Luisa, Leo Cabral from the RN[7], all of them!

***

I jumped into a ditch out of sight, but I didn't fit. If I lay down, my feet stuck out. If I squatted, my head was exposed. I was trying to figure out how to get all of me in when I saw a Hughes 500 helicopter — the wasp, they call it — coming just like a car, nearly scraping the ground of the field in front of us. It went by about ten metres from my ditch.

As I started getting over my initial fright, I heard our machine-gunners firing at the helicopters. At the command post, as an anti-aircraft defence, we had two M-60 machine-guns. Even though they were at a great disadvantage, at the first turn they managed to shoot the pilot of the wasp in the ass. We heard that on their communications.

"They busted my ass," the pilot reported. "I'm wounded."

That helicopter left, but another took its place. Then a Push-and-Pull showed up. It also shoots rockets and roars loud enough to blow your nerves to bits. As soon as they knocked out our two machine-guns, the landing would begin, so we had to get ready for combat. There was no alternative. You might be a great broadcaster or technician, an atheist or a true Christian, but at that moment you had to pick up an automatic rifle and deal with whatever came at you.

From my little trench I managed to see another ditch in a bamboo grove where Santiago, Marvel, Ana Lidia, Estenia and others had hidden. Suddenly, a bright flash lit up the bright day and a rocket fell right there, right where my comrades were hiding. I saw blue, red, yellow, a hot breeze burned my face, a cloud of smoke... I felt stunned, knocked silly. I got up and checked myself over. No blood. I looked over to where they had been and saw no one. After the smoke dissipated, I still saw no one, but now I heard screams.

"Wounded! Get out the wounded!"

A horrible feeling came over me. My comrades!

***

Our security plan called for all of us to squeeze into a drainage canal in a bamboo grove. Fear or lack of discipline had led Marvin to another ditch farther off. He was all alone, though we could see him from our shelter.

The rest of us, nearly all the Venceremos team, were stuck in that sewer which was about a metre high with water and mud flowing around our shins. Next to me was Santiago with his backpack full of recorders and cassettes. Then came Ana Lidia, who was so plump she could barely fit, and Estenia, who had lost all her upper teeth and would shout "Long live the inteshnashional psholetashiat!" Chila, from the monitoring team, was also there. Under a rain of bullets, Julito Perica and the rest of the security squad finished picking up our things and getting them ready for the march. Now they were engaging the enemy, firing and protecting us. Julito was standing just outside the canal, right there next to me. A volley hit him and he fell to the ground. When I saw Julito fall, I tried to leave the ditch to help him and right at that moment the rocket hit. I saw the blast as I stood there, with my eyes open, paralysed by the roar. When I could react, I heard Santiago say: "They fucked me!"

I turned around and saw Santiago with a bloodstain here on his chest.

"Me too," said Estenia.

I turned towards her and saw that a piece of shrapnel had sliced open her ear, it was bleeding terribly. Chila stood up and started walking slowly. Maybe nothing happened to her, I thought. I looked at Julito, dead. The rocket finished him off. I turned back to Santiago, opened up his shirt, wiped him off and saw that it was nothing, a scratch near his throat.

"How are you up there?" asked Leti, who had taken cover a few metres away.

"We've got wounded here!" I answered. "And Julito..."

"All of you come down here, but don't get out of the canal!"

* * *

I could only hear the screams of the wounded. I left my little ditch to see what had happened, and I ran into Hernán. He was lying face down in a puddle. I turned him over, he looked at me with a face like a corpse, and said: "They've killed me."

I started checking him over and there was nothing at all wrong with him, but the wave from the rocket blast had knocked him down and he was practically drowning in that puddle. I tried to pick him up but the bastard weighed more than a bull. Then I tried dragging him but he kept slipping out of my hands. I was beginning to get desperate when I saw another plane coming: a C-47 that shoots enormous fifty-calibre bullets out in a fan. The shooting was crazy, we were drenched with lead. Bullets, rockets, bullets, rockets... All the fire was concentrated in a radius of, I don't know, maybe 250 square metres.

Where could I take Hernán? He started to wake up a bit but he still couldn't walk. Renzo from the security squad of the command post turned up, one of those fighters who knows how to do everything from firing a missile to delivering a baby.

"Have the *cuilios* disembarked yet?" I ask him.

"No way! They wouldn't dream of it. Our two gunners are keeping them at bay. Let's see how long we can hold out!"

"What should I do with this guy?"

"Try to take him to the house in El Amate. I'll see you there!"

"Okay."

Once Renzo left, I realised that I didn't know how to get to El Amate.

***

We advanced down that sewer of stinking mud, with water up to our waists and bullets flying over our heads. Santiago, Ana Lidia and Chila were having a lot of trouble walking; Estenia was bleeding badly; Milton had the Venceremos motor on his back... We were moving too slowly.

"Get out of that damned puddle! Walk on the outside!"

We climbed out and started moving more quickly. The ditch led to another larger one that became a big pipe where it went under the street. There we met up with Mauricio and the rest.

"Those who can, go on down the ravine."

While we were deciding who was too wounded to go on, two catechists from the base communities, who never carry arms, turned up. They were on their way back from preaching in Joateca when they got caught in the shit and ended up in the same pipe as us. Because of the wounded, we had a few extra rifles.

"Two for us," the catechists said.

"You?" Mauricio said doubtfully.

"Christ took up the lash because he had nothing else."

They helped us carry Moisés, the Venceremos System soundman we called Chicken Tongue — Skinny Gustavo's assistant. He'd caught a bullet right here above his heart. We knew it had pierced his lung because of the way he breathed through the wound.

"You've got to walk," Mauricio told him.

"It hurts a lot..."

"Use your balls, *compa*. You're a man."

You use your balls when your body has nothing left to give and only your conscience keeps you going. Chicken Tongue got up and joined the column. It was about ten in the morning when we started marching.

***

I was struggling with Hernán when I saw a tree running. Shit! The only one who knows how to camouflage himself like that is Adolfo, the cook.

"Adolfo!"

"What is it?" the tree asked.

"Help me with Hernán, and tell me how the fuck you get to El Amate."

"I don't know."

"I do!" at long last Hernán woke up.

We decided to stick together. Hernán in front as the guide even though he was still dizzy, Adolfo in the middle dressed as a tree, and me in the rearguard with my M-16. All this time the helicopters up above continued shooting, the C-47 kept on tossing rockets, and our two machine-gunners kept the troops from landing.

We tried to get out along a ravine. We were pushing, pushing, pushing up a hill when boom! A rocket exploded right there in front of us, right in our path. It still gives me the shivers when I remember, because it was a question of seconds. A few steps more and it would have fallen on our heads.

"We saw her close up but we didn't get to talk to her!" Hernán laughed.

"The plane's spotted us. Marvin, take off that shirt!"

Adolfo claimed my white shirt was too bright. I pulled it off without touching the buttons.

"You're too white, buddy," Adolfo insisted.

"So what do you want me to do, pull off my skin too?"

"Wipe mud on yourself. Get down and roll around like a pig."

At last we made it to El Amate. Behind a tree I met up with Skinny Gustavo, the skinniest guy I've ever met, and also the best cameraman.

"Hey, Marvin! I'm here!"

Our trio arrived — a space cadet, a tree and a pig — and Skinny, who names himself commander wherever he goes, started giving orders.

"You and the wounded guy go to Balta up above. Marvin, stay here with me to keep them back."

"Keep who back?"

"If they land, it'll be on this flank. We've got to stop them."

"You and me, sonofabitch?"

"Of course. As long as there are people down below we can't pull out from here."

"Are you serious?"

"Get ready."

"Oh my God!"

We took cover behind a miserable little fence and since Skinny has long skinny arms like an extra-terrestrial, he started pulling in stones from all around to finish building the trench. There we were with our pair of crumby rifles when we heard the motors of the Dragon Flies approaching. The last thing we needed! The A-37s with their 500lb bombs!

The bombardment began and the noise couldn't have been more deafening. From our position I could see the planes right in front of us, diving, dropping those bombs that look like propane tanks spinning and whistling in the air... boom! Then the world trembled.

"Rat-a-tat-tat," our machine-gunners responded.

Our guys were shooting in bursts of four bullets because we didn't have much munition. Imagine the inequality: electronic machine-guns throwing out four thousand shots a minute and our little volleys limited to four! Even so, they couldn't do it. Another plane would come, diving once again, another bomb blast... Now they've fucked us, I thought.

"Rat-a-tat-tat," our two gunners responded.

What resistance our machine-gunners put up! One of them is named Farabundo, but everyone calls him Fara. If you saw him you'd think he couldn't hurt a flea — a peasant hick with all his ribs sticking out. You can count on him for anything, from digging a latrine to taking a message to El Tigre Hill, but he does it at his own pace, calmly. He doesn't lose his cool even when a plane dropping bombs is flying right at him. There goes Fara with his rat-tat-tat. It can go on for a day, a week, a month, and Fara will still be there until Germán tells him to pull back. Fara never even got scratched.

That day his assistant was Alejandro, a pretty boy evil as Satan, who at that time was in love with Martina. Since the girl wouldn't give him the time of day, he didn't give a shit if he lived or died. Alejandro took off his packs and started shooting and singing *"la vida no vale nada"*[8]. They say he was the one who busted the wasp pilot's ass.

The other machine-gunner was Isrita. He's like a saint. He was like a saint. He was killed in combat last year. If you asked Isra to cut off his arm for the revolution, he'd cut it off, but he was no fanatic. No, he was convinced the revolution was just. He was a *campesino* too, and just as skinny. If he appeared at your door you'd want to give him something to eat or some spare change. He was humility itself in shoes. His assistant that day was Melecio Meléndez, who was so toothy he always looked like he was laughing. Maybe that's why he was always in a good mood even in the midst of the worst shit.

This time the shit lasted until 4.30 in the afternoon. Luckily it started to rain and the planes had to fly off, mad as hell. The army had the entire flotilla of helicopters in Osicala, ready to jump on us and land troops, but as long as there was resistance on the ground, they couldn't do it. And they couldn't. From nine in the morning, and they couldn't do it!

***

We walked until way into the afternoon, but it seemed like forever. There was a terrible stretch up through a cactus field, and Chicken Tongue was tiring fast. He wouldn't ask us to carry him but he just couldn't make it up the hill. We got to a small abandoned house, tore off the door, and put him on it like a bed. We waited there until it started to rain. The helicopters continued passing overhead the whole time, turning above us to get a better angle of fire. With the storm, they left. They couldn't land troops in a downpour. Then we sent someone to Arambala to see what had happened, where the rest of them were, and to find out which way we had to go. Soon he came running back and said: "Back where you came from".

We retraced our steps, entered Arambala through the cemetery and there we saw the disaster, the bomb craters, everything flattened, everything stinking of gunpowder. They told us nothing had happened to the commanders, and that the wounded were in the hospital. Chila had caught two pieces of shrapnel in her tail, but they didn't reach her spine. That's why she had walked so slowly, but it wasn't serious. They were already operating on her. They told us that Julito was dead, and soon after, Chicken Tongue died too. The bullet went down from his lung and perforated his intestine. There was no way to save him.

We got back to Arambala after five o'clock. By then the town was cleansed of any sign of our presence. The army didn't know who they had run into. They attacked us as they would have any other guerrilla camp, so the security team made an exhaustive search to be sure that not a piece of paper, not one battery, not a hair would allow them to deduce it had been Venceremos and the general command.

"Hurry up," Atilio called us. "You've got to broadcast the programme today at six, as if nothing happened."

We got the equipment out of the packs, and set everything up. You won't believe it but when we were setting up the microphone we saw that it had been hit right on the mesh, a piece of shrapnel from a rocket was embedded right on the tip where you talk. Even the Venceremos mike caught its piece of lead! But we tested it and it worked.

"Where's Santiago?" Atilio asked.

"In the hospital. He's got a scratch here on his throat."

"If he can talk, get him to talk. So the enemy won't have any reason to suspect they ran into us."

We set up a link and Santiago, from the hospital hut, gripped the shrapnel-encrusted microphone and started out like every other day giving the military news:

Helicopter assault on Arambala turned back! We've just received a news bulletin recounting how several columns of the Francisco Sánchez Northeast Front heroically repelled an attempted aerial troop landing near, it seems, the abandoned village of Arambala...

I don't think even today they know they ran into us that Monday, 16 September. When they read this, that's when they'll find out.

Barbed Wire Radio

The attack on Arambala changed our lives. Up to then we had moved about all together — the command post, Atilio, the commanders, us from Venceremos, the monitoring team, the orange communications team, the green team that scanned the enemy's communications, the security squads for all these teams, the logistics people for the ones in charge and the ones they were in charge of, the cooks and *tortilla* makers to feed everyone. It was impossible. The helicopter assaults made the war much more mobile, and to run it the command post had to be truly agile. How could we do it?

To begin with, we abandoned El Gigante, where we were quite vulnerable, only ten lousy minutes away from Perquín, and we moved to more protected camps. That was the end of open-air plays and big-screen TV's and living in houses as if our camp were a town. We headed off into the bush.

We also had to rid ourselves of such a large and cumbersome structure, so we split up. One group went off to more secure terrain, where it took on most of the production tasks. With Leti in charge, the broadcasters and half the monitoring team went in that group. They took along the tape recorders, the archive of cassettes, and the minimum technical team required to put together a programme. Let's say they became the Venceremos recording studios.

The other group, a much smaller one including the rest of the monitoring team, with Marvel in charge, stayed with the command post. They were to be the bridge between the commanders and the studios, passing back strategic information and the editorial line by radio to Leti's group, who in turn would send an FM signal to the big shortwave transmitter hidden in the rearguard.

I think it was after Duarte's election in '84 that we decided to leave the big transmitter in one spot, a place deep within our territory that the army could never reach. It was too dangerous to be carrying that huge 2,000 watt beast all over the place, so with the double hook-up we overcame the problem of distance. The command post was connected to the studios, where the programme was then put together and bounced to the transmitter, which in turn sent it out on air by shortwave. Problem solved.

Solved? Like a poor man who finds a sandal without any straps, as the saying goes. Because those were the days when the goniometers, the fearsome goniometers, went into action.

In February of '86, the first of February to be exact, the Arce Battalion and others from Military Base Number 4 launched an operation in Morazán. We, that is the Venceremos studios, were on Pericón Hill. The billiards trick of bouncing information from the command post to us and then from us to the shortwave transmitter via FM was working perfectly. We were broadcasting the night-time programme live, cool as could be, when the *compas* scanning the enemy communications picked up the following message:

Location of Radio Venceremos signal on coordinates such and such.

Shit! That was our exact position! We ended the programme, packed up the equipment and roared out of there. A few minutes later the planes were flying over Pericón Hill, ready to turn us into mashed potatoes. How had they located us so precisely? The answer was the goniometers.

A goniometer is a gadget they used in the Second World War, an apparatus that indicates where a radio signal is coming from. The goniometer's needle moves towards the source of the broadcast, like a compass for sound. Then all it takes is triangulation: They put one goniometer here and point it this way, another over there and point it towards the same spot. Where the two imaginary lines cross is the source of the radio signal, the station. Maybe not exactly, but close enough. If there is nothing in the way, since the FM signal travels in a straight line, those fucking goniometers can determine the source with absolute precision. (With short wave — for those of you thinking of getting into this business! — you don't have to worry. Shortwaves are very diffuse and can't be detected by planes or anything else. We didn't find this out until later, and until then we were worried about our big Viking.)

We figured they had to be using goniometers to track down the station, and our military communications as well, since walkie-talkies broadcast on FM! How the hell could we solve such a ball-buster? Wherever we put the radio operators, they found them. They knew their voices, they knew which operator worked for which commander. They located the signal and in three minutes you had a helicopter assault on your hands. What could we do? How could we fight those phantasmagorical goniometers? We couldn't sabotage them. They must have been high up on Aguacate Hill, or at the Aerial of Cacahuatique, or who knows where. They might even have been on specially equipped helicopters.

The first thing we did was broadcast and run. As soon as the show was over, we'd take off like fugitives. That method didn't work. It was like playing with fire. Had we kept it up, in a month either our nerves or our legs would have given out.

We tried something else: We moved the FM hook-up to a nearby hill, about two hours walk away. Then we recorded a cassette and gave it to a messenger with wings on his feet and he carried it to the hook-up. He gave it to two other *compas* whose job was to broadcast it and pray to the Virgin of Lost Causes. They had to stay there all by themselves, holed up on that dark hill, watching the cassette turn and waiting for the helicopters to show up and start bombing. They couldn't leave the cassette on its own; they had to stay for the entire broadcast, to make sure it went on. As soon as it was over, the two of them raced down the mountain. The next day they'd get that damned cassette again, set up the link, and have another brush with death. It was incredibly stressful. I was with them on a couple of occasions and I smoked an entire pack of cigarettes just thinking about the first rocket exploding on my head.

The other problem was the delayed broadcast. It's not the same. Live, even though you make mistakes, it's hot, you feel that you're talking to an audience. What's more, you can give them the latest news. I don't know, that business of sending a messenger back and forth sapped our spirit. How could we crack it? Apolonio, Mauricio, El Cheje, Abel, you're the technicians. How do we do it?

Mauricio racked his brains until one day he let out a cry of Eureka: "Barbed wire!"

Mauricio had taught mechanics in San Salvador. He made bobbins, relays, that sort of thing. He's very Salvadoran, a kid with the wildest creativity and the most infectious spirit for work I've ever seen. He and Apolonio were an explosive combination for keeping the station running out in the mountains under the most adverse conditions.

"Barbed wire!"

The *compas* in the Venceremos workshop were really special. In the middle of an awful swamp they'd perform feats of high-tech engineering. They'd repair radios, build integrated circuits, tune motors... I've seen them make Venceremos work with strips of cloth. Once I thought Genaro, another technician, was going to take out his maracas and dance around the transmitter to make it work. One way or another, they always fixed it.

"Barbed wire!"

It's incredible how many pastures there are in El Salvador. In such a small country, there is no place that doesn't have a fence, usually where you least expect it. Such a little country for five million inhabitants, the most overpopulated country in all Latin America! You should see the number of barbed wire fences in Morazán. Mauricio realised that barbed wire is a good conductor, like a telephone line the goniometers couldn't pick up. He started experimenting with short-range barbed-wire communications. He tried voices, he tried music, and it worked. The more powerful the tape recorder that sent the signal, the longer the line could be. We did tests with two kilometres of wire, then four kilometres, then eight, then twelve... You could hear it! And it couldn't be detected!

"Get ready!" Mauricio warned us. "Tomorrow you're going on air via barbed wire. Careful you don't cut your lips!"

So we started broadcasting live again. It was great! After two months of recording for delayed broadcast, we even got nervous about making mistakes — maybe I'll have time left over, maybe my mind will go blank. We'd got used to saying, "Stop, let's do it again."

"How does it sound?"

"Good, but too many pork rinds."

Since it wasn't a genuine coaxial cable, during the broadcast we'd get a lot of noise that sounded like people chewing pork rinds, so we had a battle to the death with the pork rinds, until the people in the workshop discovered a resistance or something. I don't know what the fuck it was, but it totally did away with the problem. The quality was still inferior, but not that bad. The music did sound a little metallic, that was the worst.

We began by connecting the studios and the transmitter with a kilometre of barbed wire, but we never stayed in one spot. They would launch an operation and we'd have to move. As soon as we'd arrive at a new position, exhausted from carrying enormous loads on our shoulders, the *compas* of the security squad would be laying out barbed wire. They didn't wait to eat or sleep or anything, they just grabbed as much wire as they could find nearby and started laying down the line. That's what we called it: *laying down the line*, only in this case it wasn't the political line, it was barbed wire! We'd ease out the line from wherever we were to an intermediate point that was already hooked up to the transmitter. Imagine unrolling barbed wire through gorges, over peaks, across rivers, bushwhacking through thorns and thickets... Sometimes it was as much as ten, twelve or fourteen kilometres long. That's tiring work, exhausting, but that's how we started winning the war against the goniometers. Only started, because even though we'd solved the problem for the station, it didn't help with military communications.

Like I said, we could count on all the fencing of the pastures of Morazán. Practically anywhere, we could tie a cable to the nearest fence and communicate with another *compa* plugged into that line. For the system to work, we had to adapt the brown, box-shaped National radios that most people used. In the back these have an on-off switch. In our workshop we made a new circuit and converted these into intercoms of sorts, like they use in modern buildings where you push a little button to ask the guy on the tenth floor to open the door. In one position the radio worked like a radio, and in the other like an intercom; on the front we called them "carpenters". How are you going to send this message? By carpenter, we'd say, and it always worked. At the agreed hour, you show up with your little radio, push the switch on the back, and attach the positive cable to the line, that is, to the barbed wire fence. The other cable is a ground. If you pee, the call goes through better, because the wetness makes a good conductor. You pee, stick a knife or a piece of copper in the puddle of pee, and attach the second cable to it. Ready, Freddy.

"What's up dummy? Can you hear me?" a *compa* says in Torola.

"Great," replies the other from Perquín, and they have their chat. The advantages were twofold. Not only couldn't they locate you with their goniometers, but they couldn't listen in on your conversation. You could speak without codes! Do you know what that means in a war that was growing more and more complex? Codes are always slow, and cumbersome for sending and deciphering, but now we could talk as if we had private telephones without anyone listening in!

Within weeks, Morazán became a gigantic system of internal communications. There were system networks and restricted networks, and the central switchboard was in Perquín. From anywhere at all, you could tie into a line and talk to Perquín. It was incredible! Of course, we had to set up a schedule and lines for different command posts. The guerrilla combat units continued using walkie-talkies, because if the enemy showed up they could fight them off. Anyway, the army wasn't interested in finding a six-man unit. They had the goniometers to find the big camps, but all the camp communications were done by carpenters.

Cows became our worst enemies. You'd be talking and bang! The line would go dead.

"What shit of a cow just broke the wire?"

Then a patrol, like the ones from the phone company, would head out to repair the line. Isra must have tied up thousands of lines broken by cows and fallen trees. We also had to make connections from one pasture to the next. Our *compas* would go to the gates in the fences, which are made out of wood, and make a wire bridge up above. Every peasant knew not to touch the connection.

The invention worked brilliantly in summer, but in the winter when it rained it was dangerous because each of those wires is a powerful lightning rod. It was ridiculous how many carpenters got burned out; the workshop couldn't keep up with the repairs. Instructions: as soon as the storm begins, turn off your carpenter and use other systems, or just sit down and wait for it to stop.

The carpenters quickly spread to other fronts — Guazapa, Chalatenango, everywhere. All the FMLN military leaders used them. We Salvadorans took the gringos' fancy goniometer trickery and shoved it up their asses.

A few months before, General Blandón, the defence minister, had told a press conference: "Gentlemen, we are capable of carrying out lightning strikes on all the subversives' camps. They'd better get ready, because their days are numbered."

He was referring to the goniometers. It's true, at first they did manage to do us some damage by combining the goniometers with helicopter assaults. From that moment on they talked like the war was over, but our homemade wires threw them off balance just as their sophisticated technology had done to us. Venceremos still went on air every day! That was the mystery! They didn't know what the fuck was going on; they couldn't find the signal on their goniometers and they couldn't find any signals from our command posts. One fine day the front went mute. I love to imagine the conversation among their intelligence radio operators: "Nothing?"

"Nothing."

"What do the needles register?"

"I don't know what bullshit these peasants did, but we aren't reading anything."

"Could they have all deserted?"

Not even a burp turned up on their scanning equipment. Meanwhile, Venceremos was inexorable, broadcasting live every day at six! We kept the barbed-wire trick secret for months, but of course, once everybody was doing it, word leaked out. The enemy was so angry that when the *cuilios* showed up in a village, they'd cut up every wire they saw, barbed or not. Once they left, we'd come back to tie up all the pieces and reestablish communication. They got bored of cutting them up long before we did of repairing them.

We worked with carpenters and barbed wire from '86 until the end of '88. Three whole years! Today we don't use them any more. The *compas* in the overseas technicians collective invented a much better system, one that does away with wires, fools the goniometers, and gives a crisp clear sound. But let's save that story for later.

One Pole, Two Poles, Three Poles...

The target audience of Venceremos is quite varied. The station addresses friends and enemies, kids on the street and soldiers, peasants, the bishop and the gringo ambassador. Venceremos talks to them all, and all of them, if they wish or if they dare, can talk on the radio. But Venceremos *belongs* to the combatants. The *compas* feel that it's theirs. It *is* theirs! So if you receive a war dispatch via radio and you stick it in your bag and forget about it when it's time to do the programme, you'll have the radio operator from that zone calling you up the next day: "Listen, what happened to the dispatch we sent you? About the electrical pole..."

"Oh yeah, *hombre*, we didn't have time. We'll put it on tomorrow."

Then with all the comings and goings and your bag stuffed with papers, you forget again.

"Look, what happened? I didn't hear it yesterday either."

"Yes, *hombre*, forgive me, what happened was..."

They won't let you go. Like a dog nipping at your ankle, they won't leave you in peace until you broadcast a report of their action, even if it's nothing to speak of. The same thing happens if you make a mistake and instead of saying "in the village of Juilijuiste," you say "Juilijueste".

"What were you thinking of? It's Juilijuiste!"

And a little while later: "It wasn't one pole, *hombre*. It was two!"

The *compas* carry out an action. When the radio reports it, the mission is completed, but until then, it's as if they hadn't done a thing. For the fighters, a military action is only over when it goes out over the radio, when everyone knows about it. Even if COPREFA reports it, if Venceremos doesn't it doesn't count.

When the militia began to grow, Fidel, the commander of the Torola zone, told us the story of a few new *compas* who went to Carolina to dynamite a couple of electrical poles. They came back about 5.30 in the afternoon.

"We did it," the boys reported, and without telling anyone else, they turned on the radio and sat down to listen to the programme. When it was over, they went to complain to Fidel: "Why didn't they mention the poles?"

"What poles?"

"The ones we just knocked over."

"But did you write to Venceremos?"

"No."

"First you have to write the dispatch and send it to Venceremos!"

They thought it was automatic, that the radio wasn't only the voice of the people, but the all-seeing eye. The relationship between the station and the fighters got so intense that they don't say "This happened in February of '85" or "in March of '86". They'll say: "It was during Idiot One", because once when the army launched an operation called "Victory One", Santiago called it "Idiot One". The next he called "Idiot Two". Even their frame of reference for time is set by the names the station uses for operations or the stages of the political or military struggle.

The way the fighters identified with the station was undoubtedly very encouraging, but it brought complications. The same old story: how to edit so much information? The electrical poles are a good example. When we launched a campaign to sabotage the electrical system, you can imagine how many guerrilla units and how many militia members were mobilised across the country to leave it in the dark. The next day a mountain of dispatches started arriving, and all of them were more or less the same. Of course we had to tighten up the information, to make it more fluid, more digestible, not least because it literally would not fit in the space we had.

What did we do? First, since we don't have computers or anything of the sort, Marvin came up with a system. We put them on little papers all cut the same size and filed in different boxes. Everything about poles went here; engagements went over there; ambushes in this other box and so on. Just before the programme began, we'd grab the pile of "poles" and order them by front. Then we'd summarise: on the eastern front, 17; on the central front, 20; on the paracentral front... a total of 96 poles knocked down in such and such regions." Did that do the trick? No way, it was no good.

"What about my pole?" the first complaint would come in. "We blew it up at three o'clock in the morning at the turn-off for Yucuaquín."

We couldn't collectivise it, but what a deadly programme reading a series of 96 dispatches on sabotage actions against electrical poles, all of them the same. The final sabotage was against us, for the crime of boredom!

Lately we've lengthened the show to over an hour and spiced it up with other things, but it doesn't make any difference. Now it isn't 96 poles they knock over, it's twice that, so our show is just as bad or worse.

If an electrical pole arouses so much expectation, what happens with a casualty? Never mind an ambush! If you forget to read it on air, they might strangle you, and the *compas* are right. Suppose you were a member of the militia: You leave your house today, catch a few hours bad sleep in the woods, march through the middle of the night, lay an ambush with your unit, spend the whole day hiding. You've left your wife with all the kids, your brother taking care of everything on the farm, you've had to make up half a novel to get away from your village without anyone suspecting. Now there you are in the bush, your stomach grumbling, getting eaten alive by mosquitos, scared but working up your courage... and at last you pull off the ambush! Then after so much effort some jerk on the radio forgets and all that effort doesn't get recognised, doesn't get aired so that everyone will know, so that all the militia who took part can hear it and say, "I was there".

The political officers tell us that the section we do on the military map, when we read out all these small heroic deeds, helps them a lot. Above all, it helps them consolidate the new recruits. We don't simply give the information cold just like that. We greet the *compañeros*, congratulate them for the courage they showed. Flattery for a *macho*, that's what it is, but when we complain that that long sausage of a section isn't a very journalistic way of doing things, they shut us up right away: "Who is the programme for? For the press or for the fighters?"

If we compress the information it isn't of any use to them, because when it's time for the next ambush and the political officer goes to the militia man's house, he'll find him a bit reluctant: "Brother, I'll see you tonight at such and such a place. You know what for."

"Look, I... I can't. My kid's sick."

"Don't tell stories, *hombre*. What's the matter?"

"Well... I knocked over a pole and Venceremos didn't say a thing!"

General Tutti Frutti and Colonel Crazy Pig

The document is entitled "Low Intensity Conflict". At the beginning, the gringos say that they ought to learn the methods used by Che Guevara, Mao Tse-Tung, and other revolutionaries. One method is to use radio, like the stations which in many countries of Latin America and the world have accompanied wars of liberation. In Vietnam the gringos had one called The Voice of America in Vietnam; in El Salvador it's Radio Cadena Cuscatlán.

Cuscatlán, which is run by the C-5 unit of the Armed Forces High Command, first appeared in '85, broadcasting 24 hours a day on AM and

FM. They hired a huge staff of psychologists, lawyers, comedians, announcers, journalists... all of them quite professional, even though you could tell they didn't really believe what they were saying. And that they didn't know how guerrillas think. For example, their psychologists tried to drive wedges among us — Coca-Cola propaganda — to sow doubts and break our morale.

> *Combatant of the FMLN, you there in Jocoaitique: Your commanders mistreat you ... Escape!*

The combatant, who had never been hit by anyone except his girlfriend, laughed when he heard that.

> *Combatant of the FMLN, you there in La Laguna in Chalatenango: The Cubans there are making a fool out of you... Escape! Turn in your rifle! The Armed Forces will protect you!*

What Cubans? There weren't any. The only Cubans were at Cadena Cuscatlán, where they'd hired a few pieces of shit from radio stations in Miami to work as advisers.

On the fronts we discussed whether to stop people from listening to Cuscatlán, and decided that people should listen to whatever they wanted. What could possibly be gained by banning things? What's more, Cuscatlán played some great tunes that the *compas* really liked, and the disc jockeys... At night there was a woman who was terrific. She had real spunk! They gave her the early morning shift so she could kid the *cuilios* and raise their morale:

> *Get up, get up, get up! What's happened to those boys in the Belloso Battalion? Get up,* hombre, *don't be lazy, they'll leave you without even a hut! You know what they say, one Indian less is one* tortilla *more...*

She'd put on a hot rumba — ba-bada, ba-bada, ba-ba-ba-bada — and she'd start singing along with the record. She was totally nuts, but a really nice chick. They said she was screwing three captains and two lieutenants, but it wasn't true. That was just gossip.

What was true was that she put her foot in her mouth in June '86 when we took the Third Brigade. Our special forces streamed into the fort, got as far as the officers quarters, and caused so many casualties that San Miguel's undertakers ran out of coffins and had to bring in more from another town. It turned out that at the very moment when our *compas* were tearing the enemy to shreds, that girl, who knew nothing about it, was sending greetings and a big hug to Sergeant Gurri and his troops:

This is for you men of the Third Infantry Brigade, there in San Miguel.
You're always happy, always prepared. It's especially for you Sergeant
Gurri, with all my love — here's a hot cumbia!

The next day at Venceremos we wondered if Sergeant Gurri, who was well known for his atrocities against the civilian population, had enjoyed his *cumbia* in the last cauldron of hell.

At Venceremos we weren't specialists in psychological warfare, but I think we were able to come up with some really popular things, like the soap operas and the nicknames for the army's top officers. That was a trick that destabilised them, like in school when they call you "fartsy" and the more it bothers you the more they repeat it.

The head of the army at that time was General Vides Casanova. We called him Tutti Frutti. That general was one of the best strategists in the enemy's ranks, one of the very few officers who understood the dynamics of modern warfare, the political side of it, but calling him Tutti Frutti made his life a misery. It got worse when we invented a big black guy called Lothar. Tutti Frutti had to do battle with another officer to win Lothar's affection. It's interesting: Vides Casanova is not gay, but he's well educated, elegant, has green eyes, and to top it all gave himself the pseudonym of Emerald. In other words, we had all the ingredients for branding him a faggot, and that's the role he played over and over on the "Subversive Guacamaya" show — a faggot. From so much ribbing, in the end even the soldiers believed it and stopped trusting their commander.

Monterrosa got hysterical when we called him Little Pig-Face. He could never live down the nickname and all its variants — Piggy, Little Pig-Prick, Snout-Face. Monterrosa starred in all our Guacamayas from the moment he was named an officer until the day he died. We did twelve soap operas on him! In the thirteenth — bad luck! — our hero died. The last soap about Little Pig-Face was the one about his helicopter blowing up in the air and the murderous colonel knocking on the doors of heaven and then those of hell, but neither Saint Peter nor the Devil would let him in. Certain political friends of ours complained, saying it was disrespectful to the deceased, but we were thinking more of the thousand deceased of El Mozote.

We got at General Blandón through his wife, Pelancha. From our intelligence reports we knew Blandón was a toper, a real bibber, you know, an alcoholic. He drank day and night. Other officers warned him to let up, but one reason he never could was his Pelancha, a gal who had quite a life of her own. While the general made war, she made the rounds of the officers. Afraid he was losing her, he'd turn up at the house unexpectedly and when he didn't find her, shit! He'd get so upset he'd start drinking — right in the middle of an operation he was commanding! So we'd repeat it every day: Keep your eye on Pelancha, General Blandón. Watch out she isn't, as we say in Morazán, doing what she does best!

It was Jonás who gave General García the name Crazy Pig. The Torogoces even wrote songs about his nickname. The fact is that García is really fat and he's got a mole right here. He looks just like a little pig. Méndez got the name Little Doll, and it bugged him like a louse. We bugged them all, right in their weak spots. Was that the right thing to do? I think so, in a war anyway. Maybe in a civilised political campaign it wouldn't be very ethical, but the crimes these guys committed were worse than a bit of ridicule, don't you think? If upsetting them keeps more crimes from being committed, long live nicknames!

Of course things got out of hand. Once we put Monsignor Gregorio Rosa Chávez in the cast of the Guacamaya. At the time he was a belligerent Duarte supporter and he never missed an opportunity to attack us. We debated with him, we argued with him, and in the end we decided to punish him with the lash of the Guacamaya. I think we had him in a motel room with Pelancha. Yes, it was a mistake and we got a lot of flack.

Another time we were reproached when the Challenger exploded. In an incredibly thoughtless and mistaken broadcast, Venceremos said something like, "What's the big deal? Seven gringos less, while here hundreds die every day and nobody says a thing." Ana Guadalupe called us right away and told us we were nuts: How could we be so short-sighted as to think that deaths are quantities to be compared? That was an accident that had nothing to do with our war, and it doesn't matter if they were gringos or Chinese, seven or one or four hundred. She said she didn't agree with that sort of casual dismissal, and if it reflected the way we really thought then it was even more serious. That was one of the political stupidities that got by us on Venceremos.

Let's get back to psychological warfare. What else have we done? We used ridicule, but we also used fear. Just last year we got word that in a village called El Resbaladero the civil defence — people armed by the army — was raping girls and committing other evil deeds, so we challenged them on the air:

Members of the civil defence in El Resbaladero, you have 24 hours to lay down your weapons. If you fail to do so, you will suffer the consequences.

The next day, we were told, those guys, white with fear, turned in their guns and fled the town. We put the same pressure on abusive mayors.

So and so, you'd better resign. If you don't, we can't be held responsible for your security.

The next day that guy put a padlock on the mayor's office. "Venceremos asked me to resign," he said. "I'm no fool, I'm not going to risk my neck." At least twenty mayors left office that way during the last term.

For the army bases we combined broadcasts with other mischief. For example, two of our radio operators might go near Santa Rosa and allow the enemy to pick up a conversation suggesting that guerrilla columns were advancing on that town. A few exploratory footprints, a few cigarette butts left on the ground... Simultaneously, Venceremos would jovially drop a little banana skin:

We're all happy because we'll have some big surprises in the next few days. As a matter of fact, greetings to all our friends in Santa Rosa...

A little while later we'd hear on the green radios:

Red alert in Santa Rosa! Reinforce the positions!

They'd send troops down from San Francisco to Santa Rosa and kaboom! We'd let loose on San Francisco. We've used these boxing techniques plenty of times — fake here and punch there — it gives us a double advantage; the soldiers in Santa Rosa shit their pants, while the ones in the other bases relax thinking the fight won't be with them.

Suppose you plan to attack San Miguel, but it turns out there are four battalions stationed there. Wouldn't it be great if we could get one of them off our backs? So on Venceremos we'd start mouthing off about "liberated zones": do a report on the dairy farm we had, offer a commentary on popular power in our zones of control, call a press conference in Perquín to show we control it... We'd provoke them, and soon enough the enemy would get so mad they'd send a battalion to Perquín and bring in the journalists to take pictures. You see, the army can't admit there are liberated zones in such a tiny country because, according to international treaties, the FMLN could be recognised as a belligerent force. Colonel Vargas would be singing like a bird in the town square of Perquín: "Who said there were liberated zones?"

As soon as he'd say it, a crushing artillery barrage would fall on his base back in San Miguel, while he's posing for pictures up north with his main reserve force!

Thirteen Years Organised

It was 7 March, the day before international women's day.
"Let's do a special programme," they said. "Marvin, go find one."
"Find what?"

"Whatever, but something new. And upbeat. We can't be so solemn every year!"

"Okay, but what do we do? Where? Who with?"

"Don't ask so many questions! Get out there and bring it back today so you can edit it in time."

Where shall I go? Maybe to Perquín. I climb up Gigante Hill, an hour and a half uphill under the noonday sun. I'm walking along, trying to think of a woman to interview. What could I possibly do that hasn't already been done? Suddenly I hear the murmur of laughter coming from around the bend. It's forty women, all *samuelitas* — young radio operators — taking a course. This is a miracle, I tell myself, a gift from heaven.

All the girls are laughing and joking around, trying out their equipment and trying on their battery packs. All of them have tits like this and tight shirts, really tight shirts. That's the way guerrilla women strut their stuff: they leave the top button ready to burst at the slightest breath. There's no makeup here, no Max Factor, no mascara. Here tits are tits, hands are hands, lips are lips, and you flirt with whatever you've got. But let's not get off the subject — concentrate Marvin, you've come to do interviews.

***

We didn't have battery packs at first. I'd tie eight batteries up with masking tape and connect it to the communications radio, but in the middle of a battle it would all fall apart. The *compas* would come back to the workshop all upset: "Look Apolonio, this gadget doesn't work."

I'd tie knots and patch them up, but it was no good, so we came up with battery packs. We made all sorts: wooden boxes, plastic ones, leather... In the end, Abel designed a special battery pack, part of the cartridge pouch. You slip your belt through it, the cover makes the contact, and a wire goes out to the radio. That's what you call quality.

Battery packs have been high fashion throughout all these years of war. Most of the radio operators are women, girls, and the battery pack is one of their prized weapons: the way they wear them, the way the radio hangs — if the cable isn't spiral then nobody wants it. Spiral cables! Once, just before we launched an offensive, we needed more battery packs. Since Mauricio had run out of regular cable all he could do was cut the spiral cable off an old telephone we had in the workshop and put it on the last walkie-talkie. Time went by, the radio operators would bring in their broken cables, and the only one who never complained was the one who had the spiral cable. Her battery pack put up with all the pulling and twisting, and since it was prettier, everyone else was jealous. So every time we'd go into town and sack the telephone company office, we'd take a whole bunch of those little phone cables with us. Little by little, all the radio operators in Morazán were equipped with these modern battery packs. Nobody wants the ones with the old duplex cables. "It's the same thing!" Mauricio tells them, but they all want spiral cables. Their radio is their way of flirting: the aerial out, the cable rolled up over here, the cartridge pouch towards the side, halfway down the thigh.

***

In the middle of that crowd of radio operators, I took out my tape recorder and all I could think of was one question, so I asked them all the same thing, like a poll: *Why are you fighting?* I was biased, I admit it. Those girls were bound to say something silly, but since they were just kids, the audience would at least find it amusing. I start with the first:

"I'm fighting", she tells me very firmly, "because here in El Salvador we are living under a capitalist system that exploits us. We want to destroy the old state to build a new socialist state."

I was lost for words. She was a little peasant girl, you understand? I go on to the next: "So why are you fighting?"

"Because that guy Reagan, the president of the United States, wants to take advantage of us because we're a small country. But the mouse can chase the cat, you know. If all the little mice get together we can beat him. Isn't that right?"

Whoa! And the best part was that they said this as naturally as could be, giggling, without the gooey DJ voice I used for the questions. I go on to the third: "Look, we're peasants, and we want the land to belong to the tiller. But the bourgeois state and the military..."

"Wait a minute," I interrupt. "Do you know what a bourgeois state is?"

"Of course. When a handful of rich folk own everything and live on the backs of the people."

Incredible! I was completely taken aback. I go on and I find a skinny little kid with a big nose and a long braid going down her back, who looks terrible, hopeless.

"What's your name?"

"Leonor Márquez."

"How old are you?"

"Thirteen."

"How long have you been organised?"

"Thirteen."

"What do you mean, thirteen?"

"My mother lived in La Guacamaya when she was pregnant. Just after I was born the *cuilios* burned her house and we've had to keep moving ever since."

I finished up my interviews and went back to the camp thinking about this new generation, these women who had war for a school.

Chiyo and His Brothers

At night he'd put on a brown sweater that covered his hands and he'd lie there, curled up, sleeping on a bench. He looked more like a hairy little rat than a child, one of the thousands of orphans left by this war.

When I started at Venceremos, Chiyo was barely thirteen. Leti trained him as a radio operator and then brought him to the station to help with the monitoring. Pale, short, his eyes clear and clean, the kid had only been able to reach first grade. At the station he learned about everything, from debating politics to falling in love, and he cheered us all up. Chiyo became the camp mascot, always happy, always willing. Every day he had a new story or a new joke.

There were times when we saw him as a child, other times as just another member of the Venceremos team. His work would get criticised like everyone else's, but he never took any of it badly. He'd even laugh at his mistakes, and if he was eating a mango, he'd give you half so he wouldn't have to eat alone.

Years before, when nobody imagined he would join the Venceremos staff some day, Santiago did a striking interview with him. It must be in the archive.

"What's your name?"
"Lucio Vázquez, but they call me Chiyo."
"Where are you from?"
"Osicala."
"And your family?"
"My family is all split up. Two of my brothers died in a massacre the cuilios *committed during a demonstration in San Salvador. We never saw them again because they were buried in El Rosario cemetery. We heard that on KL."*
"How did your mother take it?"
"My mother told us to cry, but not to lose faith, that's the way the struggle is."
"Where is she now?"
"The cuilios *killed her last year. I was with my brother, Pajarillo, and we were bringing the calf in. It was about prayer time, and getting dark when we heard the shots. The two of us took off for the house. When we got there the* cuilios *had already left. My mother was dead and my sister too. My mother was on a bench, leaning to one side with her head full of blood. My sister was in the hammock, her head blown open, with another pool of blood. We were alone because my father and the others had fled days before. The army was looking for them. So Pajarillo and I cleaned up the blood and we lay them down on the beds."*

"Did you ever find out who did it?"
"They came with a sergeant from Gotera."
"Where did you go after that?"
"After that, everybody left the villages because they were killing off whole families. Crowds of people went to the refugee camp with the few possessions they could carry. I went with them, but halfway there I decided to turn back."
"Why?"
"I didn't want to go. When they noticed I wasn't there, they were already far away."
"What are you going to do now?"
"I'll go to elementary school. Maybe I'll learn something."
"How old are you?"
"Nine."

Radio Venceremos, June 25, 1981

Chiyo had eight siblings. Two of them were killed in the capital, at a demonstration; another named Hubert was killed at the battle of Moscarrón; one more was killed somewhere else, I can't remember where; his mother and oldest sister were murdered by the army. The only ones he had left were his two little sisters and his last remaining brother, Pajarillo, who was his best friend. Years ago, Chiyo and Pajarillo were the announcers when the schoolchildren took over the radio for the day. Pajarillo sent him letters, messages, and Chiyo always wrote back. Pajarillo was the leader of a guerrilla unit in Jocoaitique, a fair way away from Venceremos.

In '87, after an all-night march, we reached Volcancillo de Jocoaitique. Someone came, I don't know who, and told Chiyo: "Pajarillo's dead. He fell in combat yesterday."

It devastated the kid. He didn't eat that afternoon, wouldn't speak to anyone, stayed up the whole night. We didn't know what to do. We'd never seen him sad; he was the one who cheered up the whole camp. What can you say in a case like that? "My heartfelt condolences?" I was writing something for the radio and I watched him from a few metres away, sitting on a log, alone, hanging his head, scratching doodles in the dirt. Then Martín, another teenage fighter a little older than Chiyo, came over. He stood there watching him. Then with a tenderness I'd never heard before, he said: "Don't be scared Chiyo. I'm your brother too."

Chiyo looked up, and he smiled.

Footnotes

[1] Universidad Centraoamericana "José Simeón Cañas," a Jesuit-run college in San Salvador.

[2] Combatiente Organizador del Pueblo (Combatant as Community Organiser), a course offered to guerrilla fighters in the FMLN's school founded in 1984.

[3] The Spanish acronym for the Army's Long-Range Reconnaissance Patrol.

[4] A small mammal similar to a badger.

[5] Secretary General of the Salvadoran Communist Party and a member of the FMLN General Command.

[6] A few days later, Inés Guadalupe Duarte, the daughter of the president, who had been kidnapped by the FMLN, was exchanged for Commander Nidia Díaz, Commander Américo Araujo, and safe-conduct out of the country for a group of wounded combatants.

[7] National Resistance, one of the five member organisations of the FMLN

[8] 'Life is worth nothing'

Section V
On to the Cities

Meeting Our Colleagues

They keep saying Venceremos is in Nicaragua, that we broadcast from Nicaragua, that Daniel Ortega is our godfather and keeps us sitting pretty in Managua. We laugh when we hear that. We know Morazán like our backyard, we've broadcast from every square inch of it. But journalists are like Saint Thomas: they have to see to believe.

During Easter week in '88 four foreign journalists travelled up to Morazán with some UNICEF personnel who had come to vaccinate children.

"Do a live broadcast from Perquín," the commanders told us. "That way those journalists will see where Venceremos really is."

After the show, we sat down to shoot the breeze with the journalists — one from NBC, another from the BBC, one from the *Washington Post*, I can't remember the fourth. Atilio had already given interviews in '85 to the *New York Times*, *Le Monde* and other foreign media.

"The Salvadoran press is a bit resentful," they told us. "You only talk to journalists from other countries."

It wasn't who we wanted to talk to, it was a question of security. A Salvadoran journalist could put himself in a tight spot if he came to do a live report on us. Anyhow, we figured it was up to them to cover their own asses, so we called a press conference right in Perquín, 'the rebel capital', as the journalists liked to call it. We sent out invitations — personal ones, through our own channels — to the director of YSU, the guy from KL, the TV news reporter, the anchor from the other channel, and the correspondents from UPI and the other news agencies. About fifteen local media and a few foreign ones were invited, and nearly all of them accepted gladly. They came up in a caravan and didn't even stop in Gotera to ask the army's permission. They showed up in Perquín happy as could be and bursting with curiosity.

The idea was to hold a press conference with the commanders first, and then let them witness a live Venceremos broadcast.

"We've got to publicise the station," Atilio told us. "In the coming period, the station is going to play a very important role."

"So?"

"It's time you got known. Let your colleagues from the other media know your names, see your faces. Get rid of the station's grey image."

"So?"

"So start by doing something about your looks!"

We lived in the woods, so our pants were all patched and re-patched, and we had mud up to our ears. A bath, a shave, a nice haircut. They sent brand new black uniforms for the whole collective. We shined our poor old shoes for the very first time in the whole war. Deodorant! It was years since I'd used deodorant! All we could find was women's, but it didn't matter, the point was not to stink like a wildcat. I felt like I was in disguise when we left our camp on Gigante Hill and set off down the path to Perquín.

"There are the ones from Venceremos!" somebody yelled when we entered the town square.

A cameraman from Italian TV started filming our delegation: Leti and Marvel, Santiago and Ana Lidia, Yaser — the poet of Torola — and me. At about three o'clock we arrived at the house where all the journalists had gathered.

"Carlos Gallo![1] I've met you at last!"

"You must be the famous Marvel who was filming in San Salvador a few years back in a van?"

"Leti! You're just as pretty as I thought!"

Since Venceremos is a guerrilla radio station, broadcasting every day from the mountains for so many years, we had earned a certain respect, even among those who didn't like us. They greeted us enthusiastically, touching the legend with their very hands. We were excited too. We had monitored them for so long, listened to them, watched them on TV — and now we had them right in front of us, in flesh and blood! It was like those couples who get married by mail and know each other without ever meeting. Santiago made like he was everybody's pal.

"Your voice! I listen to you every day!"

A meeting of colleagues, that's what it was. No formalities, just a few cups and a bit of juice passed around. We asked them a hundred questions, and they asked us a thousand back.

"How have you bastards managed to hang on for so long?"

"Who writes the 'Subversive Guacamaya'? That's what I like best! It kills me!"

"When are you going to do the live broadcast?"

"At six. Like every other day."

The press conference began. Skinny Gustavo, who never misses a chance, did the introductions: "From left to right, ladies and gentlemen of the press, Commander Roberto Roca and Commander Joaquín Villalobos (Atilio) from the FMLN General Command, Commander Mercedes del Carmen Letona (Luisa) and Commander Jorge Meléndez (Jonás)."

They asked about politics, about the impending demise of Duarte's regime, the rise of ARENA, the presence of FDR leaders Ungo and Zamora in the country, the massive mobilisation of the UNTS union movement, the stalemate in the war... I remember Jonás talking about the gringos' obsessive distrust of the FMLN: "We have nothing to do with Russia! We are

Salvadoran. We have our own ideas and our own traditions — like that, for example!"

At that very moment an Easter procession led by Fathers Rogelio Ponseele and Miguel Ventura was passing right by the door. The cameras all whirled around towards the street to film the old peasant women singing off key: *"perdón, ooooh Dios mío, perdón e indulgencia."* It looked like a setup, but it wasn't. It just happened.

At six, Venceremos went on the air live with a studio audience. We went ahead to set up the equipment and to ask a woman to lend us her house. "Of course!" she said. "But I don't have electricity."

"Candles will do. We've broadcast that way many times!"

Ana Lidia sat at the mixer, Santiago at the main microphone, Leti and I on either side of him, Marvel as producer. We all got a terrible attack of stage fright when we saw that pack of TV cameras, regular cameras, thousands of tape recorders, everyone waiting for us to open our mouths. The opening music rang out and Santiago took off:

Radio (- a rain of flashbulbs, pop, pop, pop -) Venceremos, the official voice of the FMLN, transmitting its signal of freedom from Morazán, El Salvador, Central America, territory in combat against oppression and imperialism!

We were dizzy from all the flashes, but Santiago didn't miss a step. He spoke with the same conviction he had on 10 January 1981.

We begin today's programme with a greeting to all the journalists who have come up from San Salvador!

I started smoking like a chimney, Leti broke a pencil into little pieces, but since the anchor sets the tone for everyone else and Santiago was his usual self, Leti relaxed too and even started smiling. They'd drilled us: Don't be so stiff! You've got to radiate strength. In this business, you don't just have to be a certain way, you have to look that way too.

We finished the show and the congratulations began — and more questions, and advice, and brother don't forget us, say hello once in a while in code.

"I'll tell you the same thing I told Colonel Castillo[2]," Atilio said in farewell. "We don't ask for praise, just tell the truth."

More hugs, kisses, until we meet again. On the way back they were detained in Gotera and all their things were confiscated, but they kicked up such a fuss that in the end they got back all their stuff: cameras, film and cassettes. Ever since then, Venceremos has had a face. Every blessed day, whenever they broadcast news of us, they put on the pictures they took that day in that little house in Perquín.

Become a Guerrilla in Twenty Easy Lessons

Our guerrillas, who are mostly country people, had to win support in the cities. Sure, we had a lot of urban commandos in San Miguel, San Salvador, Santa Ana, San Vicente, in all the saints of our not-so-saintly country, but we needed to recruit a lot more young people, and above all we needed to teach them how to fight.

"Venceremos should train them," Commander Chico suggested. "Like a radio school, but teaching people how to use homemade weapons."

"A guerrilla correspondence course?"

"Call it whatever you like."

When we began working on the format, I remembered something we came across in Morazán: the Costa Rican almanac called *A School for All*. Even in the most unlikely hut you'll always find that almanac. One of the things we'd do whenever we took over a town was to collect books from the libraries and town halls to give to schools in the countryside. I always picked up copies of that almanac, but we could never keep up with the demand. Even later on, when we started setting up mobile libraries all over the front to support our literacy efforts, one of the most popular books was *A School for All*. Well, I thought, if it's so successful, it must have something. I got hold of the collection, read quite a few of them, and discovered that the secret lay in the language: simple, direct, very accessible. That's where I found the inspiration for our little programme, "Let's Learn How to Use Weapons".

Musical bridge: "Armed Guitar"
Male Broadcaster: Attention guerrillas and clandestine militia!
Attention students! Attention brother workers!
Female Broadcaster: Get ready to learn about using weapons!
Male Broadcaster: Get out your tape recorder or paper and
pencil, because we're about to begin!
Female Broadcaster: Compas, are you ready?
Male Broadcaster: In the first in our series, we're going to
give you some ideas for getting in shape.
Female Broadcaster: We should exercise every day to improve our
resistance and agility.
Male Broadcaster: Resistance and agility: these are the two principal
objectives of getting into shape. If we have resistance and agility we
can walk long distances, run without getting out of breath, jump over
walls, crawl under fences, use our popular weapons safely and skilfully.
Female Broadcaster: One important way of improving our agility
and resistance is to play a sport every day.
Male Broadcaster: It could be soccer, basketball, karate or swimming.
Female Broadcaster: Listen up, these are sports that you can practice

legally on the field in your neighbourhood without any problem. What's more, you can do your training as a team, or at least in groups of two, outside, without having to hide. Training as a team you'll be able to keep going when you're tired and encourage each other so that no one gets left behind.

Male Broadcaster: Everyone can play sports. Only you will know that you are also training for combat.

Sound effect: Running feet.

Male Broadcaster: In our training programme we're going to include the following exercises.

Female Broadcaster: Jogging and running.

Male Broadcaster: Knee-bends.

Female Broadcaster: Sit-ups.

Male Broadcaster: Push-ups.

Female Broadcaster: These are the main ones, but remember that any exercise is good.

Male Broadcaster: And this is going to be your slogan. While you're jogging, repeat it in your mind...

Sound effect: Several people jogging: "We're training to win! We're training to win!"

From the almanac and the radio schools I got the trick of asking questions at the end of every episode to leave the guerrilla apprentices with work to do from one day to the next, and to get them to write down a few things they shouldn't forget.

Female Broadcaster: Our next instalment will be on firearms.

Male Broadcaster: Small arms, rifles, assault weapons.

Female Broadcaster: What is calibre? What are munitions?

Male Broadcaster: It's a good idea to clip pictures of different kinds of weapons from newspapers and magazines. It will be useful in our next lesson.

Female Broadcaster: You can also watch gringo police shows on television. Besides seeing how stupid they are, you can look at all sorts of arms and watch the ways of advancing which we studied today.

Male Broadcaster: And one final recommendation: watch the cuilios in the street, take a good look at the soldiers, at their rifles, their equipment, their uniforms. Those details will be very useful.

Female Broadcaster: Listen up: now you're observing the arms in the hands of our enemies. Tomorrow you're going to take them for yourselves!

From the third lesson on we started explaining how to make and use homemade weaponry: blunt weapons, firebombs, explosives, home-made gunpowder, Molotov cocktails, shooting stances, camouflage in the country and the city... All in all, an entire course. We even included the Biblical weapon of David, which is quite common among our *campesinos.*

Female Broadcaster: The weapon we all know about is the slingshot, and if we practice systematically, we can learn how to aim it really well.

Male Broadcaster: With a slingshot you can use stones or ball bearings.

Female Broadcaster: The slingshot is also easy to make at home and it's great for shooting large steel marbles. We can even learn to use it to throw incendiary grenades, contact bombs and other objects that weigh up to half a pound.

Male Broadcaster: You can make a slingshot with two pieces of thick cord about 85 centimetres long or a bit longer. You make the pocket out of leather or cloth. You can even make it out of string, as long as you weave it tightly like a burlap bag. The pocket should be shaped like a miniature hammock.

Female Broadcaster: Let's tie the strings, one to each side of the pocket.

Male Broadcaster: To use the slingshot put the marble in the pocket, pick up the ends of the strings, tie one string to your thumb, and wind the other around your index finger. When you're ready, start twirling it in the air until you get up a good speed.

Female Broadcaster: Then let go of the string you have wound around your index finger when it's pointing in the direction of your target. The other end will stay tied to your thumb so the slingshot won't get shot out along with the stone.

Male Broadcaster: With a slingshot you can shoot as far as 75 metres.

It's difficult, not to say impossible, to do a military training programme over the radio. The real training of urban commandos was done in person on the spot. Even though we did teach things, these little programmes were more to keep our comrades company, so they would feel like they were part of something. It helped motivate people to use the simplest of weapons, which is how the FMLN was built.

Female Broadcaster: As we said before, there are different uses for homemade weaponry in street combat. With a mechanic's sledgehammer we can break the padlocks that hold back the people's rebellion.

Male Broadcaster: With workers' picks and shovels we can dig trenches to detain the enemy tanks.

Female Broadcaster: Don't forget compañeros, *when the revolutionary movement took up armed struggle as the just and correct*

path to power, the first small arms — pistols and revolvers — were recovered from the enemy using shovels, stones and knives.
Male Broadcaster: That was how we began to arm ourselves. With sharp weapons we recovered small arms, and with small arms we recovered larger weapons. The guerrilla army didn't start out with rifles or artillery or machine-guns like we have today. In the beginning it was blunt and sharp weapons that launched the struggle. In the great street battles that are approaching, these weapons will play an important role once more as part of...
Several: Homemade weaponry!

The episodes lasted 15 minutes and went on air every day. For each new weapon we played the appropriate sound effect: explosions, gunshots, rifles being cocked — and guerrilla marches. Teenagers in the cities loved it. They asked us to repeat them, which doesn't happen very often on Venceremos.

A Typical Day at Venceremos

At 5.30 in the morning everybody's awake. Ready? We stand in formation. We do calisthenics for about half an hour. An icy bath in the river and a cup of hot coffee.

***

Coffee is a ritual in Morazán. No matter what time it is, there's always coffee. At three in the morning they put on the first pot. You fill up your gourd and serve the whole crowd.

***

From six to eight in the morning we do the monitoring. We listen to all the stations in the country, the TV channels, the Voice of America and the Honduran stations, which usually have a lot of news. The camp is a beehive of activity, a pile of radios all turned on, every one of us in his or her tent, deep into our assigned station, taking notes. If you want to find out what's happening in the world, go to Venceremos and ask any of these journalists without diplomas.

Those of us on the broadcasting side get together for a few minutes to decide on the day's work plan. We divide up the tasks: I'll do the editorial, you finish the soap opera, he'll help Chiyo do the monitoring.

***

In the camp you could find everything from *Revolutionary Theory* to *Love in the Time of Cholera.* From Marx to Márquez, whatever you wanted. The newspaper comes every day. The country's political magazines like *ECA*, the *New York Times* every so often, *Newsweek*, Omar Cabezas's novels, Sergio Ramírez's latest, *Perestroika* by Kiva Maidanik, *Perfume* by Suskind... The library is quite large — only for long periods we have to hide it or split it up among several locales.

***

At eight o'clock we have breakfast. If you've got a deadline to meet, someone will bring you *tortillas*, but it's better to go down to the kitchen, because it's the heart of the camp, the best spot to be. There we have another cup of coffee and get the latest gossip, we run into Atilio, talk about the news, we run into Luisa, we laugh, and we don't go back up to work until old Germán tells us what he saw in the night.

***

We built Vietnamese kitchens which have a system of underground tubes that cool off the smoke and dissipate it near the ground as if it were mist. That's the first rule if you want to keep the helicopters from seeing you from up above.

***

Nine in the morning and the sacred monitoring meeting. The entire staff gets together and each one reads out his news. Let's see, you, YSU. If there is something worth discussing, we stop and discuss it. Remember that the monitoring was being done by peasant boys and girls who didn't even know the earth is round, yet there they were debating Reagan's foreign policy or the foreign debt. Once, one of them got Lebanon all mixed up. He had the Palestinians fighting the Italians and the French — an awful mess, nobody understood a thing. Somebody suggested we drop it and go on to other items.

"Just a minute!" the *compa* protested. "If you don't explain Lebanon to me, I can't continue monitoring."

Incredible discussions and long-winded explanations make the meetings interminable, but these daily debates are the best political school by far. They force us to dig up the sources if we're going to explain, among other things, what the devil is happening in Lebanon.

***

The monitoring team liked to have its idols. When Tripoli got bombed, Khaddafi was the hero. At Venceremos people talked a lot about Khaddafi and it was like touching God's ass. When the war against Nicaragua was really hot, Humberto Ortega was the man. Khaddafi had already fallen from grace because he vacillated at the meeting of the Non-Aligned Nations. After that, everything was Humberto. Then Humberto went to Sapoá for talks with the contras. Sure, we tried to explain to the *compas* about the need for flexibility, but even so Humberto fell off his pedestal — and Gorbachev climbed up. Everybody started talking about Gorbachev, and since we have a lot of names that start with "ch", people started saying Gorbachiyo, Gorbacheje, Gorbachila, Gorbachela — a whole fan club. Heroes were rising and falling fast! Alan García was the star for a short while. Alfonsín had a few points in his favour, but lost them quickly. Several heroes always held their stature: Fidel Castro, for example. All the *compañeros* on the monitoring team really admire and respect Fidel.

***

At that meeting we decide on the programme: the subject of the editorial, the military news, news from the popular movement... Since we don't have many typewriters or enough time to transcribe it all, we just staple together the handwritten pages from the monitoring team, write up a summary to go on top and send it all to Atilio. If he doesn't get to read everything, at least the summary gives him an overview, and if a story interests him, he can dig it out from the pile. It's all there: opinion pieces from the US press, commentaries from Radio Havana, summaries of panel discussion shows, the national and international news — a daily mountain of information.

There was a time when Atilio would stop whatever he was doing at twelve sharp to meet the broadcasting team, go over the programme, and discuss all the issues. He'd give us his opinion on the political approach to take, but how we actually did it was our problem. As the war became more complex, the meeting got shorter and shorter. Sometimes he'd just check the programme over with Marvel and delegate more to the team, but if you read over the scripts at five o'clock and thought something might cause political problems, you could always go to Atilio and he'd take the time to read them over and suggest another approach. Venceremos always has access to Atilio.

Once we get the green light from Atilio, we have lunch.

***

In the kitchen there are two big pots. One is where they cook up the corn for *tortillas* — there's always plenty of corn. The other pot is for what we call the "withwhat". You've got to eat *tortillas* with something, haven't you? You don't eat something with *tortillas*; it's the other way around. *Tortillas* are the meal. That's how *campesinos* (and guerrillas) eat: our diet is *tortillas*. The withwhat could be beans, rice, cheese, meat, vegetables, whatever. But the proportions are always a lot of tortillas and a little withwhat. Isra can put away six or eight *tortillas* in a single sitting, depending on the work he's been doing. We've got one *compa* we call Juanito Twelve Chengas. A *chenga* is the same as a *tortilla*, only *chengas* are thick and the size of a dinner plate. Juanito would chow down with a dozen at every meal. You've got to be a horse to eat a dozen *chengas*.

***

After lunch, some of us nap for half an hour. Then at 2.00 or 2.30, each of us scuttles off like a crab to his cave to write up his piece for the show. To write in a guerrilla camp is no mean feat. Forget about having a desk where you turn on the lamp and sit down to pound the keys of a typewriter. What you do is pick up a pencil, find a rock to sit on, and start scribbling. When it rains it's a disaster. The paper gets wet, you can't find anywhere to sit, everything gets muddy, even your thoughts, and you can't remember what you were going to write about.

We don't only write. Somebody goes out to do an interview, another makes up jingles, or attends to the comments of some visitor.

***

Jonás turns up one day and says: "So how are the apparatchik today?"

"What apparatchik?"

"You. You're a bunch of old fogies. Squares! Venceremos is boring!"

"The best criticism you can make of a river is to build a bridge, don't you think?"

"Precisely. That's why last night I dreamed up something that'll be a lot of fun. Here's the script. Let me know if you like it."

"A script for what?"

"Well, it's a series. A series, but it's not serious. It's called 'The Little Squirrels'."

"What's it about?"

"There are two characters: a little squirrel who's very political, and another who thinks he's hot shit."

"We can't do that. Which of us can talk like a squirrel?"

"Jesus! You're not even apparatchik. You're just a piece of shit! Don't you have a tape recorder with a speed control?"

"Yeah."

"Well, record the voices normally and then speed it up so it sounds like squirrels talking. Let's do it, *hombre!*"

"But you see..."

"Go jump in the river!"

Before Jonás became a guerrilla, he studied art. He was an actor on the stage and taught acting technique. He's a fierce critic of the straight-laced thinking that often comes across on Venceremos.

***

At five o'clock everything should be ready. It has to be. Those of us on the broadcasting team get together to decide who will read what, what music we'll use, any last-minute news. We organise the programme and check the scripts one last time. We all agree on what to do — or we start fighting.

***

We called Yaser "Menéndez y Pelayo"[3] because he reads the dictionary and he's a real master of syntax, metaphors, parasynthetic adjectives...

"People aren't going to understand that word, Yaser."

"What word?"

"That one, 'plaudits'."

"You're nuts."

"Nor this one, 'uberous'. I don't even know what it means."

"Go look it up in the dictionary."

"Where are the listeners going to look it up?"

"You underestimate the people. You think they're all ignorant."

"It's not that. People don't know what uberous means."

"They should learn. That way they'll get educated."

"You just said they weren't ignorant. Who has to get educated, them or us?"

"Simple language makes people stupid!"

"Flowery language makes them think they're stupid!"

"Come on, cut the bullshit. It's almost six — and the programme's going to come out shituberous!"

***

Six o'clock. On air. The national anthem. Every one at his post. Ready? "This is Radio Venceremos, voice of the workers, peasants and guerrillas!" Broadcasting live for an hour straight is really stressful. Not only because a bomb might drop on you, but because the responsibility weighs on your shoulders. After all, this is not just any old radio station. You've got to choose every word with care, because you know the next day the Voice of America is going to reply. You have to make sure the tone is right for psychological warfare. You have to improvise knowing full well that the enemy is monitoring you and will take advantage of any slip-up, and above all, the *compas* are listening and if you show any lack of conviction it affects their combat morale.

Afterwards we do a quick evaluation and then go to supper.

***

All of Radio Venceremos's programmes — from 10 January, 1981 to this day — have been saved and are safely stored somewhere in the world. Not one cassette has been lost. We've got thousands of hours of tape of leaders dead and alive, interviews with combatants, the daily military news... The oral history of the revolution is right there! We just have to write it up. Anyone fancy the job?

***

At night we have a few things left to do, the most important being to waste time gabbing with our friends, but sometimes there is a political meeting, or we have to monitor foreign broadcasts. We usually all get together to watch the eight o'clock news, which is one of the best. For me, and I think for everybody, sitting there watching television with everyone is the best part of the day.

"Listen to that bastard Ponce[4]!"

"His ears will burn tomorrow, because we'll answer him right back!"

"Are you recording that shit?" Atilio asks.

"Yes."

"Let's do a Guacamaya with Ponce. He deserves it!"

Then everybody comes up with a joke or an idea. It's a lot of fun.

***

Some people go to roost early with the chickens. Or because of the chick waiting in his tent! Others stay up to watch a movie on the betamax or to tell stories about *La Ciguanaba*. For a while, when Luisa was in charge of the station, we were up all night playing a card game called *matraca*. Playing that game with Luisa was really tricky because she played to win. You could hear us shouting all the way to the mountains of Honduras. Isra would get mad as hell at all the noise and laughter, but what else could we do? *Matraca* is the official game of Venceremos. Anybody who doesn't play it doesn't love his mother.

***

Too bad for the guy who has to stand watch. Good night, tomorrow's another day.

The Last Shy Guerrilla

Love begins with messages by courier. That's the rule among lovers in Morazán — so much so that the desire to write your own messages became one of the greatest motivations to learn to read and write for our peasant *compas*. I'm glad they learned because I couldn't find the time to write all of theirs as well as my own.

"Well it's that... listen, I..." Servando says one night. "It's that I'd like you to do me a favour."

"A message, right?"

"But don't tell anybody."

It's always got to be a secret. Even though most of the time everybody already knows, you've got to have a touch of mystery and the complicity of a procuress. Or a procurer, in my case.

"Who's it for?" I ask in a whisper.

"For Butterfly, *hombre*," Servando breathes. "Lately I can't sleep for thinking about her."

"Okay, go ahead."

Servando dictates and I fill up the lines of a page of my notebook. Sometimes the wooer will ask you to write in big letters, easy to read, so the sweetheart won't miss even a comma.

"You don't think it's a bit pushy to say `my dear comrade'?"

"It depends."

"Then take it out, would you? Better later on when the mango's ripe."

The letters are written studiously, weighing the implication of each and every word. They're long, kilometric, filled with country-and-western romanticism and words borrowed from the radio soaps. They're also illustrated.

"Do you know how to draw birds?"

It's a very common question in Morazán. You see, love letters are supposed to have two birds in the corner of the page, their beaks kissing, and hearts with arrows through them.

"Will you fold it for me, or should I find someone else who knows how?"

There are two ways to fold a letter. There is the utilitarian way you use if you're telling Luisa to send some cassettes up to Venceremos. Then there is the other way, the artistic way, for when a man is in love. How you fold the paper is part of the message: like a flower, like a little *tamale*, in the shape of a heart, so that when your lady-love opens it she feels the first flush of heat. It unfolds like a rose and inside she finds the nectar of your words: "*Compañera*, please forgive my being so forward, but ever since that afternoon when I saw you in Perquín, my days have been without sun, my compass without a north, my *tortillas* without salt..."

If they answer your letter, there's hope. You sprout wings. That Sunday, early in the morning, you meet Servando by the stream. He's washing his things.

"So, it worked..."

He wants to look good because he's off on a visit. He bathes, combs his hair, puts on his clean clothes, his tight shirt. All resplendent, he sets his cap or his hat on his head just right. A man can't go out bare-headed. I spent several years with my head uncovered until my girlfriend couldn't stand it any more: "I can't go on with you like that."

"I've got a big head. No hat will fit me."

So she went to a tailor and ordered one made to my size. You see, a man without a hat is worth nothing. The first thing a man gets and the last thing he loses is his hat. To go bare-headed in the countryside is like going barefoot in the city.

"Good luck, Servando!"

The usual thing is to make like a cat. The beloved goes to the camp where the girl is staying. He doesn't say he's going to see her of course. He's come to talk with one of his buddies, or any excuse at all. He yacks on and on, and it gets late. They invite him to eat and it gets later. Once night falls, he makes like a cat. As a good guerrilla, a good *campesino*, he knows where the girl sleeps and how to get there surreptitiously in the dark, to the tent where she awaits him. In absolute silence — because a lot of people are sleeping nearby — he goes inside, stays with her, then he leaves. Nobody finds out, only the guard. You've got to be a hell of a good cat to get by the guard unnoticed, since he's a guerrilla and a *campesino* just like you!

***

Is there time for love among the guerrillas? It should be the other way round: Could you possibly do this without love? No way. We love like crazy in the guerrilla camps. Love here is as common as bullets flying by, and there are good reasons for it. Going off into the mountains is a supreme act of rebellion for a young kid. By going against established society, he or she assumes a lot of responsibility from a young age. Responsibility about life, about death, about political decisions. They know that what they are doing will determine the future of the country, no matter whether we win or lose. They feel they are part of something so big it can change the course of the entire country. Some do this more consciously than others, but everyone shares in this feeling of absolute rebelliousness.

So what happens when you're 14 or 16 and you discover that you are in control of your life and your actions? Who is going to tell you yes or no? Your father and older brother can't rule your life any more, so you can love with incredible freedom. You break free of all the social conventions, all the prejudices, all the proper ages for doing one thing or another. You break free and that liberates your capacity for love. Among the guerrillas, you're always in love with someone, and you're always trying to get someone to fall in love with you. Always, day in day out, there's someone waiting for you who wants to make love to you.

This freedom we've won meets up with the oldest of traditions and it's quite a mix. You see, all the moral crap about courtship — sin and staying a virgin and sleeping with somebody else — all that gets buried in the great act of rebellion, but the beautiful rite of love remains. The peasant way of being remains, the little birds in the corners of the page.

✳✳✳

You get all kinds, from the most romantic to the most pragmatic — and the shy.

The romantics go and stand by the wall. I don't know how it is, but when people fall in love there's always a stone wall and she always manages to be sitting there with her eyes lost on the horizon, and he's there, at a prudent distance, rhythmically pounding the mouth of his rifle with the palm of his hand.

"Well yeah, at home we had a little cow... You know, once it got worms and we didn't know what to do..."

Our Romeo talks on and on, telling stories, waiting for the decisive moment to declare his love.

"Well you know, I've been thinking about you a lot and I'd like for us to be together, that is if you would too."

Acompañarse. That's the matrimonial word. To become *compañeros.* Father Rogelio might even end up involved if it's a formal *acompañamiento*, which is the guerrilla equivalent of a wedding. The romantics always use that strategy, promising a stable relationship and eternal love, no matter whether such a thing is at all feasible in this crazy shit.

Not the pragmatics. The pragmatics skip the protocol and get right down to business.

"Okay, let's both go in this column, then I'll come by your place tonight. Tell me where you're going to be."

"Jesus!" she gets a bit frightened. "Who do you think you are?"

"I don't have a partner and neither do you, right? I'll be there."

"Hang on, don't be in such a hurry."

"But that's the way things are. I'm a man and you're a woman. Why say no, eh?"

"I haven't said that..."

It's a form of wooing imposed by the war. We're here today, tomorrow who knows? The man doesn't mince words. The only problem is if she doesn't like the guy. If she does, if he's sparked a feeling, it doesn't matter if his approach is romantic or pragmatic.

Then there are the shy ones. I'm in that category, but I don't know if anyone else is. If there were others, they didn't stay that way for long. Really, I think I may be the only shy man left in this war. Or rather I was, because something as surprising as it was unstoppable happened to me. Want to hear about it?

***

Then there's the other side of it, the fierce competition. Among the guerrillas, love is always a wrestling match. You see, in the military force there are far fewer women than men. Among the rank-and-file supporters, in the communities depopulated by repression or unemployment, women predominate, but in a guerrilla column the proportion is seven men for every woman. Seven snipers have got that woman in their sights. Seven crocodiles ready to fight over her in the war of love, the little war within the larger one.

In reality, since the supply is so much greater than the demand, it's not the men who decide. She does. The woman selects the one she'd like to *acompañarse*. That's the way it is. It's matriarchal, feminist, and detestable, but what else can we do? They pick one and leave six. Among the guerrillas, women have all the luck.

***

So, one fine day after five years of working together at Venceremos, of learning all the good, the bad, and the ugly about each other, of her being the party rep in the radio collective, the one charged with bending our minds to the right path, after five years with her as my boss and political officer, Leti stood before me as a woman. I was getting some papers ready for the afternoon show, and when I looked up I saw her and her two big boobs. Leti didn't say a thing and neither did I, but she made me feel her presence. You haven't stopped to look at me the whole war, have you? Well, from now on you're going to have to notice me, understand? Because what's standing before you, above all, is a woman. All that I photographed in her shining eyes.

Down that path I went, my thoughts caught up in the vertigo of my shyness, terrified of putting my foot in my mouth. Was I mistaken? After five years, why does she do this to me? That very evening, I had to take a truck to Perquín because the army was threatening to launch another operation. On the way back, at a crossroads, I ran into Leti. She was waiting for some mules to take the radio equipment up into the mountains. I stopped the truck.

"Don't you look elegant!" she said to me. "I knew you could drive, but I've never seen you at the wheel before. Bye-bye!"

My confusion was growing, I had a bunch of spaghetti between my ears. Could it be true? Suppose I send her a letter and she tells me to go to hell? I could never stand the humiliation!

The next day, I was the one who got a letter. As soon as I saw it folded, my heart started pounding. It could only be her.

Remember, you've got to take along the Venceremos hook-up and change the frequency every other day...

It started off with a rather obvious comment, since I'd been doing that for five years and I didn't need anyone to remind me of anything. I carried that equipment in my sleep. The letter went on and right in the middle of the pretext she slipped in a phrase:

You looked so elegant last night! I wish I could have gone with you.

Then on it went giving directions for the hook-ups and the cables, but by then I was already thinking about other hook-ups and connections.

The army operation turned out to be a false alarm, so the commanders brought us all together in El Manzanal, at the foot of Gigante Hill. That's a lovely camp, filled with apple trees, not the apples they have in other countries, but little yellow fruit that here we call fart-apples because they're full of air and when you bite into them — pppfff — they sound like a fart. Well, it was there in that Salvadoran paradise, under those huge green leafy trees, that Eve tempted me with her apple, even if it was a fart-apple. Right there Leti launched her final offensive. It began in the morning in the Venceremos air-raid shelter, a very narrow tunnel where only one person can enter or leave at a time. On my way out — what a coincidence — I met Leti coming in. I clung to one side and as she passed by with her eyes on the ground, her tits brushed against me, just the nipples. Two boobs this big! I was left breathless, my mouth dry. I still didn't know what to do because I wasn't sure. Suppose she laughs at me, suppose she answers me with a guffaw? I was so shy I wanted to bury myself in that air-raid shelter and never come out until the war was over.

Later on, when I was putting up my tent, Leti came by: "It's a pretty tent, Marvel. Big for one person, small for two."

You could have knocked me down with a feather! I was going nuts. That night I made up some excuse and went to see her. She shared her tent with Dina, so we just talked in whispers killing time until the other girl fell asleep. Once Dina was snoring — or pretending to snore, I'll never know — I took Leti's hand in mine. It was electric, like picking up a live wire. She pulled me towards her and we kissed a long French kiss that was more like a bite, panting too loudly all the while.

"What's the matter?" Leti whispered. "When you taught me broadcasting you didn't take so long."

Shit! But the other girl was right there. How could we do it? Of the three of us, one had to go, so I got up and went outside. I went back to my tent to sleep all alone and dream about the stars.

At dawn a letter arrived:

Let's talk. You must be wondering about things.

More than wondering, I was horny as hell. I was sure I wasn't wrong.

"I want one thing to be clear," Leti began. "It's crazy what we're going to do. As for me, I want to do it. If you do too, great, but don't get the idea that we're going to stay together."

"Whatever you want," I said. "At this point in the championship, any penalty will do."

The worst thing was that the second night Isra was on guard duty. To sneak by without Isra knowing is like asking for the moon. Isra hears things a kilometre away, he sees in the dark, neither special forces nor elves can get by him. But I had to get around him because — and I haven't mentioned this so far — at that time Leti was Mauricio's girlfriend, and Mauricio, the technician, was my good friend, a friend who had the bad luck of being sent to another front for a few months.

The TV news was over. Everybody went off to their tents and all the lights went out. Alone at last, we started kissing passionately, but we were right next to the television, in the camp's meeting place.

"Let's get out of here," she says, already burning.

"Yeah, let's go."

"Where are we going?"

"Uh... I don't know."

"You haven't thought of where we're going?"

"Afraid not."

How shameful! The tom-cat is supposed to have everything planned out, the time and the place, but just having kept my nerves in check enough to do my usual tasks was plenty for me. Luckily, the she-cat saved the day.

"I know a place," Leti told me. "Isra won't see us. Come on."

She took me to her place, and there we hugged, made love, bit each other, we let loose... All the verbs and all the dirty stuff that I'm too shy to tell you.

***

There's no movies for the guerrillas, no cafés and no discotheques. Love is what there is. Love is what helps you find, not meaning — you've got meaning — but colour in life. Love and the whole drama leading up to it: did she look at me, she said yes, yesterday I got a letter, today I touched her foot under the table, I put my finger here... All that give and take gets you excited. It makes you happy to be alive.

We don't have Mondays here, or Tuesdays, or Sundays, or anything else. Every day the monitoring at six in the morning, every day the programme at six in the afternoon, every day the enemy might get you. Day or night, in mountains or plains, you live with the terror of a helicopter assault. You live in a brutal, violent world where you've always got to be ready for whatever comes, where you're not at home. You live with death at your side. So a girl bathing in a stream, a well-put compliment, a button poorly fastened, puts colour back in your day. It makes it different.

In my diary I wrote up a vision. One day I was sitting on a stone watching Lidia de Licho and two other women bathing. I was there for an hour, as if watching a movie. The *compas* were pouring water on themselves, laughing, soaping up their naked bodies, no bras. They weren't flirting with me nor did I have any desire to go after anyone. I was just watching. Watching a woman. Watching beauty and forgetting the gunpowder and screams.

***

I'm from the asphalt city of Caracas, educated in London. I've visited a hundred cities, but I had no idea what a peasant woman from Morazán is like when she makes love. I've seen a lot, but in all my wanderings about the globe Leti is the most erotic woman I've ever known. Erotic. No inhibitions. She can enjoy a relationship, enjoy sex in a way I hadn't found in any other woman I'd ever met. She's from the *barrio* of Azacualpa. Her most cosmopolitan experience to date had been selling clothes between San Miguel and Usulután, but Leti knew infinitely more about love than I. She knew, among other things, about the importance of words. With Leti, love is spoken, the entire love-act is filled with words. Sensual words referring to this love and to a love we might invent, to shapes, to smells, to tastes. With Leti, love is never limited to hands or mouths or anything else. I never imagined this peasant woman's way of making love. It destroyed my preconceptions — and put an end to my shyness.

In the morning, while we were drinking coffee, Isra winked at me: "You look tired, Marvel," he said and I knew right then that he knew, and that I could count on his silence.

***

Here, people have dropped all their traditional ways of behaving. Nobody cares if a woman has had several husbands. Why should it matter? If today she breaks off with one and tomorrow she starts up with another, does that diminish her moral qualities, her capacity to be a good person? It's not a question of promiscuity. I understand promiscuity to be when a woman sleeps with her husband's son, where everybody's getting it on with everybody else. That doesn't happen on the front. If Santiago is with Ana Lidia, she isn't going to lay a finger on me. Somebody's girlfriend is his girlfriend, and people respect that.

People respect homosexuality too. Take the case of Nando, the tailor who made uniforms for half the BRAZ. Nando asked permission like everyone else and made like a cat to be with his friend. Nobody reproached him for being gay. The only problem with Nando was when he wanted to measure you for a pair of trousers — careful with that hand! There was one guy here who called himself Lucha Villa. The *cuilios* would come and he'd shoot at them like everybody else. There were lesbians. Who didn't know about the turbulent love affairs between Trini and whatever her name was? So what? Pluralism has to be the rule in love too.

***

I discovered how to find eggs, cut bunches of bananas, ripen sapodillas. I learned to make the best tents in the camp; I learned which poles should be bent and which shouldn't. I got hold of a big nylon sheet — matrimonial size. Even though it weighed a ton in my pack, with it we could make love all the way up and down and to either side, and we didn't fall out. Our tryst under the fart-apple trees led to a steady relationship. Leti and I became a couple, publicly acknowledged. What we never institutionalised was love itself. In the mountains, there is always a place to make love, and we always want to.

Backroom Heroes

I've never liked the Venceremos posters. Most of them are pictures of the broadcasters, or at most, of the production team, but there are hundreds of other people who are involved in this project and who make it possible.

The station is a collective project. What the hell could Santiago use to start up the generator if Odilón didn't bring the gasoline? No matter if we have tons of gasoline, where the fuck could Mauricio hang the aerial if there weren't people ready to give their lives to defend it? And where would we find people ready to give their lives to defend others if there weren't mothers who had read the Bible with Miguel Ventura or Rogelio, and who decided to raise their children to be so generous?

These are the people who don't go on air and aren't on the posters. The logistics team, for example. Let's not worry about the *tortillas* or the medicine or the thousand other things you have to have on a guerrilla front. Let's just talk about gasoline. How do we get gasoline for Venceremos? Little by little, we built up a network of young men who buy a bucketful in Osicala, peasants who carry a litre in their shoulder bag, drivers who store a few gallons in a house in the town of Sociedad... They have to work with small quantities, like ants, because there's no way to hide or justify taking a whole barrel up to Perquín.

Quincho was the first one to weave the network. He trained Odilón, Roque, all his loyal troops. Then as the war grew more complex, so did Venceremos. We needed more and more gasoline. On top of our six o'clock show, we started doing another at eight. Later on, we added one at six in the morning, then a fourth at noon. From a half-hour programme we went to forty-five minutes, then an hour, and at one god-awful point we were doing an hour and a half or two hours straight. From a small generator we went to a big gasoline-driven one, then to a big diesel generator, plus the FM generator, and another little one to charge the batteries for all the FM repeating stations. It became a big operation, but the logistics were always based on grassroots organising, on an immense machinery of people who made sure each little cog worked.

When the BRAZ was strong our gasoline operation wasn't so humble. Once, during the campaign when the butcher Medina Garay was killed, we set up a barricade on the Pan-American Highway at a place near El Semillero. Hundreds of vehicles got held up, among them two big tanker trucks, one full of gasoline, the other carrying diesel and kerosene. When we went to take that treasure, the drivers didn't even get mad.

"Take whatever you like. It doesn't belong to us."

With the sort of brazenness typical of the BRAZ, we left the battle in a caravan of twelve buses carrying our troops, a jeep in front, another behind, and a third for the logistics chief guarding his two tanker trucks. Just like a regular army!

Since kerosene is the fuel peasants use for their lamps, we handed it out along the way. Every time we came to a town we started yelling: "Kerosene! Come and get it! It's free!"

The whole village turned out, lines of people with buckets. The diesel also became a party. We filled up all the buses and cars we came across, any Christian on wheels. The gasoline, of course, was ours. We took it to Carolina on the banks of the Torola River, and from there our immense grassroots network took over. We had drums stored in the homes of dozens of supporters who risked their lives to make sure Venceremos could go on air.

Other people who don't go on air are the *compas* of the security team: Walter's men, Ismael's, Germán's — these people are there one hundred percent. They've become incredibly efficient. We arrive somewhere and in the time it takes you to have a catnap they've already set up the infrastructure for the radio and the command post to function. They believe that every minute lost is a gift to the enemy.

It takes years of experience to pick the best place for a camp. It has to have enough routes of escape. It has to fulfil certain conditions for cover and communications. For example, Germán and Isra might go out early in the morning because we have to move. They head off and soon they're back.

"How do you like the spot?" Manolo asks them.

"It's pretty, very pretty."

"What kind of trees does it have?"

"Oak."

"Have they lost their leaves?"

"No. They've got them."

"Did you test the television?"

"Yes."

"Can you get all the channels?"

"Yes."

"How does channel two come in?"

"It's the worst of them, but you can see it."

"We won't have problems with the monitoring?"

"No."

These are requirements that Che would never have dreamed of, right? Guerrillas with television sets!

Once a site has been selected, we start moving in. First comes the kitchen. Germán takes an advance team to set it up. Then we dig the air-raid shelters: two enormous holes about three by five metres and two-and-a-half metres deep — one for Venceremos, with its built-in table and bench, the other for strategic communications. You lay a double row of tree-trunks and earth on top so even a rocket couldn't cave it in. Then you dig trenches for all the fighters. L-shaped trenches so that if a bomb falls into it the shrapnel won't get everyone. Digging trenches is exhausting work, but the security squad finishes them off in no time. Later on, while everyone pitches their tents, they finish setting up the Vietnamese kitchen, the table for the command post, the place for the television set, all the while making sure that the camp can be taken down as fast as it was put up, or even faster, and that the enemy won't be able to tell who was here.

That's the other condition. When we leave a place, we can't leave behind any clues. The smell of gasoline is suspicious. A miserable little piece of paper with Santiago or Marvel's handwriting means that Venceremos camped here. We've meted out serious punishments for having wiped our asses with a monitoring sheet. That's absolutely prohibited because the first thing the enemy does when they find an abandoned camp is to dig out the latrine and search for papers with writing. If they find out it was us, they'll follow our tracks. That's why the policy is never to leave a camp in place.

Everything has to be left as we found it. The security squad even marks off paths for walking which you can't go off, and when we leave you have to cover them with the same sticks and dry leaves that were there before and that we piled up at the edge of each path. It's impossible to leave it so they won't know someone was there, but they shouldn't know who or how long ago.

Of the original Radio Venceremos security squad, only Isra is left. The rest have all died in combat defending the station, or in other battles defending the people. I have especially fond memories of the Pericas. Minchito, the youngest, was a kid I watched grow up, from the station's messenger to a special forces volunteer. He died heroically in an attack on the base at Gotera. Just before that, his brother Julito died when we were attacked at Arambala. Just after that, his other brother Payín died covering the retreat of several *compañeros*. A few months later Chepito, who was our first cook at Parra de Bambú, died.

Of the Pericas, only the women are left: Marinita, a hard worker who's with Marcela in the press office; and the sixth sibling, the youngest, in Colomoncagua with her parents. Halfway through the war she fulfilled the dream of all young girls who grow up in the refugee camps in Honduras and who listen to Venceremos from afar: She became old enough to return as a guerrilla, to become a radio operator on the front lines.

Six brothers and sisters, six revolutionaries. The Pericas' commitment was made as a group; the father, who was from a very Christian family in La Laguna de Villa El Rosario, volunteered with all his children, all his family, all his cousins and friends. Everything he had, including his life, he gave to God, in other words, to the revolution.

There are many families like them in Morazán and all over the country, and overseas there are innumerable brothers and sisters who work in solidarity: Germans, Swiss, French, North Americans, Nicaraguans, Mexicans and Swedes, a pack of white folks who have helped us generously. What would we have done without the German friends who for ten long years sent us the tubes for the transmitter, each of which costs 3,000 dollars?

All of them, outside the country and in, those who died and those who still fight, they are the ones who have made this station possible. They are Radio Venceremos.

Multi-media Revolution

Right from the start we worked with an array of different media. Even before we had the station, in the days of the COMIN international committee, we made videos and put out the magazine *El Salvador*. Of course we did all this outside the country, though we had a small telex inside for sending information overseas.

Once the station got under way, COMIN focused on supporting whatever Venceremos was doing in Morazán, with the station coordinating all the publicity work. That's when we launched the magazine *Señal de Libertad*, an international Radio Venceremos review, which was even published in German, and lasted for quite a few issues before we suspended publication under an agreement with the other forces of the FMLN.

We also started making movies — features and shorts so people could follow the war as it developed. They've all been documentaries, but a kind of documentary that broke with the classic form of a narrator stringing together a series of images. We worked with a group called *Cero a la izquierda*. The reality they filmed was so eloquent and the montage so well done that no narration was necessary. Check out "Letter from Morazán", "Will to Win", "Time of Audacity". The cineastes gathered in Havana for the Tenth Latin American Film Festival were so impressed with this way of making documentaries that, in addition to the prizes they had awarded us in previous years, they gave Venceremos' productions special recognition. Documentaries about the Salvadoran revolution, which revolutionised the genre.

For the movies and videos, people on the inside — Skinny Gustavo and his team — would work with others who came from overseas to help with the filming and then went back outside the country to edit. The commanders always made a lot of time for them. María, Chico, all the big-shots got involved in writing the scripts, reviewing the clips, the whole process.

The videos weren't only for foreign consumption. They were often shown right in the camps and when we took over towns. Later on the Venceremos Cultural Brigade added skits and dances with Los Torogoces musical group. We even took photo exhibits on bamboo stands all over Morazán. You didn't know which to admire more, the incredible pictures of the combatants or the faces of the combatants looking at themselves; actors and spectators at the same time.

Of course, the station always came first, demanding the greatest effort and the most resources. We didn't only broadcast on short-wave. To reach an audience in the cities, since '82 we broadcast on FM. In '84-'85, right in the midst of the dispersal of the guerrilla forces, we decided to disperse the station too. The idea was to have a lot of small FM stations connected up to the main Venceremos transmitter. They weren't to be just repeating stations — we'd tried that already with the Devil's chain and the four hook-ups — this time each was to have its own local 15 minute programme. The challenge was to reproduce the same interplay of political and military elements, the double dimension of having a real presence and doing mass communications, at the level of guerrilla units. We even had a slogan for that stage, *Venceremos is on your front!*

Apolonio and his German friends figured out how to adapt some tiny little FM transmitters which could put out about 100 watts. They were incredibly compact, wonderful little gadgets. Some day they'll be on exhibit in a revolutionary museum. But we ran into a lot of problems with such small autonomous stations. It's not enough to have the equipment, you've got to train the people who are going to do the broadcasting and produce the local shows. We also had to turn a thousand pirouettes to evade the goniometers. What was worse, the war escalated. In Guazapa, for example, the saturation bombing during Operation Phoenix put an end to our efforts to reach the capital via FM. It all became so complicated that we opted for a powerful FM transmitter hidden in Morazán that could reach the whole country.

**

The large FM transmitter is a big responsibility for Ricardo, Toni and Marcela's cousin who's called Chiri. Chiri and his team keep that FM substation going with nothing but their balls. They have their own supply network for gasoline, their own logistics operation, their own base of support, their own security system. We don't often see them because even though they are in Morazán, they aren't close to us. Where are they? I'll tell you about the miracle, but not the saint. Let the enemy find them with their fancy goniometers!

They're underground, of course, like armadillos, but don't think it's just a little air-raid shelter; it's a whole underground room, with ventilation, a generator, a transmitter — a real feat of engineering. The only thing outside is the armadillo's tail, that is, the aerial, or rather the mess of aerials, because there's one that receives from us, another that transmits, one that bounces the shortwave signal, another for internal communications, still another hook-up we use, and a new aerial we're going to install soon to boost our FM signal so we can reach the youth of the city who don't listen to shortwave because of the damned interference or because it just isn't their thing.

And television. The plan to have a TV Venceremos hasn't been shelved forever, not at all. Any day now we'll surprise you because we've already learned that we don't need fancy long-range equipment. Do you know how we'll do it? With simple equipment, but installed in a mobile unit. It's possible. That way you can broadcast a television signal right from San Salvador, right in the belly of the capital, and the enemy won't detect you since you're in constant motion from one side of the city to the other.

As for the radio station, we have plans for that too. Now we have FM equipment that's very portable and quite powerful. There are thousands of ways to hide it in the city: You could put it in a park, or inside a tape recorder and broadcast with the recorder's aerial; the equipment could be a booby-trap at the same time. You could install one of those gadgets inside a police car and they wouldn't even notice! There's also a way to put a clock inside so that several small stations can broadcast in sequence, like a relay.

The first one transmits for five minutes and, while the enemy is trying to find it, it stops and the second one continues the broadcast on the same frequency but from another site, and then comes the third, then the fourth... The *cuilios* will go nuts playing blind man's buff, while the audience won't even notice that what they heard on one channel was a dozen different broadcasts. With brains you can do anything!

***

We keep a close relationship with our sister station in Chalatenango, Radio Farabundo Martí. Farabundo went on air a year after we did, on 22 January, 1982, to accompany the FPL's[5] struggle on the central front. They've developed a different communications system to promote their work, using telexes, very professional press releases, cassettes, solidarity festivals — truly audacious initiatives.

On several occasions we set up a simultaneous broadcast. Either we broadcast their programme live or they broadcast ours, but hooking up like that was not easy. We had to adjust the aerials, find better heights for receiving the FM signal, and expose ourselves to the goniometers.

In any case, both stations, each in its own way, one in Morazán and the other in Chalate, played an extremely important role, not only for the combatants and their supporters inside the country, but also for the refugees. In El Salvador there was a commercial that said "It's a fact that you can't live without a radio". For people in exile that's the truth. The stations have been umbilical cords keeping people on the outside in touch for ten years.

***

In '80 a group took over the Panamanian Embassy in San Salvador. They were protesting against the repression and since they were going to be repressed as well, the takeover ended up in asylum. About a month later they managed to leave for Panama. There were a lot of them, about 300. Torrijos[6] was very hospitable, but he sent them to live in the middle of nowhere in the jungle on the Atlantic Coast.

"Salvadorans are like ants," the general said. "Wherever they go, they make their way."

Sure enough, when Torrijos went to visit them a few months later, the Salvadorans had built wooden houses, planted corn, fixed up a runway, the place had come to life.

"What do you call the town?" the general asked.

"Ciudad Romero. For the Monsignor."

"What do the people of Ciudad Romero want?"

"Give us a shortwave radio so we can hear Radio Venceremos."

"I'll send you three, but listen to me: when you get nostalgic, don't come tell me you want to go back. I won't let you go!"

Torrijos laughed, but it was true. The station has fulfilled a social and emotional function beyond keeping people informed. All the refugees have family on the fronts. They hear on the station when their relatives die — did you listen to Venceremos? Juancito died, Doña Mela's son. In the cooperatives, in the refugee camps, people listen to the station every night to stay abreast of the overall situation and to find out about their small circle of friends. Of course it makes them nostalgic, but it also cheers them up, it reminds them that they are Salvadoran. Because after ten years outside your country, without any news of what's happened, anyone could lose interest in returning. Instead, these people are like the day they left, with their suitcases packed.

***

Though we had a lot of problems, we managed to set up a support and marketing network overseas. Venceremos's correspondents acted as distributors for the products of the whole system: radio, video, film, music. Several of our people in France established a relationship with the free radios in that country, who produced their own programmes in French calling themselves Radio Venceremos. It caused a diplomatic row because the Salvadoran government protested vehemently to the French. How could France allow subversive groups to install aerials on its soil? They thought we had an international link-up, when it was just a few crumby cassettes that a handful of people broadcast over the free radios!

We also did good work in Mexico. We even had a PO Box there, 7-907, where we got letters from listeners all over the world, including people who wrote to us from inside the country, since they had no other way to reach us. We announced that box over Venceremos every day. Later on we couldn't keep it because the political situation in the region changed.

We've done exchanges with community radio stations in Quebec and Vancouver in Canada, and with a few local stations in Los Angeles and San Francisco, who rebroadcast Venceremos programmes for their Latino audience. The relationship with progressive stations in Latin America has been more difficult, because they are very exposed to repression from the government, the army or other powerful groups.

From Quilapayún to Madonna

Santiago is from the Andes and he's already gone over the forty-year hill. He likes the flutes on "*El Cóndor Pasa*" and marches like "The People United". Latin American music is his thing. Marvel, on the other hand, likes jazz, reggae, a good tango. Marvel studied in London and developed a fine appreciation for music. Don't talk to him about Mick Jagger and his awful screeching. "To me rock is like a kick in the balls," Marvel says. He hates it — and if it's *heavy metal*, even worse. Leti doesn't see much in it either. Leti's thing is Perales, Julio Iglesias, a few in English like "Sealed with a Kiss", ballads like that.

I confess I love rock. I'm from a *barrio* in San Salvador where people listen to rock night and day. Rock and salsa. Atilio, who also comes from that sort of noise, writes his political analysis with a Walkman on. He puts on his earphones to forget all about the world, listening to Frank Sinatra, the Beatles... if you say something bad about John Lennon, watch out! Atilio defends the Beatles as if they were the ideological principles of the party! Modern ones turn him on too, like Tina Turner, Tracy Chapman, Springfield... Once there was a meeting of the political commission at the same time as a TV special with Donna Summer.

"Shall we continue after Donna?" Atilio asked.

"All right!" some applauded.

"How could you suggest such a thing!" others grew indignant.

Each of us struggled to impose his taste on everyone else. It wasn't a problem because we washed our dirty linen at home. Regarding Venceremos the consensus was absolute. On Venceremos, *never*. Venceremos was something else. The fact that it was a guerrilla station defined the music we could play, which remained practically unchanged since '81. What was it? "The People United Will Never Be Defeated." Quilapayún, Mercedes Sosa, Los Guaraguaos, songs with a conscience, hymns of protest. Nobody questioned it, not even me. I love rock, but it never would have occurred to me to put it on Venceremos.

Last year in December Atilio left the front for a tour of Latin America. Balta was left in charge of the station. Balta likes rock, and besides he's a perestroika type from head to toe.

"That editorial is too long," we told him.

"You're right," Balta agreed. "Cut it."

"What can we use to fill in the time?"

"Put on Pink Floyd!"

"What did you say?"

"Pink Floyd, *hombre*. It would sound great, wouldn't it?"

Even I got scared, but Balta started arguing that if we wanted to reach people in the city, we'd have to update the record library.

"What record library? Since '81 we've been playing the same old cassettes! We don't even know what music young people in the capital like."

"Well ask them. Ask them to send it to you."

With Balta's encouragement, we put out a call to the youth in San Salvador to put together some recent music and send it to us at the station. Shit! A week later we had a pile of 60 cassettes of groups we had never even heard of! And they came with commentary: "dynamite", "hot", "very *nais!*"

We led off with "Star Wars". For the military news we put "Star Wars" on in the background.

"At last!" said Chiquito, a man without dogma.

"It's like a different station!" said Jonás, happy as well.

If the combatants didn't approve, at least they didn't complain. So we pushed it a little farther. We started giving the programme highlights with rock in the background, and the military report too, then we'd compensate with a song from Los Torogoces, but as soon as "In the North of Morazán" was over, vavavoom, another rock song.

"No, no, no, no," Santiago would scream. "Too much of that noise. Turn it down! Ana Lidia!"

Ana Lidia, at the mixer, was a great rock-and-roll fan, and she'd be in ecstasy tapping her feet and keeping the controls up high.

Santiago also had to leave the front at that time, so I seized my chance. Maybe I went too far, I admit it. Anyway, I thought "I can't imitate Santiago. Santiago talks and people sit up and listen. Not anybody can do that, especially me with my high-pitched voice like a market-woman without any customers, so I'll talk like I talk." That day, given the success of our first musical experiments, I abandoned the traditional opener ("We begin this broadcast with a salute to the combatants of the FMLN!") and opened with an incredible *swing*:

Yo, brothers, what's up? What's happening? Here's Madonna with her hit "Like a Virgin!"

I still blush when I think about it. People had heart attacks, protests came in by mail, people wanted my head. The hostility was so great that I was scared to leave the camp.

"What kind of shit is that?" one *compa* growled at me. "What the fuck is happening to you people?"

"You don't like it?" I asked, scared shitless.

"Of course I like it! But not on Venceremos."

Santiago came back and he looked like Christ throwing the merchants out of the temple, "What have you done with my station, you sons of bitches?"

"The problem is you're too old, Santiago."

"The problem is you're alienated, Marvin."

"The kids in the city like it."

"If they want to hear rock they can listen to La Femenina! There are sixty stations that play rock!"

"But we've got to win over the youth."

"At the cost of losing the station's character?"

"What character? It's your character Santiago, you just don't like rock, that's all!"

"It's because we are Latin Americans, not gringos!"

"I don't know why you criticise her so much, you're just like her."

"Like who?"

"Madonna. Like a virgin. You're just like a little virgin, except what you're trying to hang onto is your ideological purity!"

"Sonofaguava!"

"Sonofabitch!"

"Cut it out," Leti butted in. "Let's take the argument on air."

Friends, we have a problem with the music. We can't agree on it. The comments you send us are all over the map and we haven't been able to find a way to satisfy them in a show that lasts barely an hour. So, since it never rains to everybody's liking, we've decided in a democratic manner that each member of the radio staff will have a ten-minute space for music in the middle of the programme. You can listen to the one you like.

I took rock and salsa and I called it "The Music Lover". Santiago's was "We Sing", Latin American protest songs. Marvel called his "Do you like it?" — the best of each genre, all exquisite. Leti and a lumpen kid decided to do "Salvadoran Songs", and they put on the San Vicente band and other bar-room music. Between "The Little Bitch" and "Mommy I Like Pupusas?", they congratulated people on their birthday or played requests dedicated to somebody's girlfriend. I don't know if it's because of the greetings or the music, but that's the one people like best so far. Oh yeah, the fifth one, on Friday, was a special with Los Torogoces. If we didn't play Los Torogoces, who are like the Beatles for this war, I think the combatants would lynch us — the peasants too, even the students.

That's how we settled it. We're still fine-tuning it, but at least with this mosaic people are more satisfied, and we're not so angry.

We are Latin American, tropical countries that have lived under the cultural influence of the United States. Our culture is a hybrid of our Indian, black, and Spanish roots, and the Saxon culture from the North. This cultural characteristic is directly related to our climate, our traditions, and the most powerful influences on our continent. We can't deny it, because that is our culture and the tradition that our peoples accept, understand and like.

The fact that nearly a million Salvadorans live in the United States (besides the economic value) is an enormous cultural influence on our society that cannot be erased.

Our greatest cultural identity for historical reasons is with Latin America and the United States, and we identify little with Europe (except for Spain) and even less with Eastern Europe.

The revolutionary generations of America have grown up under the influence of rock, Hollywood, salsa, Mexican romanticism, and the

Christianity brought by Spain. There is a process of cultural fusion under way between Latin America and the United States. The socio-cultural developments occurring throughout the continent are transforming it into an important centre of universal culture. We cannot nor should we try to ideologise cultural influences. That would be dogmatic, an extremely backwards way of thinking which would not give proper interpretation to the feelings of our people and would not allow the process of revolutionary change to grow forth from our own historical roots.

Commander Joaquín Villalobos,
"The Prospects for Victory and our Revolutionary Plans"
March 1989

It's the law of habit. After ten years it isn't easy — for the listeners or for ourselves — to go from the "Guerrilla March" to "Star Wars". It blows your mind! Luckily, now that we've negotiated our five little programmes, we can start laughing at ourselves. When Santiago puts on his Andean laments, I say, "Pardon me, I'm going outside for a cry", and when I put on Madonna, he says "Excuse me if I cover my ears. I want to save myself from imperialism's sewage."

It's funny, but lately I've heard Santiago humming soft rock tunes under his breath, and he claims, though I don't believe him, that at night he hears me whistling *"El Cóndor Pasa"*.

The Stubborn Izote Flower

Manolo gave us the news: "The commanders have decided to launch an offensive, the biggest of the whole war."

"When?"

"Soon."

After nearly ten years, there are more than enough reasons to want to end the war. The country is worn out, in ruins. People want peace and so do we. We don't want to make a career out of being guerrilla fighters or living in the hills. The way the world is changing favours a negotiated solution, but neither Duarte nor, much less, the Army High Command is going to negotiate anything unless we pressure them militarily. That's the only language they understand.

"We're going to take the war to the cities," Manolo continued. "We're going to take all the experience we've gained over the years, all our weapons, all our men and all our strength — pull it all together in one big ball and throw it at San Salvador. That way they'll either understand or we'll bust their ass."

That was towards the end of '88, around September. At Venceremos we were put in charge of preparing our combatants psychologically for an all-out offensive with no retreat, so we formed a commission and racked our brains for the right slogan.

"For social justice and democracy, everyone unite to fight the oppressors until the final victory!" suggested someone, whose name I won't mention.

"Too long, *hombre*. By the time you finish saying it, the bombs will be landing in your mouth."

"Crush criminal fascism!" suggested somebody else, who will also remain anonymous.

"Too heavy."

"Let's build peace!"

"Too cold. Listen to how the Nicaraguans do it: 'Everybody all out!' Why can't we do something that has a bit of Salvadoran flavour to it?"

"Salvadoran?" Santiago piped up. "How about, 'With the finger of unity up the enemy's ass!' You can't get more Salvadoran than that."

We all laughed, but we couldn't come up with a slogan. Finally, Marvel spoke up: "What does an officer say when he gives the order for a final assault?"

"We're going all the way!"

"Okay, that's the best slogan: 'All the way!'"

"Doesn't it sound too militarist?"

"Not really. It's erotic too. When you're with a girl, don't you try to go all the way?"

"All the way — and what else?"

"All the way, period. This is all coming to a head, isn't it? So we want to put an end to this whole thing."

Of love and war, it stuck: *All the way, period!* With that accomplished, feverish preparations began: training for urban commandos, the formation of insurrectional detachments, concentrated operations on the war fronts. On the air we stoked the fire.

"When?" we wanted to know.

"Soon."

The munitions, the organisation, the entire plan for the offensive was ready, but we had to time it right politically. It was going to be ugly, and the people had to feel that the FMLN had exhausted all possibilities of working things out by peaceful means. In a gesture as unexpected as it was audacious, the FMLN General Command announced they were willing to participate in the upcoming elections, as long as the government could guarantee they would be clean, subject to international supervision, and postponed until October, so the FMLN could campaign under the same conditions as the other political parties. The proposal was so logical even the gringos accepted it, but ARENA rejected it outright. After hesitating at first, Duarte agreed with ARENA, invoking "constitutional order".

Given the long history of electoral shams and the likelihood of another, we called on the population to stay away from the polls. On 19 March 1989 the abstentions won with 62 per cent of the vote, but since paper-ballot democracy doesn't take the people's rejection into account, the presidency went to the ARENA candidate, Alfredo Cristiani, who got slightly over half the votes cast. In other words, Cristiani took office representing barely 17 per cent of Salvadorans old enough to vote.

"Is the offensive on or isn't it?" asked our combatants, who'd been left hanging.

"And when?" we asked at Venceremos, getting impatient as we kept turning up the heat. Once more, the commanders took the initiative in seeking a peaceful settlement. Doesn't Cristiani say his government is democratic? Then let's sit down and talk, and sit down they did, in Mexico at a high-level meeting with Shafick Hándal and Joaquín Villalobos from our side. Unfortunately, ARENA sent a second-rate commission with no power to take decisions, so the only result of that September meeting was another one in October, this time in San José, Costa Rica. There it went even worse. Military officers were on the second floor of the house where the talks took place, spying to make sure the government commission wouldn't say or sign anything without consulting them first.

A few days later, a bomb exploded at the FENASTRAS[8] union office, killing Febe Elizabeth, the UNTS[9] leader, as well as ten other union leaders. More and more places were being searched and more people put in jail, evermore paramilitary repression against the popular movement. It was clear that Cristiani didn't have the slightest intention of negotiating.

"Get everything ready for 11 November," they told us. "Now those bastards will find out what the FMLN is made of!"

The offensive was to be launched in the country's five major cities: San Salvador, Santa Ana, San Miguel, Zacatecoluca and Usulután. Besides these strategic points, we would hit a whole range of smaller targets. Venceremos was to continue broadcasting from Morazán, but from underground installations. Only a small group of us would stay behind, practically without any security because the war was going to be fought down in the South and nobody would bother with us. Not even buzzards would be flying over Morazán.

11 November arrived, as we checked the connections and went over the entire transmitting and audio system for the umpteenth time to make sure that absolutely nothing would go wrong. When night fell we were underground, sitting behind the microphones, surrounded by the tiny lights of all the military communications radios. A few minutes before eight, Atilio called in: "We're up on the bronco," he said. "There's no turning back now."

"Any orders?" we asked.

"If you know how to pray, do it."

***

If you weren't there, you would never believe it. On Saturday 11 November, in the neighbourhood of Colonia Zacamil, there was a wedding where the bride dressed in white, the groom in coat and tie, the best man and bridesmaid, the guests, the musicians, and the drunks, all of them were urban commandos. The guns were wrapped up as wedding presents. It was all a set-up to bring people together, hand out arms and take over a sector of the city.

At a soccer game in Mejicanos all eleven players on each team, the referees, onlookers, women selling home-made popsicles, the bus they came on and the one on which they left, all were part of a disguised troop movement to take over that sector.

At a house in Colonia Metrópoli, young couples started arriving at five in the afternoon, girls and boys with their arms around each other, laughing and making way for the cars full of guns that kept coming and going. Those weapons still hadn't been oiled because they'd just come out of caches where they'd been stored for months.

In that house 46 young people from different neighbourhoods gathered. They were university students, union members, all sorts of people. Three of them had combat experience. The rest had never touched a pistol in their lives. Sure, they'd been getting ready with courses, radio programmes and pamphlets, but they'd never had a shoot-out with anybody. At six in the afternoon, those in charge started handing out the hardware and giving basic instructions on using it.

A National Police vehicle pulled up and parked across the street from the house. The cops got out and began to patrol the street.

"The police!" warned one of the young men. "Either somebody ratted on us or we've got the worst fucking luck in the world."

Commander Choco, who was in charge of the group, put on a smile when the police knocked at the door.

"Good evening friend," they said. "Could you give us a little water?"

"Sure, just a second."

Inside, in the next room, 46 urban commandos were oiling a pile of guns. Had a neighbour noticed something? Was there an informer? The police drank their water and took off without so much as sticking their noses inside the door. Maybe they did suspect something, but didn't want to get into a fight when it was almost the end of their shift.

At eight in the evening, Choco brought all the new combatants together: "The time has come, guys. Everybody into the street!" The door opened and the whole crowd of guerrillas rushed out, brandishing their new guns, to take over that part of the city. This was their first encounter with the *cuilios*, whose truck was still parked only a few blocks away.

***

All hell broke loose, the biggest bang in ten years of war. Thousands of men and women poured into the streets of San Salvador. In the *barrios* of the northern part of the city, they opened fire, dug trenches, put up barricades, and completely took the army by surprise. The *cuilios* had smelled something coming and prepared a large operation in Guazapa to keep our troops from entering the city, but we were already inside! The FMLN was fighting in Colonia Zacamil, Mejicanos, Ciudad Delgado, Cuscatancingo, Soyapango and Ayutuxtepeque! The guerrillas were attacking the capital of the country!

In San Salvador, the offensive began with a simultaneous attack on fifty enemy positions, including army headquarters and Cristiani's own home, but at Venceremos we were playing dumb. We said we'd heard about "some attacks" here and there, but we didn't want to kick up a storm or use the word "offensive" until we saw how the wheel was spinning. Suppose something went wrong and they drove us out of San Salvador that same night? We played it cool.

The other stations didn't swallow it. At 8.15, KL set off its alarm:

News Flash! Heavy fighting is taking place in the northern area of the capital. Practically all the poor neighbourhoods have become the theatre of one of the FMLN's most violent onslaughts. We have also received information from Zacatecoluca, where the guerrillas have attacked...

The Army High Command didn't believe these were mere skirmishes either. Just two hours after the attacks began, Ponce[10] decreed a state of siege and set up a national emergency radio and television network.

On Sunday the twelfth, at six in the morning, we went on air like the evening before, without making much noise. A short while later Atilio gave us the green light: "The rice is cooked," he said. "Tell them it's an offensive!"

Now everyone was talking about the big FMLN offensive. The guerrillas had always attacked at night and withdrawn before daybreak, but now the sun was high in the sky and our people were still going at it in the streets of San Salvador, Zacatecoluca, Usulután, in downtown San Miguel. The urban commandos who had opened fire from within were by now joined by the FMLN's real military force, the peasant columns that took advantage of the army's disorder and entered the cities. There was fighting going on in every part of the country. That's when Venceremos let loose.

We'd set up three stalls with radio equipment to get the military news straight from all our command posts: Facundo reporting, Carmelo reporting, Dimas reporting. From every corner of the country, dozens of radio operators were sending us dispatches on their 40-metre orange units, the "Spilsburies". Their transmissions went to any of our three reception stalls, which were spaced far enough from each other to avoid interference. There was a radio operator in each stall, and next to her a messenger, a boy with winged feet. The radio operator had pieces of paper all cut and set up with carbons to make three copies. As the information came in, she wrote it down as fast as she could, kept one copy for herself, and gave the runner the other two. Then the kid took off like a fart for the underground studio. Before jumping into the hole, he gave a copy to the girl sitting at the entrance, who had 14 folders, one for each of El Salvador's departments, to classify the dispatches. All out of breath, the boy then raced to the back of the shelter, where we were broadcasting. Santiago grabbed the piece of paper and switched on the microphone:

A few moments ago, at 10.35 in the morning, our forces destroyed an armoured car on the corner of...

We had a fourth stall, a special one, for overseas communications. Don't ask me how or where because I can't tell you. Let's just say it's the last place the brass would ever think! We set Marvel up in an office with telephones, computers, all that modern shit. Just as day was breaking, Marvel would call us on a direct line: "This is Mouse calling. Look, I've got a *New York Times* editorial that's just come by fax. Here goes, I'll translate it for you."

Incredible! At six in the morning, a contact would buy the paper in New York. At 6:05 he was faxing it to Marvel. At 6:10 Marvel was translating it to us on a secret band, and less than a quarter of an hour later we were discussing it on air. Down in our pit in Morazán, we were getting the stance of the US press sooner than a gringo sitting in his office in Manhattan! We also followed the Spanish and German press and monitored all the important TV news programmes in the world via satellite. Since we expected the government to decree a state of emergency and a news gag, Marvel spent his time watching foreign TV with his satellite dish. Then he lent us his eyes.

"Marvin, I'm watching the troops from the Atlacatl Battalion all crowded around the headquarters of the High Command. They're wearing camouflage uniforms and their faces are painted. They look really nervous. They don't know which way to point their guns..."

Marvel narrated everything he picked up over NBC or CBS, down to the smallest detail, and we reported it as if we were right in San Salvador. That's how that fantastic hook-up worked.

From Monday on, we broadcast non-stop from six in the morning until eleven at night — exhausting marathons for only four announcers. We did shifts of six and eight hours, which left Santiago voiceless and loosened Leti's tongue. They ruined my nerves and finished training Herbert, the Venceremos rookie who at that time wasn't too good at improvising.

Everything had to be improvised. You didn't even have time to scratch your ear. When a dispatch came in, you had to come up with your commentary right on the spot. Santiago and I would forget all about the microphone and talk as if people were sitting there in front of us. Other times we'd challenge the rich, calling them by name and insisting they come out of their mansions. One afternoon Santiago started to pick on William Walker, the gringo ambassador in El Salvador and the namesake of the other swine from the last century[11]:

Aren't you ashamed, Mr. Walker? Where did you learn diplomacy?

He raked him over so hard, and the ambassador's nose was so out of joint, that the State Department sent a message to the FMLN through our Political-Diplomatic Commission: "Let's make a deal. Stop insulting our personnel, and we'll stop calling you terrorists."

All right. The next day we reined in Santiago and they removed our little nickname. Venceremos had them worried because during those days even the deaf were listening to it.

In ten years we'd never had such a big audience. People tell me you could go into Metrocentro[12] and hear Venceremos at full blast in all the stores. We were monitored constantly by the middle class, the press, the enemy, the gringos, even Cadena Cuscatlán, the network all the stations in the country had to hook up to. Santiago would report that we took over such and such a place, and a couple of minutes later the Cuscatlán commentator would furiously deny it.

We tried out new formats to reach even more listeners: hourly news bulletins, sketches, comic dialogues, jingles based on tunes everyone knows.

***

I'm not going to tell you what people said, just what they did. On the night of the eleventh when the guerrillas arrived, people came out to support them, but they were still a bit afraid. The next day there were more people. By the fourth day, everybody was busy making food for them and giving them clothes. One young *compa* said to a lady: "Ma'am, would you happen to have an old pair of pants you could lend me? Something your husband doesn't wear any more? I just need them until my uniform dries. You see, I've been sleeping here in the trench with wet clothes for two nights now."

That's all it took. The news travelled all around my community and the neighbouring ones. A clothing commission was set up in each district and people showed up with tons of clothes, saying: "For the guerrillas!"

Even the poorest people brought over a little dress, a skirt, panties, underpants, socks, everything a guerrilla could want, and all that guy wanted was one pair of dry pants! But the neighbours got together and piled up a mountain of clothes. You see, people felt happy. We'd been told that the guerrillas were foreigners: Nicaraguans, Cubans, Vietnamese, from who knows where. So we were watching to see how they looked, right? When people saw them come marching in, they called out, "Hey, it's so and so!" They were old friends or family they hadn't seen in years, and everyone was giving each other big hugs.

"Nephew, were did you crawl out from?"

"My brother-in-law, we thought you were dead!"

So it turned out that the big bad foreigners were from our own neighbourhoods. Only the doctor, a tall white fellow, looked like a foreigner, the rest all looked as Indian as the rest of us. Something special happened with that guerrilla doctor. Since nobody in our neighbourhood has money to pay for health care, people started to hang around when they found out that a doctor and a nurse were there.

"What's wrong with the little girl, ma'am?"

"She's got a bit of a fever, doctor. She didn't sleep a wink last night."

"Come on over here."

They took her into the little shelter they'd set up. It was a field hospital of sorts. By the time she came out, another little girl was waiting. The guerrilla doctor began to treat all the sick people in the neighbourhood. People started lining up, a huge crowd. There were people with diarrhoea, bad nerves, epileptic fits, people with so many ailments that the poor doctor couldn't take care of his wounded buddies because he was too busy seeing people from the *barrio*. People were grateful, and they started bringing him coffee or a few *tortillas* or a pair of shoes. Since nobody had any money, they gave the doctor whatever they had.

"No ma'am, keep the food for your son. If not, you'll be bringing him back to see me again soon. It's hunger that's making him sick!"

People started to feel at ease with the guerrillas. You can talk with these soldiers, they said. We can have a smoke together. We can take them into our houses to eat. Not like the *cuilios*: you shake just to look at them because you never know what the fuck they'll do to you.

That's the way my neighbours talked. In my *barrio* we were happy just to go to the store or the supermarket to buy things for the guerrillas. We brought them sugar cane and lots of things so they could hang in there. More than anything else, we hoped they would never leave. As things turned out, it was the other way around. We were the ones who had to escape. When people heard about what the air force was doing in Soyapango and Zacamil, bombing people's homes, they left in a hurry, grabbing whatever they could. People were crying as they headed off carrying their few belongings, and when they turned to look at the guerrillas who stayed behind, they said: "You poor kids! May God forgive me, but I have to go."

You see, the planes were already coming.

***

By Wednesday, 15 November, we were within a hair's breadth of defeating the army and winning the war. The *barrios* had become FMLN strongholds, each building was a fort. The enemy came in with armoured cars and troops behind them, trying to recover terrain and exhaust our munitions, but they failed to do either. Instead, as time went by, so many people were joining us, and the army was falling apart so quickly, that on Wednesday evening, fearing a general insurrection, the Army High Command called an emergency meeting at its headquarters.

Much has leaked out about that sinister gathering where the thirty most senior officers of the Salvadoran Army decided to escalate the war, no matter what the political cost of the ensuing genocide.

"It's them or us," stated one of the colonels.

That's where they decided to use the air force against the civilian population: helicopter gunships against the *barrios*. They also decided on a night of long knives: that very night they would murder those they considered to be the brains behind the revolution. At the head of the list were the Jesuit priests of the Central American University. They say when the meeting was over, the officers joined hands and prayed for the success of their crimes. A few pairs of gringo hands — the CIA advisers — helped complete that macabre circle.

Thursday the sixteenth dawned. I was still half asleep when I thought I heard them say it on the radio.

"They killed Ellacuría," Ana Lidia confirmed.

"That can't be," I said. Santiago was yawning and getting ready to start the broadcast. A terrible look came over his face when he was told.

"It's true. And Segundo Montes and Martín Baró and..."

Santiago turned on the mike and began to speak. Since the first offensive back in January of '81, I'd never seen him so angry — or so sad.

To make soup for the guerrillas here in Morazán, the girls who work in the kitchens go out to look for izote flowers. They cut them off at the stem and throw them into the pot. Every time it gets cut, the izote shows its incredible instinct for survival. It grows back immediately. If you go back in a month, you'll see the izote sprouting anew. Even if the machete cuts it off at the roots, the izote always comes back. It always insists on blossoming again, on staying stubbornly alive.

Ignacio Ellacuría is like those izotes. Martín Baró, Segundo Montes, Amando, Juan Ramón, Joaquín López, they are all like the izote flower, stubborn to die and irrepressible in their refusal to stop growing.

Why do we say this? Because there's something Cristiani didn't take into account: all of them were teachers. They spread their knowledge to the thousands upon thousands of young people who studied with them. They spread the moral values of Christianity, that are so compatible with the principles of revolutionaries. Today the moral values these priests taught have become thousands of seeds. They weren't the brains behind the revolution. They were part of our national conscience, the critical, scientific conscience that searched for the roots of the conflict by researching our history, to try to find a path to peace and national reconciliation.

We know our people will take up this izote flower, symbol of the Salvadoran nation. We know the Salvadoran people will raise it in their fists as a symbol of the irrepressible yearning for peace that flowed in the veins of the murdered Jesuit priests. And we know that on the day of victory, which is approaching at a dizzying pace, people will pour into town squares from all four corners of this nation, to raise the izote flower of Ignacio Ellacuría and the seventy thousand Salvadorans who have died. People will fill the plazas of the country tumultuously, like a river in the rainy season, to pay tribute to these brothers of ours who died for the sake of peace, to these brothers who were born in Spain but were more Salvadoran than their assassins, that pack of criminals with no patriotism in their hearts.

On the day of victory, the mothers of the fallen, their brothers and sisters and children will all be there. This struggle has seventy thousand martyrs. The barbarism has touched millions of Salvadorans: those of us who have lost a brother or a sister or a friend, those of us who have lost Ignacio Ellacuría, those of us who have lost Monsignor Romero. In their name, let's find the road to peace!

Santiago, 19 November, 1989
Day of the Jesuits' Funeral

They bombed the cities. In San Miguel, the Third Brigade turned its 105mm cannons on the slums where people had joined the insurrection. Colonel Vargas gave the order to open fire and the shells blasted the little wooden houses to bits. Afterwards, all you saw were dead children, corpses, pieces of people trapped in the rubble. Helicopters finished the job.

They bombed the civilian population indiscriminately. They destroyed San Salvador's poor *barrios* so thoroughly that we had to change our plans. In a night-time manoeuvre we moved into Colonia Escalón.

"Let's see if they bomb the rich!" said Chico, and he set up his command post in a huge mansion.

The bourgeois lady almost fainted when she saw thirty guerrillas invade her house.

"What do you want? What are you looking for here?"

"Take it easy, *señora*," Chico said, trying to calm her down. "You just go on as usual."

"And what are you going to do?"

"For the moment, we're going to eat. We're hungry."

"Here, there's no..."

"Sure there is, and it's not stealing because you've got more than enough to eat."

"All right," the *doña* acquiesced, and she started to call her servants.

"Oh, no," Chico stopped her. "You're the one who's going to cook."

"Me?"

"You."

"That's ridiculous!"

"This way, even though it's just for a few minutes, you'll experience what other women go through every day in the kitchen. Boys! What'll it be?"

"Fried eggs!"

"Beans!"

"Take care of them," Chico told her. "The menu's simple enough, isn't it?"

You should have seen that old lady grabbing pots and burning her hands on the grease, but she cooked. A woman from the oligarchy served lunch to our guerrilla fighters.

The takeover of the Sheraton was directed from that mansion. We attacked the big hotel because it was the highest point in the neighbourhood, but we had no idea who was inside: none other than the secretary general of the Organisation of American States, João Baena Soares, who was in El Salvador to learn about the war and ended up seeing it up close.

The takeover of the Sheraton turned into the plot of a comic film. On the top floor there were a dozen gringo Green Berets scared shitless and barricaded behind mattresses because the guerrillas had slipped into the hotel. On the first floor, the army was watching every exit — even the sewers — to make sure the guerrillas didn't escape, and we were in the middle, competing with a few *cuilios* to see who could do the best job of protecting Baena Soares.

After a few very tense hours, negotiations got under way and Bishop Rosa Chávez came to ensure the agreements were adhered to. The OAS secretary general left the hotel without so much as a scratch, then our guys and the soldiers withdrew. The last ones to pull out from the hotel were the fainthearted gringos. They sneaked out the back door with their faces covered, carrying little white flags just in case. They looked horrified by the whole thing, which could only have taken place in the kind of violent country their Pentagon sponsors.

Back in Morazán we broadcast everything as if it were live: all the commotion at the Sheraton as well as the takeover of Escalón and the other rich neighbourhoods, which naturally the army of the rich decided not to bomb. Marvel used his eyes and we provided the voices. We also broadcast news flashes thanks to our network of military radio operators in other cities where the fighting was just as fierce as in the capital. We hooked up with our sister station, Farabundo Martí, to tell people far and near about the most impressive military offensive ever waged by a Latin American guerrilla movement.

After 14 days on the offensive, we began our withdrawal from San Salvador and the other cities, a decision which had a lot to do with the ruthlessness of the air force. If we'd had missiles, a different cock would have crowed, don't you think? We had a lot of explaining to do to convince our combatants to pull out, because they wanted to hold their positions, but there wasn't much point in holding on to trenches in bombed-out neighbourhoods after the people had evacuated. Anyway, we won the main battle: strategically speaking, the apparent stalemate was broken.

See You in San Salvador

No one would have bet a cent on us before the offensive. The huge battles we waged in the countryside were invisible in the city. When we stopped all transport or blew up electrical poles, it affected the entire population, but feeling the effects of sabotage is nothing like seeing the bullets fly. People hadn't really felt the war in San Salvador. Out of sight, out of mind, and their propaganda starts to have an effect. Drop by drop, news item by news item in all the mass media, they reported what hadn't happened and omitted what had. They portrayed the FMLN as weak and hurting, and ended up believing their own lies: "There are barely a handful of guerrillas living along the Honduran border. They're racked by desertions; they don't have any weapons; nobody supports them..."

That's why we weren't making any progress in the negotiations. You don't negotiate with people who are on their last legs. They figured they could stall until we faded away all by ourselves, and what happened in Mexico and San José was just a lot of talk. Cristiani wanted to stall for time and improve his image. The talks also helped justify more US military aid to liquidate the last remaining pockets of guerrillas. You see, the gringos also thought we were out for the count.

The November offensive changed all that. Who would have thought we were capable of laying siege to the capital for almost a month? When had an oligarch from Colonia Escalón ever dreamed he'd see fighting on his own block? Now they've smelled the powder and heard the explosions, not even their grandmothers still believe we're just a handful of guerrillas hiding out in the hills. We took the war to the cities, right into the very heart of El Salvador's national life.

We lost 401 lives. One by one, we read every name over Venceremos, starting with Commander Dimas Rodríguez. The great majority of our casualties were men and women who had just joined our ranks and hadn't had much combat experience. The FMLN's military structure remained intact, while the army suffered its worst defeat in all these years of war. They lost nearly 3,000 men and another 3,000 deserted. In January, when rumours circulated about a second offensive, another 1,300 soldiers fled the barracks. A lot of people signed on with us. We now have more urban commandos than ever before, more unit leaders; hundreds of young people withdrew with us; and thousands more sit at home trained and waiting for our next call.

The political victory was even greater than the military one. The offensive ripped the mask off the fascist army that rules our country. In its desperation, the army had no qualms about assassinating the Jesuits and bombing civilians in full view of foreign journalists and representatives of the UN and the OAS.

Above all, the offensive forced them to negotiate. That's why we did it: to wipe the smirk off Cristiani's face and get the US to sit down at the negotiating table. They're decisive in all this, the owners of the circus, and now even Thurman[13] admits the Salvadoran Army "cannot defeat the FMLN". At least they understand that much.

In San José, when we raised the issue of purging the armed forces, Larios[14] said it was absurd and ridiculous. Now it's at the top of the agenda. When we brought up agrarian reform and reforms to the judicial system, they ignored us. Now Cristiani himself talks about negotiating. Fine. By military action we dispensed with a military solution to the war. That was the offensive's finest legacy.

Sometimes the enemy loses touch with reality and falls into a fantasy world. They take heart from the invasion of Panama and the electoral defeat of the Sandinistas in Nicaragua. They pluck up their courage with the fall of Eastern Europe. They get all excited and start dreaming about a quick and dirty solution in El Salvador. Well, a mule only understands the stick, so if November's offensive wasn't enough, we'll give them three more. Unfortunately, to make sure they negotiate we have to maintain the threat of a new offensive.

Venceremos is on the agenda in the negotiations. They want us to return to civilian life, do they? Gladly, but we're taking all our equipment with us, because that's how we'll take part in public debate. They want us to register for truly clean elections, with full guarantees? Then one of the things to be guaranteed is the freedom to broadcast our point of view. A station hidden in the hills won't fill the bill any more. Venceremos has done its time as a guerrilla station. In the new political situation, Venceremos needs to operate legally, out in the open.

It's time we dealt with all the interference by getting a broadcast license, instead of using barbed wire. We have a right to offer our opinions to the public and to have media at our disposal for that purpose just like the rest of the country's political forces. The time has come for the FMLN and its radio station to take part in legal public life and to vie for power on those terms. That's what we're proposing: Radio Venceremos in San Salvador, with its doors open to the public. Are these mad ravings? Not in a country where the people have fought for the right to democracy — and won.

What are we going to do in San Salvador? The idea isn't to transplant our guerrilla programming to the capital. To meet this new challenge, we'll have to reinvent our style, transform the way we communicate.

***

Frankly speaking, we haven't attracted as large an audience as we could have over the past few years. The issue isn't about politics, but actually being heard. We've had a weak signal with lots of interference, and our programming hasn't been the best either. But it's also true that the message of Venceremos goes beyond what we say on air. It's the fact that we exist. If we're still there, it's because we're strong, because we hold terrain, because we've got people's support.

When the first big army operation was launched in Morazán, the objective was to resist, to show them that the FMLN could hold territory, that those zones were under our control. The station's first political message was to let our friends and the enemy know that we were there — shouting any damned thing, but there we were. We spent those days broadcasting under mortar fire. On countless occasions we've broadcast underground, under the rain, right in the *cuilios'* faces, with helicopters overhead, with the greatest determination to go on air ever displayed by a radio station anywhere in the world.

Can you imagine what it meant to keep a station like this going for ten years in a tiny little country like ours in the midst of a full-scale war? You can count on your fingers the days we missed going on air — some of them by our own decision. When the station went dead in '84 it was in order to kill Domingo Monterrosa, and we had to warn all the guerrilla fronts so they wouldn't be demoralised by our silence.

Now we're at a new stage. Today's challenge is much more than resisting: it's competing. What's your message? What are you going to say? Moreover, how are you going to package it? How can you reach everyone: guerrillas and non-guerrillas, peasants and city dwellers, believers and the unconvinced? Especially those who aren't convinced.

So it's time to change, to change everything from boosting our signal to opening up our minds. What's done is done. Did we do the right thing? Things were different then. I don't think Madonna would have been of much use when we were fighting to take over Cacahuatique. Now the winds have changed.

***

the poor of the *barrios*. People who before had only Monsignor Romero's voice to speak for them will soon be able to speak for themselves. Let's listen to them. They have spent centuries waiting in line to have their say.

Footnotes

[1] One of Santiago's pseudonyms.

[2] Colonel Francisco Adolfo Castillo, undersecretary of defence, captured by the FMLN in 1982.

[3] Marcelino Menéndez y Pelayo, a twentieth-century scholar of the Spanish language.

[4] Gen. René Emilio Ponce, head of the Salvadoran High Command.

[5] Popular Liberation Forces, one of the member organisations of the FMLN.

[6] Panamanian President Gen. Omar Torrijos.

[7] Traditional Salvadoran dish of stuffed *tortillas*.

[8] The National Union Federation of Salvadoran Workers

[9] National Union of Salvadoran Workers, a broad-based federation of popular groups.

[10] Colonel René Emilio Ponce, head of the Salvadoran Joint High Command

[11] An American adventurer who invaded Central America in 1855 with an army of mercenaries.

[12] San Salvador's largest shopping mall.

[13] Gen. Maxwell Thurman, ex-commander of the U.S. Southern Command, headquartered in Panama.

[14] Defence Minister Gen. Humberto Larios.

[15] Members of National Resistance (RN), one of the five member organisations of the FMLN.

[16] Salvadoran poet Roque Dalton, an ERP member and a bitter opponent of the sectarianism that rent the left in the 1970s, was murdered, apparently by his own organisation. After the murder, ERP dissidents left to found RN.

[17] Leader of RN.

Epilogue:
When the Fighting Stops

Eleven years after that first, much-loved, Viking transmitter made its secret journey from San Salvador to Morazán, one of its successors made the same journey, again in secret, but this time in the opposite direction. On 16 January 1992, Santiago and a small team arrived at the capital's outskirts to join thousands of peasants, workers, students, and members of religious organisations, many carrying FMLN banners, converging on the Square of the Martyrs. They hurriedly climbed the tower of the cathedral, connected up the console, and with their sister radio station, Radio Farabundo Martí, started reporting the celebrations below.

An all-too-familiar noise momentarily interrupted the festivities. A Hughes-500 helicopter, the killer of several *compas* in the war, began to circle overhead. Santiago raised two hands towards it in the victory salute. This time it didn't shoot. Peace really had broken out.

The FMLN took the city, not by force, but in an outpouring of jubilation and relief that after twelve years, and 75,000 dead, the civil war was over. Agreements brokered by the UN and signed in the Chapultepec castle in Mexico stipulated that five US-trained elite battalions were to be disbanded, including Colonel Monterrosa's infamous Atlacatl; the army was to be cut by half; a new police force was to be created under civilian control; a Truth Commission was to investigate the worst abuses; and there was to be land redistribution for former combatants of both sides.

For its part, the FMLN was to demobilise fully its 8,000 guerrillas, and turn itself into a political party. Its main achievement was to have won the right to participate openly and legally in the political process; its main aim was to take part in the elections of March 1994 and beat the ruling right-wing ARENA party. But could it broaden its appeal beyond the already committed peasants and trade unionists? Could it balance the demand of its militants waiting for land and training, with the exigencies of fighting an election? Could it demobilise but also keep alert to ensure that the right stuck to the accords?

In the event, the FMLN-Democratic Convergence coalition became the second political force in the country, beating the Christian Democrats into third place in the first round of the elections. In the subsequent second round run-off, widespread irregularities accounted for some of Arena's large margin of victory, but divisions between the different political organisations within the FMLN did not help their campaign, and healing them remains a major problem.

Radio Venceremos reflected the changing priorities and difficulties of peacetime. From the start, it declared it was no longer the official organ of the FMLN. In August it received its broadcasting licence, and a year later the party that created it, the ERP, officially adopted social democracy as its ideology. Its commander, Joaquín Villalobos, announced that the ERP now believed in a market economy, the progressive business sectors and the honest military officers.

In peacetime the radio faces difficulties far more complex than being bombed by A-37s, hunted by the Atlacatl battalion or jammed by hi-tech wizardry. It must adapt, and adapt quickly, from being the official mouthpiece of a guerrilla organisation to being Archbishop Romero's — commercially successful — voice of the voiceless in the *whole* of Salvadoran society.

At least one task is easier. Foreign visitors seeking to visit the radio no longer have to lobby suspicious army officers for permission to cross the River Torola. The main obstacle now is the non-stop traffic in San Salvador, which taxi drivers curse as an unwelcome by-product of peace. The site chosen for Venceremos' new offices is tucked away — not in a bat cave, but in a quiet, leafy middle-class district. By one of those frequent ironies of Central American politics, the building is rented from a prominent member of the right-wing Arena party.

These days, Santiago sits in an office, no longer the bearded, thin, bedraggled guerrilla, but a smartly-dressed and well-groomed civilian with a neatly-clipped moustache. The voice is still honey-toned: "The danger now comes not from the army wanting to destroy us, but from ourselves not understanding the precise historical moment," he insists. "What El Salvador requires now are professional, pluralistic and democratic radio stations."

To mark the shift, Santiago's first interviewees in San Salvador were two of the FMLN's main enemies during wartime — the then deputy defence minister, General Mauricio Vargas, and the United States ambassador. "We can't just remain the voice of the FMLN," explains Santiago, "or we would just be a mirror for ourselves to look into. We can't divorce ourselves from the rest of society. We have to be able to criticise the right, and at times, the FMLN." New employees are not asked their political affiliation. Venceremos boasts the country's youngest radio announcer - chosen not for her politics, but for her alluring voice.

That search for pluralism has led to internal tension and soul-searching. In September 1992 five journalists at the radio were sacked after they criticised what they saw as Venceremos' drift to the right. They thought the opening up had gone too far when the radio criticised a teachers' strike for threatening the country's fragile political stability. Officially they were dismissed for not accepting the radio's new ideology, but they had also complained of the station's rigid hierarchies, left over from the exigencies of wartime.

Some have also questioned the need for the radio to attract private advertising, but Santiago is adamant. "Gone are the days when we could rely on help from solidarity organisations abroad. We have to find more secure finances if we are to survive at all."

Capitalists are reluctant to put money into a radio station with a guerrilla past, but for Santiago, that makes a break with the past all the more urgent. Some swords have been successfully beaten into ploughshares: walkie-talkies which used to crackle out warnings of army operations now direct mobile units to the news — protests, meetings, accidents.

Venceremos can no longer count on its former audience of journalists, US embassy staff, bishops, and even Colonel Monterrosa, eager for news of the war. One of its priorities is now to attract new listeners by speaking more of the poor's everyday problems, maintaining a strong social content.

Listeners responded well by bringing food, clothes and money when the radio appealed for victims of a flood in Usulután in October 1992; it joined the campaign to save Cuscatlán, Salvador's ancient pre-Colombian capital, which was threatened by one of the rich families trying to get richer by developing land for new buildings; and Venceremos provides a constant service to the community, announcing funerals, lost vehicles, and personal messages.

It also promised a popular campaign of civic education for the elections — a crucial issue for a country needing a strong civil society to reverse years of electoral fraud and shortcomings. However, the shortage of money and journalists with experience of working in peacetime soon curtailed Venceremos' ambitions to keep the social content high. They are forced to compete with other radio stations and keep much of the news short, and the music programmes long.

But what music to play? The debate has ended in clear victory for the modernists. There are two hours of protest music in Venceremos' twenty hours of daily broadcasting, but the rest of the music is requested by listeners; it's virtually all the "three Rs", rock, rap, and romantic.

Madonna too has her part to play now the target is audience figures, not the army. "Some of the *compas* have criticised us for playing rock music in English," Santiago admits, "but a lot of our listeners want good rock music. We mustn't think that it's just cultural penetration by the big powers."

Venceremos' future, like El Salvador's, is still unsure, but at least one thing is certain. Amidst the plethora of radio stations desperately competing for their market share, Radio Venceremos can boast the best jingle. *"Radio Venceremos, La más buscada en la guerra"*, Radio Venceremos, the most sought after [by the army] in the war, *"En la paz, la más deseada"*, in peacetime the most desired.

For the first few months, Venceremos continued to broadcast two hours a day from the ERP's old headquarters in Perquín, at the end of the Black Road through Morazán. The studio now doubles as a museum. Inside, on the wall, there's a reminder of the need for revolutionary commitment: "You must be the last to eat, the last to sleep, the last to own, the first to die." Outside, hangs the twisted torso of Colonel Monterrosa's helicopter, the villagers' proudest war trophy.

Yet despite the constant reminders of war, Perquín exudes peace. Children in school uniform carry books to class, buses come and go, people idly chat and eat in the plaza. You can even buy a beer, previously banned after one over-spirited *compa* gave away a military secret.

Propped up against the empty shell of the town hall, a wooden kiosk sells souvenirs and knick-knacks for the political tourist — not just books by guerrilla commanders, but ashtrays, pendants and even white designer T-shirts with the FMLN logo. Latin American, European and Japanese tourists have made the trip to Perquín, some staying overnight in the crude guest house once reserved for the FMLN's best fighters. Most visitors are ordinary Salvadorans, keen to visit this mythical village, out of bounds for the previous twelve years.

Venceremos still plays much of the country-style music of the Torogoces. Sebastián, the violinist who taught himself and all the members of the group to read, agrees with the new priorities. "Before, we sang of combat, life with the *compas*, the sorrow of losing a cherished friend", he says. "The causes of the war are still all around us, hunger, misery and disease, but our songs now have to reflect the culture of debate. We have to be armed with ideas, where previously we had weapons."

In Morazán, the mood is notably more cautious than in the city. Venceremos veterans, few aged more than 25, talk fearfully, and with justification, of the slowness of the implementation of the Chapultepec accords.

They point to the delays in purging the armed forces of human rights violators, in the creation of the new police force and the dismantling of the old, and in the full surrender by both sides of their weapons. Above all they fear the resurgence of right-wing death squads, which the FMLN accused of killing nearly thirty of its members in 1993. And many of these sons and daughters of poor *campesinos* in Morazán are still asking, where is the promised land?

By the end of 1993, only about 3,000 of the 20,000 former fighters of both sides had received land, and only eight per cent of scheduled land had been transferred. Comandante Licho, the Pipil Indian and the ERP's brilliant military strategist, decided not to join most of FMLN leadership in San Salvador, preferring to stay close to his roots in Perquín.

"Of course we all want peace," he reflects. "But there could be trouble if they don't hurry up and give us the land they're supposed to." Looking up to see who else might be listening, he adds, "and who needs reminding that land is why this war was fought in the first place?"

James Painter
June 1994

What is the Latin America Bureau?

The Latin America Bureau (LAB) is concerned with information and education about issues of human rights and economic justice in Latin America and the Caribbean. With LAB, you can discover:

* BOOKS for enquiring minds:

- Introductions to Latin American and Caribbean society and culture, economics and politics

- Country guides: Bolivia, Venezuela, Jamaica, Guatemala and Cuba are the first in the series

- A series on Latin American women's lives and experiences

- Latin American authors in translation: from street children to salsa, from rubber tappers to guerrilla radio stations

* MAGAZINES with news and analysis, covering the region week by week

* DAY SCHOOLS AND EVENING CLASSES for you to explore the politics, people and culture of the continent

* A LIBRARY AND RESOURCES GUIDES to help you dig deeper

For a FREE Latin America Bureau Information Pack write to LAB, Dept RR, 1 Amwell Street, London EC1R 1UL (fax 071 278 0165)

For details about LAB books in North America, write to Monthly Review Press, 122 West 27th Street, New York NY 10001 (fax (212) 727 3676)

New from the Latin America Bureau

In the Mountains of Morazán
Portrait of a New Community in El Salvador
Mike Gatehouse and Mandy Macdonald

"They set out on foot in the midst of the most intense fighting of the civil war. They were determined to go home, war or no war, and took with them every scrap of wood they could lay their hands on."
8,000 refugees returned to El Salvador in the months that followed their decision. On the deserted hills of Morazán, they founded Segundo Montes City, named after a Jesuit priest killed by the army.

In the Mountains of Morazán is the extraordinary story of Segundo Montes, told by the community's men and women, and interpersed with vivid descriptions of daily life in this remote corner of El Salvador. Bitter memories of the past contrast with sweet hopes for a better future, despite constant obstacles. Underpinning the whole story are thorny questions about the community's development.
Have the inhabitants of Segundo Montes managed to preserve the structures of co-operation and solidarity so painstakingly created in refugee camps in Honduras? How successfully have they become reintegrated into national life? Does Segundo Montes offer a blueprint for rural refugee returns elsewhere? Have the 1992 Peace Accords healed the wounds of a violent past?

Freelance writers, **Mike Gatehouse** and **Mandy Macdonald** have followed the community's progress since the early days of refuge in Honduras. Their story is based on recent visits to Segundo Montes City. Mike Gatehouse is author of *Soft Drink, Hard Labour: Guatemalan Workers take on Coca Cola* (LAB, 1987): Mandy Macdonald is author of *Out of the Ashes* (ESCHR, 1984).

November 1994 220 pages, with photos, map and index
ISBN 0 906156 94 7 (pbk)

£11.00 by post from Latin America Bureau, Dept RR, 1 Amwell Street, London EC1R 1UL (cheques payable to LAB)

US$ orders to Monthly Review Press, 122 West 27th Street, New York, NY 10001. Tel (212) 691 2555 (cheques payable to Monthly Review Foundation)

CURBSTONE PRESS, Inc.
is a non-profit publishing house dedicated to literature
that reflects a commitment to social change, with an emphasis
on contemporary writing from Latin America and Latino communities
in the United States. Curbstone presents writers who give voice to the
unheard in a language that goes beyond denunciation to celebrate, honor
and teach. Curbstone builds bridges between its writers and the public –
from inner-city to rural areas, colleges to community centers, children to
adults. Curbstone seeks out the highest aesthetic expression of the
dedication to human rights and intercultural understanding: poetry,
testimonials, novels, stories, photography.

This mission requires more than just producing books.
It requires ensuring that as many people as possible know about
these books and read them. To achieve this, a large portion of Curbstone's
schedule is dedicated to arranging tours and programs for its authors,
working with public school and university teachers to enrich curricula,
reaching out to underserved audiences by donating books and conducting
readings and community programs, and promoting discussion in the
media. It is only through these combined efforts that literature can truly
make a difference.

Curbstone Press, like all non-profit presses,
depends on the support of individuals, foundations, and government
agencies to bring you, the reader, works of literary merit and social
significance which might not find a place in profit-driven publishing
channels. Our sincere thanks to the many individuals who support this
endeavor and to the following foundations and government agencies:
ADCO Foundation, J. Walton Bissell Foundation, Inc., Witter Bynner
Foundation for Poetry, Inc., Connecticut Commission on the Arts,
Connecticut Arts Endowment Fund, Lannan Foundation, LEF Foundation,
Lila Wallace-Reader's Digest Fund, Andrew W. Mellon Foundation,
National Endowment for the Arts, and The Plumsock Fund.

Please support Curbstone's efforts to present the diverse voices and views
that make our culture richer. Tax-deductible donations can be made to
Curbstone Press, 321 Jackson Street, Willimantic, Connecticut 06226.
Telephone: (203) 423-5110.

Other Fiction & Nonfiction Titles about El Salvador
from Curbstone Press

ASHES OF IZALCO
written and translated by Claribel Alegría & Darwin Flakoll

"In a novel that blends politics, history and romance with unfailing gentleness, unforeseeable, explosive events determine the actions of the characters but never interrupt the work's lyrical structure...Alegría has distinguished herself to many American readers, but this novel, written with her American husband, a former journalist, will astonish even those familiar with her consummate skill."—*Publishers Weekly*

"...Rich with the insights and sounds of a Salvadoran village, with energetic, sometimes humorous insights into the lives and attitudes of the stratified population..."—*The New York Times Book Review*

$17.95cl   ISBN 0-915306-83-2 / $9.95pa   ISBN 0-915306-84-0   192pp

MATANZA
by Thomas P. Anderson

Newly revised and available for the first time in paperback, Thomas Anderson's 1971 landmark study of the 1932 communist revolt and subsequent government massacre in El Salvador is the seminal work on the origins of the current social conflict in that country.

"This Curbstone Press title...should reach new audiences with its powerful study of the 1932 uprising in rural El Salvador. The massacre continues to impact the nation's events, and Thomas P. Anderson's *Matanza* is crucial in understanding that country's past, present and possible future."—*The Bookwatch*

$12.95 pa   ISBN 1-880684-04-7   224pp

MIGUEL MARMOL by Roque Dalton
translated by Kathleen Ross and Richard Schaaf
Introduction by Manlio Argueta & Preface by Margaret Randall

Miguel Mármol is the testimony of a revolutionary, as recorded by Roque Dalton, which documents the historical and political events of El Salvador through the first decades of the 20th century.

"*Miguel Mármol* is an extraordinary literary document and political resource, a book one wants to read, think through and quote from again and again."— *The Nation*

"An insightful history that reads like an adventure novel. It ranks among the world's great revolutionary literature. Don't miss it!"—Cedric Belfrage, *The Guardian*

$19.95cl   ISBN 0-915306-68-9 / $12.95pa   ISBN 0-915306-67-0   506pp

The World Association of Community Radio Broadcasters

Known by its French acronym, AMARC, the World Association of Community Radio Broadcasters is an international non-governmental organisation serving the popular radio movement. It is a network for exchange and solidarity among community radio broadcasters and its work focuses on coordinating and facilitating cooperation and exchange among community radio projects. AMARC's ten-member Board of Directors has representation from all continents.

The international secretariat, located in Montreal, Canada, coordinates work on a worldwide level. AMARC's regional offices play an essential role providing training and other services and coordinating exchange projects.

Coordinated by José Ignacio López Vigil, the Latin American office in Quito, Ecuador, is one of the most active centres. It offers courses and evaluation for community radio projects and maintains regular contact with the region's 200 members.

In Africa, AMARC and the Interafrican Centre for the Study of Rural Radio in Ouagadougou (CIERRO), a partner organisation in Burkina Faso, are establishing a regional office for the continent.

A European office has been set up in cooperation with the Community Radio Association in Sheffield, England.

AMARC's Declaration of Principles states, in part, that members of AMARC:

- believe in the need to establish a new world information order based on more just and equitable exchanges among peoples;
- contribute to the expression of different social, political and cultural movements, and to the promotion of all initiatives supporting peace, friendship among peoples, democracy and development;
- recognise the fundamental and specific role of women in establishing the new communication practices;
- express through their programming:
  * the sovereignty and independence of all peoples;
  * solidarity and non-intervention in the internal affairs of other countries
  * international cooperation based on the creation of permanent and widespread ties based on equality, reciprocity, and mutual respect;
  * non-discrimination on the basis of race, sex, sexual preference or religion;
  * respect for the cultural identity of all peoples.

AMARC's projects and services include: its magazine, InteRadio; research and publishing; a solidarity network in defence of freedom of speech for community broadcasters; a women's network; an electronic mail users group; training and consultancies and international conferences.

For more information contact AMARC at:

3575 St-Laurent, #704   Fax: +(514) 849-7129
Montréal, Québec H2X 2T7   Tel: +(514) 982-0351
Canada   Email: amarc@web.apc.org

NOTES

NOTES